The

Canadian
Contemporary
Philosophy

Series

John King-Farlow
William R. Shea

Editors

The Challenge of Religion Today

The Challenge of Religion Today: Essays on the Philosophy of Religion

John King-Farlow

Editor

Science History Publications

New York • 1976

First published in the United States by
Science History Publications
a division of
Neale Watson Academic Publications, Inc.
156 Fifth Avenue, New York 10010

First Edition 1976
Designed *and* manufactured in the U.S.A.

Library of Congress Cataloging in Publication Data

Main entry under title:

The Challenge of religion today.

   (Canadian contemporary philosophy series)
   Bibliography
   1. Religion--Philosophy--Addresses, essays,
lectures. I. King-Farlow, John.
BL51.C48   200'.1   76-13492
ISBN 0-88202-157-5

Contents

Preface

JOHN KING-FARLOW

This collection of essays is primarily designed to meet two kinds of need in Canada today. On the one hand, for students taking undergraduate classes or seminars in Philosophy of Religion at universities and colleges, the book offers a good range of Canadian philosophers' views on the subject. Authors were invited to contribute with the intention of providing a broad spectrum of attitudes towards actual religious subjects, as well as a representative cluster of topics in the Philosophy of Religion. Some of these authors, teaching across thousands of miles in Canada, are already well-known internationally. Others are beginning to make a name for themselves in this branch of philosophy. These essays can be used by students and teachers as a Canadian supplement to their main textbook. But they may also be used as the central text by people studying Philosophy of Religion in many countries. None of these authors is a nationalist in any narrow sense. The essays are all on subjects of interest to philosophers of religion. The authors are used to writing for an international audience of men and women with a common bond of interest in religion, philosophy, and truth. Since they are also experienced *teachers*, I left most decisions to those who accepted invitations to contribute. The focus, in view of the likely readership, is mainly on questions raised by Western religions, especially those in the Judaeo-Christian tradition.

Let me turn now to the essays and how they may be seen in relation to each other. There are, of course, various ways in which they can serve to throw light on many overlapping questions in Philosophy of Religion.

Introductory Essay

Jay Newman's "The Ethics of Proselytizing" introduces us with refreshing vigour and clarity to some very old yet currently important moral questions—about preaching at others, protecting personal freedom, and showing respect for those who disagree with us about religious faith, agnosticism, and atheism. What right have we, if any, to try to change someone's religious outlook, if he does not invite us to touch upon his private life? On the other hand, if the answer seems first to be "Absolutely none," do we have absolutely no right to try to prevent others from accepting private attitudes which will lead to *their* trying to convert their neighbours? Professor Newman considers the issues

1

both from the standpoint of *Utilitarians*, who believe that some vital ends justify many possible means, and from the perspective of so-called Deontologists. The Utilitarian is likely to try to justify a moral policy as being useful, as being conducive to some good end. The Deontologist is often more interested in saying that something is right just because it is right, or wrong just because it is wrong. For example, some Utilitarians would try to justify abolishing the death penalty on the ground that an execution will not reduce present rates of crime; some Deontologists might support Abolition by saying, "It is wrong because it just *is* wrong to take human life, except in self-defence or an honourable war." Professor Newman's topic deserves far more discussion than it currently gets from those who reflect on morals and religion.

Part One: Commitment and the Problem of Evil

In the hope of easing the way for readers who are interested in questions about God's existence, yet are unfamiliar with recent moves in debates about the possibility of *rational* religious faith when the world news is so depressing, I have next offered three papers which touch on the question "Can there be a good God if parts of His alleged creation are so often cruel and horrifying?" Arguments from the existence of Evil have been used for many centuries by those who hope to show that God does not exist, or does not care for mere humans, or is somehow good but tragically limited. Others have argued from the existence of Evil and Good, that two Supreme Beings really rule our world. In our modern age the hydrogen bomb and the concentration camps of the Gulag Archipelago provide such arguments from Evil as dramatically as did raging bubonic plague and massacres by Attila or Genghis Khan. In my own essay, "Scepticism, Evil, and Original Sin: A Case for Reincarnation?" I try to cover some recently prominent types of argument about God and Evil in a way that the newcomer to philosophy can easily follow. John Leslie in his companion essay, "The Best World Possible," distills his own arguments on these matters, published over the years in leading journals, to offer the reader a philosophy of life with much practical, as well as metaphysical and religious, interest: *Cosmic Optimism*. The value of commitment to a specific religious faith can thus be compared by the reader to a more general commitment to living religiously as a believer in the supremacy of Good over Evil. Next, the exchange of "Letters Concerning Naturalist Religion," composed by Richard Bosley and myself, invites the reader to view matters in a new perspective. Professor Bosley's Ricardo offers an account of traditional religions' values when they are stripped

2

of clearly supernatural themes and interpretations. Such an account, if it is acceptable despite Jonah's protests, might make a religious community's faith utterly invulnerable to arguments from Evil.

Part Two: Religious Experience and Meaning

Time and again one hears that it is religious experience which justifies faith either in a Biblical God or in a more mysterious and impersonal "God" that has emerged from "the Death of the Old God." Such a "God" is sometimes said to be better and more evident in human experience than the Supreme or Transcendent God of many orthodox traditions. Why? Because the new kind of believer speaks of personal experience in *symbols* and makes no claim that could conflict with Reason or Science. But what is to be understood by "religious experience"? Francis Sparshott, currently the President of the Canadian Philosophical Association, is noted for his writings on aesthetics and art criticism, while he remains a practicing poet. In "Religious Experience and Aesthetic Experience" Sparshott shows in a brilliant and devastating manner how terms like *religious experience, artistic experience*, and the like are employed as confusingly in ordinary life as they are in critics' columns and in philosophers' diatribes. Although we are superficially led to view appeals to such experiences as empirically hard-nosed or respectful of individuals' insights, these appeals can be used all too easily to generate euphoric nonsense about art, religion, and personal feelings. Without careful analysis and cautious clarification, talk of *experience* can be signally unrewarding in Philosophy of Religion. In "Encounters and Metaphor" Carlos Prado argues that traditional theologians' talk of *Analogies of Being* between the human and the Divine, as well as 'Death of God' philosophers' talk of *symbols* and *metaphors*, must be mistrusted. They must be mistrusted unless the users of the analogies, symbols and metaphors indicate how to cash them in in terms of men's familiar experiences of a public, social world. When a philosopher or theologian tries to "protect" religious claims from every criticism by refusing to make them cashable in this way, then he divests those claims of intelligibility in human language. For the meanings of terms in human language cannot be totally "inner" and "private": Those meanings must be explicable to other organisms of flesh and blood who make communal judgments. Too many have sought to ground metaphorical propositions about God or "God" on mystifying assertions about utterly private Encounters with a Divine Being or Being-Itself. But such self-protective thinkers seem to succeed only in depriving their religious experience of any power to support religious claims through interpersonal dialogue.

3

Part Three: The Existence and Nature of God

"The Existence and Nature of God" offers a debate between the well-known champion of philosophical atheism, C. B. Martin and Father Frank Firth, C.S.B. Crucial texts from Aquinas, Plotinus, Dionysios the Areopagite are presented at the start. Professor Martin argues that, of all theologians, Saint Thomas Aquinas offered the least indefensible case for belief in God's existence and in God's essence of 'infinite perfections.' Alas, Martin concludes, Aquinas' case is still indefensible: Natural Theology, the attempt to prove theism's soundness by using human reason, is doomed to rot away in irredeemable contradictions and confusions. Father Firth is not convinced. He allows that Aquinas' arguments are certainly not all beyond criticism. But, he argues, Martin's new argument for atheism turns on a typical, but fatal, misunderstanding of what Natural Theologians who make serious use of Saint Thomas have held about God's existence and perfections.

Part Four: Understanding and Evaluating Faith

This section begins with an exchange between Wayne Grennan and Catherine Dafoe on the question "Can Faith be a Christian Virtue?" Professor Grennan ingeniously seeks to show that, given both Catholics' and Protestants' more prominent accounts of (religious) Faith, there is nothing morally praiseworthy about a Christian who has Faith in God—about such a Christian, that is, simply in so far as he or she exhibits and persists in holding such Faith. Thus both Catholic and Protestant theologians are seriously mistaken in construing Faith as a major virtue, or as any kind of personal virtue at all. Dafoe retorts that Grennan has not gone far enough: The men and women who subordinate their lives to Faith are probably guilty of moral laziness or cowardice.

In "Paradox and Faith in Kierkegaard," Alastair McKinnon seeks to rescue the great Christian Existentialist thinker Kierkegaard from persistent misinterpretation by friends and critics. Professor McKinnon argues from evidence provided by his own use of computing science to analyse books that Kierkegaard published under his own name and other books published under his pseudonyms. He concludes that Kierkegaard's own account of faith, as opposed to accounts of Faith offered by creatures of his imagination, is nowhere near as difficult or counterintuitive as most of his readers have believed. Professor McKinnon's main concern is not simply to explain Kierkegaard's actual view of faith, but to commend it as a powerful model of a saving relationship into which each person can enter with God. The final essay is by Dewi Z. Phillips, an advocate of reconciliation between (a) those who have traditional Faith and (b) those like Richard Bosley who adamantly reject belief in 'transcendent beings' that exist over and above the physical universe of Nature. What Professor Phillips calls the *mythic* or *story-telling* element of religions is not something to be reduced or revised until we have literal assertions about the Supernatural. Religious *stories* as *Stories* are the stuff and staff of a healthy human life. Nor does it help our understanding to move next with such literal assertions about Supernatural Beings to still more confused faith in *symbolical* or *doctrinal* propositions which some philosophers of religion and theologians try to derive from 'The Literal.' The very attempt to replace religious *stories* (the *mythic*) with "literal" claims about Transcendence or 'symbolical' propositions and 'doctrines' is fundamentally misguided. We should view human life as a story-guided pilgrimage towards ever fresh insights. We should not view human life as a sort of iron deposit vault for "doctrinal" finalities, and so restrain our personal growth. Dewi Phillips' new interpretations of healthy faith will continue, as in years before, to arouse the heated criticism of believers and atheists alike. But, as the very purpose of this book has been to stimulate disagreement, discussion, and debate about religion, it seems admirable to close with Professor Phillips' provocative essay.

I owe many debts of gratitude for the appearance of this book. Neale Watson and William Shea deserve the thanks of all Canadians for their faith in the vigour and importance of contempory philosophy in Canada. Catherine Dafoe, my Editorial Assistant, as well as Patricia Brunel and Douglas Carr of the University of Alberta's Philosophy Department, have provided me with much help and encouragement in this venture. My chairman, Dr. Peter Schouls, and my friend at nearby St. Joseph's College, Father Frank Firth, have been lavish with their kindly patience. Illness and hard circumstances prevented three expected contributors from finishing their manuscripts before my understanding but practical publisher's deadline. Hence I have drawn more on colleagues in the Province of Alberta than I had first intended. But still the philosophers in this book, like those in other volumes of the Contemporary Canadian Philosophy Series, offer a good representative sample of the thinkers who teach and learn at campuses spread widely across a great and free and peaceful country.

The Ethics of Proselytizing

JAY NEWMAN

The last time that the Jehovah's Witnesses tried to convert me (and everyone else in my neighborhood), they sent two well-scrubbed, fresh-looking young people to do the job, a young woman in her teens and a more experienced male proselytizer in his late twenties or early thirties. I liked them; they were pleasant and respectful, and I usually enjoy talking with young people about God, the Bible, morality, and other important subjects. They began by asking if I was opposed to the violence in the modern world, and when I told them that I was, they informed me that they knew the proper way of dealing with the problem of violence. I knew what kind of solution these young people had in mind, but I still listened to their little speech, with its interesting reference to certain passages in the Scriptures. Then I asked them some questions about their peculiar interpretation of some of those passages, and the answers I received were not very illuminating; so I asked some other questions: "Do you understand Biblical Hebrew and Biblical Greek?" "Are you familiar with other interpretations of those Biblical passages?" "Do you recall what Thomas Aquinas said about this passage and what Paul Tillich said about that passage?" "Don't you know who Paul Tillich is?" Soon it became clear to the three of us that our discussion was not going to be a fruitful one. I was neither learning anything nor enjoying myself; they were neither converting me nor enjoying themselves. So they gave me a strange look, thanked me for giving them some of my time, and went away. Though I rarely find such discussions intellectually exciting, I generally do not object to people's attempts to convert me to their faith. Most people slam the door in the proselytizer's face, but I am usually not so busy that I have to be rude to people, who are, I suspect, sincere and quite genuinely concerned about my salvation. I have confidence in rational discourse, and I do not think that anyone is the worse for engaging in it, especially when the subjects under discussion are important. And though I never consciously aim at proselytizing the proselytizers, sometimes that is what I seem to end up doing. Yet, most people whom I know are less tolerant of proselytizers. They look upon them with contempt and are quick to ridicule them. Even my "liberal" friends refuse to talk with proselytizers and regard them as stupid and dangerous people. At one level I can see why: There is indeed a connection between religious propaganda and religious persecution—they have the same source. As C.E.M. Joad has observed:

6

> All persecution, it is not too much to say all propaganda, arises from the curious inability of the human mind to think anything by itself. Directly we hold a belief to be true we desire to communicate it to others, directly we think such and such things desirable we endeavour to make others think them desirable also.

Proselytizers have not always been as pleasant and respectful as those that visit us nowadays. In the past, they have been prepared to take extreme measures to save men's souls; they have tortured "heretics," burnt them at the stake, and deprived them of civil liberties. The new proselytizers are in important ways descendants of the old. But there is another reason why proselytizers are so disliked and distrusted: We tend to regard them as arrogant meddlers. Most of us consider our religious (or atheistic) beliefs to be highly personal things, and we do not take kindly to people who suggest that we have been blind, stupid, or obstinate. Still, proselytizing does not necessarily involve persecution. In the pages that follow, I shall be discussing the ethics of proselytizing. Is proselytizing rooted in the proselytizer's "intolerance"? Is it always immoral? Or if it is not necessarily immoral, when and under what specific conditions is it morally acceptable or even morally advisable? These are questions worth considering, especially by those who take religious belief seriously.

Let us begin by considering the ethics of proselytizing from a utilitarian standpoint. In any given case of proselytizing or attempted proselytizing, we find a person or group of people (P) that is committed to a doctrine or set of doctrines (x) and is actively seeking to convert another person or group of people (Q) from not believing x to believing x. Q may or may not be committed to a doctrine or set of doctrines which conflicts with x; conversion does not necessarily involve abandoning some of one's older beliefs, although it may. From a utilitarian standpoint, Q's conversion is morally good if and only if it promotes the general happiness, while it is morally right for P to (attempt to) proselytize Q if and only if P's actions here are based on his *reasonable* belief that Q's believing x will be conducive to an increase in the general happiness. "Act-utilitarians" believe that we should consider each particular case on its own merits, and "rule-utilitarians" are concerned primarily with the morality of either the general institution of proselytizing or the general effort to convert people to believing x. So for the act-utilitarian, the key moral question here is whether or not P's actions do actually promote the general happiness, and for the rule-utilitarian, the key moral question is whether or not (attempted) proselytizing is, as a general rule, conducive to an increase in the general happiness. What we must consider now is how P's (attempted) proselytizing of Q can be conducive to an increase or decrease in the general happiness.

A utilitarian could defend proselytizing on a wide variety of grounds: psychological, social, and metaphysical. The psychotherapeutic value of religious belief is acknowledged even by certain militant atheists. For many people, their religious beliefs are a source of contentment or peace of mind. Religion helps them to bear the misfortunes of life, and often to feel more at ease with nature and their fellow human beings. It gives some a sense of purpose. In short, it often helps to make people "healthy-minded." And just as abandoning atheism may lead to peace of mind, abandoning one set of religious beliefs for another may also have positive psychotherapeutic results. Proselytizers do not often use this argument when they are attempting to convert people, although P might say to Q in passing, "If you believe x, you will, I promise you, find life more pleasant and more satisfying." Proselytizers tend to be more concerned with truth and salvation than with the mental health of potential proselytes, but if you asked them to defend their actions, they would probably tell you that even if x is not true, Q is still better off for believing x. Conversion can have social value, too. Throughout history many men have converted in order to be "successful" in the political, business, or professional world. In certain places, "advancement" depends partly on the church in which one worships. Of course, conversions of this kind are not always sincere. The proselytizer wants Q to believe x, not simply to pretend that he believes x. Still, a utilitarian theorist might well argue that if Q's not believing x prevents a talented man like Q from fulfilling his natural potential as a leader in some field, then P's proselytizing Q is probably conducive to an increase in the general happiness. Again, P is probably more concerned with truth and salvation than with Q's personal advancement and social utility, but if you pressed him to defend his proselytizing, he might tell you that even if x is not true, he is still performing a service for both Q and society by proselytizing. It is important to see that increasing the general happiness does not necessarily require increasing Q's happiness. P can persuasively argue that even if his (attempted) proselytizing makes Q substantially unhappier, it may still be conducive to the *general* happiness. For in addition to considering Q's happiness, P, if a utilitarian, is morally obliged to consider his own happiness and the happiness of all those who would like (or not like) to see Q believe x. Critics of proselytizers and missionaries usually fail to appreciate the psychotherapeutic value that the proselytizer's activity has for the proselytizer himself. Since the Jehovah's Witnesses do not make me substantially unhappier by vainly trying to convert me, and since it obviously makes them happy to be doing the kind of proselytizing that they are doing, their proselytizing would seem, all other things being equal, to be conducive to an

8

increase in the general happiness. When I talk with Jehovah's Witnesses, I may well be helping them to be "healthy-minded" and to enjoy peace of mind, and at a low price. But are all other things equal? The actual conversion of a person effects a wide range of people, not just the proselytizer and the proselyte. It may be a source of unhappiness to Q's family, friends, former co-religionists, etc. Proselytizers, even when they are utilitarians, rarely take such matters into consideration.

This last point is a reminder to us that a utilitarian could attack proselytizing on the very same grounds with which other utilitarians defend it. In abandoning his earlier religious (or atheistic) beliefs in favor of x, Q may have done psychological and social harm both to himself and to others. As a result of his conversion, Q may now be *less* capable of bearing the misfortunes of life. He may have alienated relatives, old friends, former co-religionists. He may have burdened himself with feelings of guilt which are an obstacle to peace of mind. Though he no longer will be regarded as a heretic by P and P's co-religionists, he will now appear to loved ones as an apostate, an infidel. Moreover, "outsiders" often tend to be suspicious of proselytes; Q may now be regarded by many as a disloyal, weak, and opportunistic individual. Some outsiders will see Q's conversion as a personal matter, but others will perceive it as a reflection of some weakness in Q's character. Some resent proselytes for the same reasons that they resent proselytizers. Educated people also often believe that there is a core of moral truths in all major religions, and they may well interpret Q's conversion as an act rooted in his ignorance and misunderstanding of his former faith.

The proselytizer's ultimate utilitarian argument is that if Q believes x, Q will be "saved." "Salvation" is a rather nebulous concept. Few proselytizers are prepared to spell out in detail exactly what happens to a person when he is saved. Still, no matter what specific benefits salvation brings, it would certainly seem to be in our interest to be saved. People are willing to be persecuted and killed if they sincerely believe that their faith will be rewarded with salvation, immortality, eternal life, or a beatific vision. Compared to such rewards, peace of mind and "success" are relatively unimportant. But how can a potential proselyte like Q be sure that P is telling him the truth when P says that believing x is the exclusive way to achieve salvation? And how can Q be sure that the religious beliefs he would have to abandon are *not* necessary for achieving salvation? For that matter, how can he be sure that salvation will actually compensate him for all the things that he will have to give up when he lives according to x? There is empirical evidence to justify the proselytizer's claim that believing x *may* lead to peace of mind and "success." But as even an amateur philosophical

9

theologian knows, it is (almost) impossible to prove that an afterlife awaits those who hold certain metaphysical beliefs. A proselytizer does have some arguments at his disposal here. If Q accepts the Bible (or some other work) as Revelation, P can try to show Q that certain passages in this work suggest that believing x is the key to salvation. P may also be able to make use of certain philosophical arguments. But there are proselytizers of many faiths making use of different interpretations of passages of many different "sacred" works; and as for philosophical theologians, almost everyone knows that *they* rarely agree.

Having considered psychological, social, and metaphysical grounds, we can see that from a rule-utilitarian standpoint, it would seem to be extremely difficult or even impossible to determine whether or not proselytizing as an institution is basically morally sound. Even determining whether converting people to some *specific* doctrine is morally sound looks like a difficult task. The act-utilitarian's job, of course, is in one way much easier than the rule-utilitarian's, for he can deal with each case of (attempted) proselytizing on its own merits. But not only does the act-utilitarian have a huge number of individual cases to consider, but determining the moral rightness of a particular act of (attempted) proselytizing may require making a fantastic number of calculations involving a very large number of factors or variables. But to turn to non-utilitarian considerations now would be premature. For in addition to considering psychological, social, and metaphysical grounds, the utilitarian must consider yet another aspect of proselytizing, which involves the specific content of the doctrine or set of doctrines in question. In many cases Q's coming to believe x will clearly make him a morally better human being. So far we have ignored the specific content of x and have thought of P and Q as two civilized men. But proselytizing does not always involve young Jehovah's Witnesses trying to convert highly civilized people. Consider, for example the case of the missionary (P_1) who knows that certain savages (Q_1) in some exotic locality not only do not love their neighbors but torture people outside the tribe, sacrifice such outsiders to their god, and occasionally eat them. Some of these bizarre rituals may reflect Q_1's religious beliefs; Q_1 may believe that if a young virgin is not sacrificed at least once a week, Q_1's god will become angry and will destroy Q_1. Now let us assume that no matter how happy Q_1 is as a result of sacrificing the young virgins, Q_1's happiness does not compensate for the unhappiness of the young virgins or others. Would it not seem morally advisable for P_1 to convince Q_1 that there is only one, benevolent God, who does not require or even like human sacrifice? Educated people often believe that there is a core of moral truths in all *major* religions, but few believe that there is a core of moral truths in *all* religions. In fact, most people associate primitive religions with barbarism. Tolerance does not demand that we condone human sacrifice, torture, cannibalism, and similar practices; if anything, tolerance demands that we *not* condone such practices. So from a utilitarian standpoint, it may well be morally advisable for *P* to attempt to proselytize *Q*, and whether it is or not depends upon how highly civilized *Q* is and what the specific content of *x* is. We would not have much use for a missionary who converted savages to Christianity by convincing them that Christianity does not conflict with the inhuman rituals that they practice; such a "conversion" would not be worth very much, even if the savages had bothered to memorize every word of the Bible. On the other hand, from a utilitarian standpoint, it may well be morally advisable under certain conditions for *P not* to attempt to proselytize *Q*, for it is not difficult to think of a case in which *Q*'s coming to believe *x* will make him a morally *worse* human being. If an enlightened missionary from the West leaves a tribe of potential proselytes, having himself been convinced that human sacrifice is a wholesome practice, the witch doctor who converted him has not done much to promote the general happiness.

In recent years, certain anthropologists and philosophers—"cultural relativists"—have argued that so-called "civilized men" are wrong to believe that they have an obligation or even a right to change the value-systems of so-called "savages." Cultural relativists cannot be expected to look favorably upon missionary activity. A *pure* ethical relativist cannot see the point of any proselytizing. But anyone who believes that there are certain ethical absolutes or ethical universals would seem to be committed—in principle—to appreciating the value of *some* proselytizing. Nor can "ethical" proselytizing be completely isolated from religious or theological proselytizing.

The last point is a disturbing one. In many cultures, failure to observe certain purely symbolic rituals is widely regarded as being just as immoral as, say, theft or even murder. Most religious people regard religious duties (i.e., duties to God or some god) as ethical duties in the same way as they regard duties to their fellow man. An important theme in Gospel is the conflict between Jesus and the Pharisees over which commandments of the Pentateuch are most important. The Pharisees described in Gospel refuse to subordinate rules concerning, say, the Sabbath to broad ethical rules relating to concern for the interests of one's fellow human beings. Throughout the centuries, much religious persecution and proganda has had its roots in minor doctrinal or theological disagreements rather than broad ethical disagreements. For example, those who sought to convert or destroy

11

the Anabaptists during the sixteenth century sincerely believed that the Anabaptists were dangerous, immoral people—relatively "uncivilized"—because of their heterodox views on baptism, religious liberty, etc. To their persecutors the Anabaptists were different from headhunters in degree rather than in kind; for in the eyes of these persecutors, rebaptism was *immoral*, even if less so than something like headhunting. We who live in the twentieth century can now see that the sixteenth-century Anabaptists were highly civilized people and that proselytizing them probably would not have made them morally better people. But the fact remains that there is no clear line of demarcation between "ethical" proselytizing and this other unnecessary kind of proselytizing. For even if we reject the pure ethical relativist's claim that there are no ethical absolutes or universals, we must come to grips with significant disagreements among people about exactly what those ethical absolutes are. So the Jehovah's Witness may well believe that if he can proselytize the Roman Catholic or the Presbyterian or the Jew, he will make that person a morally better person.

Nevertheless, the moral justifiability of an act of proselytizing does not ultimately rest on the proselytizer's "opinion" as to what beliefs it is morally advisable to hold. Few people think that beliefs about morality are articles of faith in the way that beliefs about salvation are. Rational discourse on moral subjects is quite common. A large part of being civilized is being able to give good reasons for believing that one should do this as opposed to that. If the Jehovah's Witness is going to believe that Q's believing x will make him a morally better person, the Jehovah's Witness ought to be able to discuss in a rational, non-dogmatic way about what morality and moral goodness consist. But not only are most proselytizers not moral philosophers, but most of them are terribly naive and credulous and have difficulty in carrying on an extended rational discussion on any subject. And that, alas, is why religious teaching has often given way to religious propaganda and why religious propaganda has often given way in turn to religious persecution. When one considers certain historic attempts to proselytize, like Christian attempts to convert the Jews, and sixteenth-century attempts to convert the Anabaptists, there is good reason to sympathize with the potential proselytes. The Jews and Anabaptists were rarely as irrational (or as immoral) as the people that came to convert them. If one pressed the leaders of the Jewish and Anabaptist communities, they were able to defend their ethical code with at least as much depth and grace as the proselytizers could. Aware of this fact, more sophisticated proselytizers turned to sophistry and deception, and the most sophisticated proselytizers turned to torture and murder. Now anyone who uses irrational, immoral means to make people morally better is inconsistent and perhaps even hypocritical. So it is not enough for the proselytizer to believe that he can make Q morally better; he must have *good reasons* for believing that he can, and he must be able to express these reasons when he presents his case to the potential proselyte. If the potential proselyte is wholly irrational, of course, the proselytizer will not be able to make much use of rational arguments in dealing with him. But he should be *able* to provide such arguments. Dealing with Q_1 who is irrational is obviously very different from dealing with Q_2 who is not; but in any case, P should have good reasons for believing that by getting Q to believe x he is making Q a morally better person. If they would listen to me, I could offer savages some excellent reasons why they would be morally better people if they stopped sacrificing young virgins to their non-existent god. When proselytizers visit *me*, on the other hand, I usually listen closely, but the arguments that they offer are not intellectually exciting.

Recapitulating, we find that when the ethics of proselytizing are considered from a utilitarian standpoint, few broad conclusions can be drawn. P's proselytizing of Q may be conducive to an increase in the general happiness for "psychological," "social," and "metaphysical" reasons, but for the very same reasons it may also be conducive to a decrease in the general happiness. Few if any proselytizers seem to appreciate the complexity of the utilitarian calculations which are based on a serious consideration of these various factors. The moral rightness (or wrongness) of proselytizing would appear to depend for the utilitarian on the degree to which belief in the *particular* doctrine or set of doctrines in question will "civilize" the potential proselyte or make him a morally better person. Anyone who is opposed to radical ethical relativism and believes that there is at least one ethical absolute or universal would seem to be committed *in principle* to appreciating the value of *some* proselytizing. But since "ethical" proselytizing cannot be completely isolated from religious or theological proselytizing, and since people do disagree significantly about what counts as an absolute ethical good, it is extremely difficult for utilitarians to reach a consensus about which proselytizing is morally justifiable even on these "ethical" grounds. Few of us are pure ethical relativists or are contemptuous of missionaries who try to undermine the religious beliefs of savages who have faith in a god who demands human sacrifice, torture, and cannibalism. The Jehovah's Witnesses, regarding all other religious bodies as instruments of Satan, simply believe that the average "liberal" intellectual is still too relativistic. Nevertheless, rational discourse on moral subjects is possible, even common, and a large part of being civilized is being able to give good reasons for believing that one should do (or believe) this as opposed to that.

13

Anyone who is rational enough to be willing to reflect upon the ethics of proselytizing cannot be expected to have any use for those dogmatic, irrational proselytizers whose strongest weapons are sophistry and brute force.

From a 'deontological' point of view, what is basically right is right because it is right. The deontologist asks us whether or not the proselytizer can rightly approve the proselytizing activities of men who do not share his religious convictions. Kant points out in his ethical writings that the moral wrongness of promise breaking is reflected in our inability to accept the right to break promises as a universal rule. If everyone broke promises whenever he found it convenient, the very institution of promising would collapse. Now I never cease to be amused at how the very same Roman Catholic friends of mine who look favorably upon their Church's attempts to convert Jews and Protestants express an implacable hostility to Jehovah's Witnesses, Mormons, and other proselytizers who seek to turn Roman Catholics away from the religion of the Roman Church. I suppose I am amused only because I do not share the religious beliefs of my Roman Catholic friends. To most non-Catholics, the attitude of these Catholic friends of mine must seem to be a bit inconsistent, if not hypocritical. Catholics, of course, regard their religious beliefs as true and good; but then, Jehovah's Witnesses and Mormons regard their own religious beliefs as true and good and better than those of Roman Catholics. It is interesting to note that in the Middle Ages, the same Church that zealously proselytized Jews and pagans did not permit non-Christians to attempt to proselytize Christians and actually condemned non-Christians for attempting to proselytize when these non-Christians had no interest whatsoever in proselytizing. When two groups of strong, active proselytizers meet, a holy war invariably develops. Our concern, however, is not with history, and so let us ask ourselves whether it is possible for proselytizers to have the attitude that the proselytizing activities of "outsiders" can be morally wholesome. Proselytizing is obviously not in the same class as promise breaking, and we can imagine P saying aloud, "Everyone has a right to attempt to proselytize, and may the best man win." Proselytizers rarely make such a statement, and when they do, it is usually as a means of making themselves more attractive to potential converts and "liberals." When P_2 wants to proselytize Q, the very existence of some other "outside" proselytizer, P_3, is a hindrance to P_2's being successful in his work. For at the same time as P_2 is trying to convert Q, P_3 may be trying to convert Q or even those who share P_2's beliefs. Also, Q may argue in the following way: "Why should I convert right now, P_2? Perhaps I should first hear what P_3, P_4, and P_5 have to offer in the way of rational

14

arguments. In fact, at this very moment, there are intelligent men attempting to persuade others of the reasonableness of the religious beliefs which *I already hold*!" P_2 may well believe that P_3's religious beliefs are as bad as or even worse than those that Q already holds; when this is the case, P_2 must be at least as worried about P_3's activities as he is about the fact that Q does not share P_2's religious beliefs. We should not be surprised, then, that proselytizers dislike and fear "outside" proselytizers, nor should we be surprised at their efforts to undermine the efforts of these other proselytizers.

Now try to imagine a society in which everyone was trying to proselytize everyone else. What kind of society would this be? Every time that P came to convert Q, he found that Q was also trying to convert *him*. Such a society would be strange indeed. If reason triumphed in such a society, the "best man" would "win." But *could* reason prevail in a society in which *everyone* aimed to *persuade* rather than to *learn*? I am inclined to believe that in this imaginary society, proselytizing would give way either to holy war or to radical pluralism and the abolition of proselytizing. For when people are continually subjected to attempts to convert them, they often react by becoming more "liberal" and tolerant, and proselytizing seems a silly, futile business. I have often thought that if Jehovah's Witnesses and Mormons were required to spend two years attempting to convert *each other*, they would be less willing to proselytize thereafter, and they might even end up as syncretists or religious pluralists. When we reflect upon these facts, we realize that there is indeed a kind of deontological argument that can be directed against proselytizers and proselytizing. This deontological or Kantian argument can be understood on two levels. First, from a deontological standpoint, (attempted) proselytizing is only morally justifiable when the proselytizer is prepared to acknowledge *everyone's* right to attempt to proselytize by rational means. Since most proselytizers in the modern world are not prepared to acknowledge a universal right to proselytize by rational means, they are narrow minded and hypocritical, and their acts of (attempted) proselytizing are at least at one level morally wrong.

But a person *can* acknowledge a universal right to proselytize in a way that he *cannot* acknowledge a universal right to break promises whenever it is useful. Here it is important to recognize that the argument can be understood on two levels. If everyone broke promises whenever he found it convenient, the very institution of promising would collapse. What would happen in a society in which everyone was trying to proselytize everyone else? It is hard to say. Perhaps reason would prevail, and the "best man" would win. But perhaps not. Perhaps a civil war—a holy war—would cause our imaginary society to collapse. Or perhaps people in our imaginary society would all come to regard proselytizing as silly and futile. In one way or other, the institution of proselytizing might well collapse in our imaginary society.

Our society is very different from the imaginary society that we have just considered. In our society, not everyone is interested in getting his fellow human beings to share his religious beliefs; in our society, many people are more interested in *learning* than in *persuading*. La Rochefoucauld bitterly remarked that while many wish to be pious, few wish to be humble. But proselytizing continues to exist precisely because there *are* many people who are humble enough to be willing to allow others to attempt to convert them. In our imperfect society, some are obsessed with "teaching," others are obsessed with learning, and few have found the proper balance between the two activities. One of the conditions of successful proselytizing is the receptivity of the potential convert. If everyone in our society was primarily a proselytizer and only secondarily a learner, this condition of receptivity would be lacking, and few people if any would be ripe for conversion. But we should not take La Rochefoucauld's judgment too seriously, especially in light of Nietzsche's profound observation that in the realm of religion there is a myriad of sheeplike followers for every charismatic proselytizer.

As far as the deontologist is concerned, however, these psychological considerations are less important than genuine ethical considerations. The deontologist is not concerned with the question of whether or not the relationship between the proselytizer and the potential proselyte is symbiotic or parasitic. Nor is the deontologist apt to be impressed when the proselytizer points out to him that no realist has to worry about what will happen when everyone tries to convert everyone else. To the deontologist, the fact that only certain people have an obsession with proselytizing is no more significant than the fact that only certain people are in the habit of breaking their promises whenever they find it convenient to do so. On the other hand, it is not easy to determine how seriously the deontologist's argument should be taken. Most ethical theorists are antipathetic to deontologism, and it is especially difficult to determine how much importance to assign to conflicting deontological and utilitarian arguments. Also, P_2 is likely to argue that only those who *know* which religious beliefs are true and good can proselytize by rational means, and since P_3's religious beliefs are not true or good, P_3 cannot possibly convert people by rational means and thus has no right to attempt to proselytize.

This last point leads us to 'epistemologico-ethical' considerations. ("Epistemology," of course, means "theory of knowledge.") A non-

16

utilitarian, non-deontological philosopher can argue as follows: "If x is true, then P has a moral right or even a moral obligation to get Q and others to believe x, even if their coming to believe x will lead to a *decrease* in the general happiness." Now to most of us it is intuitively obvious that it is usually morally right to believe and also to teach *what is true*. But there are certain situations in which we consciously refrain from telling people the truth; for example, we do not go out of our way to tell a dying woman that her only son has been killed in an accident, and if she asks about her son's whereabouts, we may even lie and tell her that he cannot be with her because he is on some important patriotic mission. We all know that an educator has to be highly selective in presenting ideas to fragile minds that are limited in their ability to grasp complex notions. Yet, we are rarely quick to condemn a person who acts on the principle that *no matter what the consequences*, he must believe and make known only that which appears to him to be true. In fact, we can admire such a person even though we disagree with him. But we can only admire him if he is a reasonable man who has good reasons for believing what he believes. Few are likely to respect a man who goes about trying to convince the world that the Canadian government is run by creatures from outer space; it does not matter much that he is sincerely convinced that it is *true* that these creatures control the government of Canada.

Now say that P argues that *no matter what the consequences,* he must, for moral reasons, attempt to get Q to believe what he (P) is firmly convinced is true. How are we to respond to such an argument? First, where possible, we should point out to P that in reality he is not as committed to this principle as he thinks he is (or is pretending he is). Rarely are proselytizers committed to making known the *whole* Truth. Not only will few proselytizers go out of their way to point out to a potential convert that, say, the proselytizer's co-religionists have at various times done some grossly immoral things (like, torturing heretics or excluding blacks from the priesthood), but most proselytizers *methodically conceal* truths because they feel that knowing some things is more important than knowing others. Some beliefs *are* more important than others; but if proselytizers methodically conceal certain truths, they should not believe or pretend that they are wholly unconcerned with "consequences" and other utilitarian considerations. We can respect a man who is both reasonable and frank; but it is harder to respect a man who, while claiming to be concerned above all with Truth, tells many "white" lies and systematically hides truths from us. Secondly, *when pertinent*, we should point out to P that if he does not have *good reasons* for believing x to be true, he may well be too casual in his approach to Truth. Of course, if P *has* good reasons for

17

believing *x*, and we cannot think of any better reasons for *not* believing *x*, this point is not pertinent.

Here we must consider whether or not *P* can have good reasons for believing *x* to be true. Some people who know very little about religion mistakenly believe that religious or theological beliefs are never verifiable or falsifiable. Some religious beliefs are empirical and can be verified by reference to sense-experience. If *Q* believes that sacrificing a virgin a week to some god makes the sun rise every day, a missionary can prove to *Q* that this empirical religious belief is false. On the other hand, historians have been able to verify some of the claims of the Bible. Whether or not there can also be synthetic *a priori* religious knowledge is a question which is too complex for us to consider in a study of the ethics of proselytizing. In any case, syncretists or religious pluralists who oppose most proselytizing do so partly because they believe that the most *basic* and most *important* religious beliefs either cannot be known to be true or are known to be true by people of all major faiths. The particular doctrine, *x*, that *P* wants *Q* to believe rarely appears to be an empirical or synthetic *a priori* truth. It usually appears to be a detailed speculative theory. Syncretists and religious pluralists have little confidence in the ability of Trinitarians to prove that Unitariansim is a false doctrine; and they have no more (and no less) confidence in the ability of Unitarians to prove that Trinitarianism is a false doctrine. Yet, Trinitarians do try to convert Unitarians, and vice versa. But though syncretists and religious pluralists are convinced that *P* cannot show a highly civilized *Q* that some important religious doctrine is *true*, they are not religious relativists, because they can see that it is better to hold some religious beliefs than others. Most of them regard such faiths as Buddhism, Christianity, and Judaism as morally superior to primitive religions. Now all of the major religions are different: Some expect a messiah, others do not. There are religions which seek to affirm the world, or to escape from it, or to transform it. There are religions of struggle, religions of repose, religions of majesty, of humility, of love, etc. Syncretists and religious pluralists are well aware of these important differences. But they see no point in *P*'s attempting to get *Q* to believe *x*, when *Q*'s own beliefs enable *Q* to be as morally good a person as *P* is. So though *x* differs from doctrines *a*, *b*, *c*, and *d*, the five doctrines may have something in common which makes them (more or less) equally worth believing and preferable to doctrines *e*, *f*, *g*, and *h*. Perhaps there are many roads to moral-spiritual Truth; or perhaps several different religious outlooks embody a single moral-spiritual Truth.

The views of the syncretist and religious pluralist on the nature and value of religious beliefs lead them to approve of some proselytiz-

18

ing and disapprove of most. Consider, for example, the syncretism of Arnold Toynbee, who writes:

§ If the great religions of the World are to approach one another, they must find common ground, and I believe that the necessary common ground exists.

§ We ought also, I should say, to try to purge our Christianity of the traditional Christian belief that Christianity is unique. This is not just a Western Christian belief; it is intrinsic to Christianity itself. All the same, I suggest that we have to do this if we are to purge Christianity of the exclusive-mindedness and intolerance that follows from a belief in Christianity's uniqueness.

§ What, then, should be the attitude of contrite Christians toward the other higher religions and their followers? I think that it is possible for us, while holding that our own convictions are true and right, to recognize that, in some measure, all the higher religions are also revelations of what is true and right. (*Christianity among the Religions of the World*, New York, 1957.)

Anyone who holds such views cannot have much regard for the proselytizing activities of Jehovah's Witnesses, Mormons, or Catholics who seek to turn men away from their Buddhism, Judaism, or Methodism. But these views are not relativistic, for they acknowledge the gulf between the "great" or "higher" religions and primitive religions. As for the "truth" of which Toynbee speaks here, it is not the ordinary truth which we encounter in everyday life but a moral-spiritual truth. While the syncretist thinks in terms of a single meta-religion which underlies the great natural religions, religious pluralists do not necessarily think in such terms. A religious pluralist may believe that although there is no single meta-religion, the differences between the major religions are not so profound as to to warrant the bother-some interference of proselytizers. Or he may believe that although the differences between the major religions are considerable, ethical and political principles force us to accept an often troublesome disunity. Though syncretists and religious pluralists can see the point of converting savages, they have a uniquely broad view of what kind of doctrines these savages should be persuaded to hold.

Syncretism and religious pluralism are attractive to men for ethical as well as impersonal, epistemological reasons. Explaining the popularity of syncretism, the American journalist, Louis Cassels, observes that

Its open-mindedness appeals to those who remember how much suffering has been inflicted on the human race by intolerant religious zealots who were certain that they alone possessed the true faith. Its denial that God has revealed Himself through specific acts in history appeals to those who think it unscientific to believe in any kind of miracle. Its promise of "universal" faith appeals to those who feel a desperate sense of urgency about forging bonds of human unity in a shrinking world threatened by atomic annihilation. (*What's the Difference?*, New York, 1965.)

But in Cassel's eyes, syncretism forces us to throw the baby out with the bath water. He tells us that on closer inspection we find that

> Christianity cannot come to terms with syncretism today, any more than it could in the first century of the Christian Era. You can have Christianity *or* syncretism, but you cannot have both. It is necessary to make a choice between them, because they are fundamentally and forever incompatible.
>
> The heart of the Christian faith is the assertion that God *has* revealed Himself in history in the person of Jesus Christ. The self-revelation that God accomplished in the Incarnation was unique, once-for-all, the crucial divine intervention in human affairs.
>
> When Christians try to tell others the good news that "God was in Christ, reconciling the world unto Himself," they are not laying claim to any superior religious insight. . . . They are simply delivering a message that has been entrusted to them—a message that was addressed from the start to all mankind. (*What's the Difference?*)

These lines give us a valuable insight into the psychology of most proselytizers, and not just Christian ones. Most proselytizers believe that the *heart* of their faith is not an ethical code but a concrete historical and metaphysical fact. The proselytizer's ultimate defense of his activities is 'epistemologico-ethical' and not utilitarian or deonto-logical. And though he is—at least in principle—opposed to intoler-ance, he feels morally obliged to "deliver a message," to make known the "good news." Moreover, those who recognize the assertion that is at the heart of the Christian faith see that

> there is no way in which Christians can compromise on this assertion. Either it is the most important truth ever proclaimed—or it is a damnable falsehood which has led hundreds of millions of people astray. In neither case can it be fitted into a neat synthesis with other religions. (*What's the Difference?*)

For most proselytizers, the "good news" is good because it is true. The syncretist, religious pluralist, and "liberal" think of religious belief primarily in terms of the categories of good and bad; but the average proselytizer ultimately thinks of religious belief in terms of the categories of true and false. That is why Jehovah's Witnesses go to the Catholics as well as to the savages. And we must not make the mistake of thinking of missionaries as social workers who are primarily concerned with the physical well-being of savages and others; the missionary's main aim is to pass on the "good news."

20

One does not have to be a syncretist to be able to see how naive Cassels' attitude is. It is not obvious that a complex faith like Christianity, Judaism, or Hinduism has a single, central assertion at its heart. Of greater importance, if an assertion or idea is a falsehood, it is not necessarily a "damnable" one. And if its truth or falsehood is unknowable, then that is all the more reason to think of it in terms of important axiological categories. Viewing it in terms of these categories does not necessarily involve "compromising" on it. But if Cassels has not given us a sound moral argument to support a certain kind of "exclusive-mindedness," he has drawn our attention to relevant psychological facts. Christian proselytizers (and most other Christians) have an *attitude* toward Christianity which precludes their seeing it as capable of being fitted into a neat synthesis with other major religions. It is purely a matter of speculation as to whether or not the world would be a better place if Christians, Moslems, and others had a different attitude toward their faith. In any event, given their present attitude, most proselytizers, as we have seen, cannot be expected to be very interested in speculating about such utilitarian matters.

A comprehensive study of the ethics of proselytizing requires at least some consideration of the ethics of belief, for underlying the question "What right does *P* have to attempt to convert *Q*?" is another: "What right does *P* have to believe *x*?" Most epistemologists (theorists of knowledge) who are concerned with the ethics of belief are interested in *evidence*. Proselytizers often talk about evidence, but they are not as subtle as epistemologists, and sooner or later they go back to talking about faith and Revelation. I strongly suspect that few proselytizers are themselves concerned with problems in the ethics of belief; but all I can say with certainty here is that from my own limited experience with proselytizers, it would appear that (1) proselytizers do not generally have good reasons for believing *x*; (2) proselytizers do not generally have a clear idea about what distinguishes good reasons for believing from bad ones; and (3) the theories that proselytizers want men to believe are usually highly speculative, and I am not sure myself what would be the proper way to go about verifying (or falsifying) them. There are some epistemologists, pragmatists, who are more concerned with general ethical values than with evidence in the ordinary sense; they see truth itself as an axiological category. In a sense, a pragmatic theory of religious belief can be seen as an attempt to bridge the gap between an outlook like Toynbee's and one like Cassels'. Since pragmatic epistemology is essentially an extension of utilitarianism, it reduces all questions about the ethics of belief and the ethics of proselytizing to problems of utilitarian calculation.

Whether or not he is interested in utilitarian considerations, *P* almost surely thinks that he is doing something *for Q* by changing *Q*'s

21

religious beliefs. It is possible for a proselytizer to be willing to harm a potential proselyte for the good of the greatest number. But usually proselytizers believe that if they are not making the proselytes happier, they are at least making them better by *some* standard. Even when heretics were about to be burnt at the stake, they were usually told that it was for their own good. Yet it is interesting that many who are anxious to share "good news" are not very eager to share much else. There are a few ascetic missionaries who are prepared to starve so that the children of savages can live; but usually even these missionaries are not so anxious to help those who are firmly opposed to the missionaries' religious beliefs. In any case, the proselytizers who come to visit *me* seem to be prospering materially as well as emotionally, and I suspect that they are less liberal with their property and their money than they are with their theological reflections. I have occasionally had to resist the temptation to ask them, "If you cannot save my soul, can you at least loan me a few dollars so that I can make it through the weekend?" My Marxist friends have suggested that "good news" is a cheap commodity, at least as far as the seller is concerned; but they are more than a bit unfair. Proselytizers do sincerely believe that souls are important, and in that sense they are a good deal more enlightened than my Marxist friends. The strange limitations of a proselytizer's good will do not in any way suggest that his religious doctrines are false or bad. They do suggest, perhaps, that he has not been reading the sacred books closely enough. They also suggest that he has much to learn as well as to teach.

We saw earlier that anyone who is opposed to radical ethical relativism believes that there is at least one ethical absolute would appear to be committed in principle to appreciating the value of some "ethical" proselytizing, and since this "ethical" proselytizing cannot be completely isolated from religious proselytizing, the non-relativist would also appear to be committed to appreciating the value of a limited amount of religious proselytizing. We also saw that there are probably cases in which proselytizing is clearly conducive to an increase in the general happiness and hence, from a utilitarian standpoint, clearly morally right. But we could not help taking note of the fact that even from a utilitarian standpoint, most religious proselytizing would seem to be morally unacceptable. Now that we have examined the relevant deontological and epistemologico-ethical considerations, we have seen that none of them suggest that proselytizing is morally right, and some of them suggest that it is actually morally wrong. And so I think we must conclude here that while a limited amount of religious proselytizing is morally advisable, most of the religious proselytizing that is going on in the world today is not even morally acceptable. One does not have to be either a relativist or a syncretist to realize that the time has come for proselytizers to learn that the best way to go about improving the cosmos is to be improving oneself, not to be trying to create a world in which there is only a single vision of Man's destiny.

Having stated my main thesis, I would now like to add two notes, one concerning proselytizing *within* a faith and one concerning self-proselytizing. Our attention has been focused on the activities of the proselytizer, P, rather than on those of the proselyte, Q; and it has been assumed that P's faith is significantly different from the potential proselyte's. But throughout history, many if not most, proselytizers have been more concerned with "their own kind" than with complete "outsiders." An example which springs to mind is that of "orthodox" Jews, who have little interest in converting Gentiles to Judaism but are often quite militant in their attempts to prevent Jewish "assimilation." Orthodox Jewish proselytizers care little about the religious beliefs of Gentiles but are deeply disturbed by the religious beliefs and practices of liberal Jews. Roman Catholics are at least as concerned with bringing back "lapsed" co-religionists as they are with finding new ones, and the same probably holds true for most Christians. Indeed, as anyone knows who is familiar with Aquinas' definition of heresy in the *Summa Theologica*, apostate Christians have often been feared much more than Jews, pagans, and other "outsiders." Question: Is it less immoral to attempt to convert "one's own kind" than to attempt to convert "outsiders"? Although certain intuitions may prompt us to think otherwise, reason suggests that this general question must be answered in the negative. There may well be *specific cases* in which utilitarian considerations make proselytizing "one's own kind" morally advisable. But the arguments which can be raised against "external" proselytizing can also be raised against "internal" proselytizing. Furthermore, there are no unquestionable guidelines that we can turn to in order to determine what is external here and what is internal. To a liberal Jew, the world view of the Talmudist is less congenial than that of the Unitarian. To a "lapsed" Catholic, the world view of the local bishop is less congenial than that of the liberal Jew or liberal Protestant. Many people are understandably quite surprised when certain proselytizers inform them that they are kindred spirits.

"Self-proselytizing" is a different phenomenon; here the proselytizer and the proselyte are one and the same person. Now surely, all other things being equal, a man should have the right to hold whatever religious beliefs he wants to hold. If he wants to abandon Presbyterianism in favor of Catholicism, that would seem to be his own business and nobody else's. A clever missionary could even argue that all proselytizing is ultimately self-proselytizing, for when no *force* is used by a missionary, it is the proselyte himself who makes the ultimate judgment about which religious beliefs he should hold. All other things are not always equal: Utilitarian considerations *may* suggest that it is morally wrong to change one's own faith. For example, one cannot ignore the fact that his converting may cause his parents and children to become suicidally unhappy. And "force" does not have to be physical: As we saw earlier, something like sophistical argumentation can be regarded as a kind of "force." Thus, self-proselytizing is not *necessarily* morally acceptable; and it is not obvious that most proselytizing is ultimately self-proselytizing. Changing one's own religious views is less likely to be morally unwholesome than changing someone else's, but a proselyte has just as much of an obligation to be rational as a proselytizer does, and the activities of a genuine self-proselytizer are not morally neutral.

This last point will disturb many people, who may even argue that it helps us to perceive some of the limits of utilitarianism. Some may feel that freedom of religious belief supersedes utilitarian demands in importance, i.e., that no matter how much unhappiness a person thereby creates, he has a right to change his religious beliefs. Few reflective people hold this view; it is extremely difficult to see a person as having a right to abandon civilization in favor of barbarism. But most conversion does not involve abandoning civilization in favor of barbarism. It in one thing to be worried about social justice and quite a different thing to be worried about one's family's reaction to a switch from one Protestant ideology to another. A man should not have to concern himself with an unhappiness which stems from superstition and bigotry; if his relatives cannot tell the difference between Methodism and barbarism, their reaction to his conversion need not be weighed. I do not deny that utilitarianism is an imperfect ethical theory. Still, if freedom of religious belief does supersede *some* utilitarian demands in importance, it certainly does not supersede all.

My comments on self-proselytizing will not only disturb non-utilitarians; some will see them as reflecting an untenable *conservatism* and *irrationalism*. It could be argued that my views are those of a person who is opposed to *change* and *rational persuasion*. But I am not opposed to all self-proselytizing or even to all missionary activity, and so it is not fair to interpret my position as essentially conservative. And I certainly do not disapprove of rational self-persuasion or any other kind of rational persuasion. I have argued that proselytizing is not necessarily immoral and have tried to show that under certain specific conditions it may even be morally advisable. I have not even criticized the view that we should encourage change for its own sake. Perhaps we should. In any case, *some* change should be discouraged. My attitude toward persuasion is more complex. Earlier we noted that as a general rule, we do not take kindly to those who suggest that we have been blind, stupid, or obstinate. Now it is obviously necessary to persuade people to abandon certain irrational, false, or dangerous beliefs. When we considered epistemologico-ethical matters, we saw that religious proselytizers generally do not have good grounds for believing that they alone hold rational, true, and healthy religious beliefs. And most of us consider our religious (or atheistic) beliefs to be very personal things. So persuading a person to be a Methodist or a Mormon is very different from persuading a person that more people live in Toronto than in Vancouver. Clearly there are times when persuasion is advisable and times when it is less advisable. Too much conversation is argumentative and aims at persuasion; not enough aims at the mutual enlightenment of the discussants. In his famous book, *How to Win Friends and Influence People*, Dale Carnegie rightly observed that "Nine times out of ten, an argument ends with each of the contestants being more firmly convinced than ever that he is absolutely right." Moreover, "You can't win an argument. You can't because if you lose it, you lose it; and if you win it, you lose it. . . . You have hurt [the other man's] pride. He will resent your triumph." We can win *some* arguments, but it is wise to resist the temptation to engage in rational persuasion at every opportunity.

Scepticism, Evil and Original Sin:
A Case for Reincarnation?

JOHN KING-FARLOW

In this essay I shall first look at some of the possible reasons which may lead believers in the Jewish, Christian, and Islamic faiths to abandon their traditional religious beliefs. Whether or when these reasons are sufficient to make such changes of belief quite reasonable can then be asked in an introductory way. In Part Two I try to indicate why arguments from Evil, offered for abandoning the Judaeo-Christian tradition, can appear to be valid in the eyes of some reasonable people, but feeble in the eyes of others, while still others are simply led to dilute their theology.

In Part Three I will consider a traditional line of defense against sceptical arguments from Evil. This is the complex line based on several teachings in the Bible or the oral traditions of many Biblical believers: the story of the testing of God's highest creatures, the angels, and the consequent revolt of Satan and his cohorts; the account in *Genesis* of how Adam and Eve were tested in the Garden of Eden, with the result that almost all subsequent humans were born tainted with Original Sin; the claim that those humans who cooperate with the Grace of God will be able to pass the test of Evil in this world and receive a fitting reward in the next.

In Part Four I shall argue that while such a line of defense may be intuitively acceptable to some, it should seem less harsh to the intuitions of others if it is linked with a belief in successive reincarnations, an Orphic belief in the ancient West still held by Hinduism and one branch of Buddhism in the contemporary East. That such an addition would make the coexistence of God and Evil easier to understand and accept—if true—suggests that many other sets of possible truths about a Supreme Being, truths as yet unknown to us, are available to defeat the sceptic. Thus, the reply to questions about a good God's tolerance of Evil, that *a good God may well have excellent reasons*, need not be mere whistling in the dark. In Part Five I shall conclude by relating the earlier reflections to the problem of making a rational Wager or Act of Commitment in favour of God, Freedom, and Immortality.

Part One: Reasons for Loss of Faith

A person might be *caused* to lose his belief in God by the operation of an unscrupulous but very knowledgeable brain surgeon. In another example, a child who believed in God at the age of three might lose his religious parents and then be adopted by a rabidly atheist aunt and uncle: The young child is in the habit of believing what adults say most often and most recently. The aunt and uncle do not argue or reason with the gullible child, but the child picks up atheism by osmosis and listening. His relatives *cause* him to lose his old beliefs.

In the first of these cases, we can say that the *reason* why Mr. Stansmeadow lost his religious beliefs was that the neurosurgeon took out too much of the patient's brain. In the second we can say that very early exposure to only atheist views was the *reason* for the child's becoming a non-believer. But "reason" so used is not often intended to qualify for descriptions like "sophisticated," "dumb," "logical," "invalid," and so on. If the tree burned down because lightning struck it, such a reason is not usually described as canny, cogent, profound, stupid, etc. The words "cause" and "reason" are often interchangeable, but in philosophy of religion we are interested in evaluating those reasons which belong most typically to intelligent agents when they have the ability to deliberate, analyze, argue, and thus arrive at a brilliant, sensible, or foolish conclusion.

The word "reason" can lead to still more confusion, not least in arguments about religious claims. Let us look once again at contrasting examples: (A) A repentant, highly muscular woman, six feet, six inches tall, weighing 250 pounds, is asked to explain why she recently hit her adoring, kindly, and much smaller husband five times in the solar plexus. Still more repentant, she replies: "Because I knew that would hurt him a lot." Now, she may be indicating the end or goal which interested her in choosing whether and where she would strike her unlucky little spouse. Similarly, she could tell us that her reason for bringing home "Daz" rather than Brand X was that she had just been reading about jazz which rhymes with "Daz," and that she felt like choosing by a bizarre principle. Here we get two cases of description or indication of what lay psychologically behind actions that were deliberate and not the inevitable result of emotional compulsion.

(B) A doctor explains in court that he slapped a patient who was laughing uproariously because he *thought* that the man was dangerously hysterical and needed slapping, and because he *thought* that the man had a weak heart which could be damaged by hysterics. This doctor gives these reasons to explain why he struck the man, even though the doctor now knows and everyone now knows that the man was not hysterical and had no heart condition. The doctor offers these reasons to *justify* himself *as acting honourably, though mistakenly.* In the circumstances, he pleads, he made an *entirely* or *largely excusable* mistake. Indeed, given the background and confusion, what he did, he insists, was in a sense *quite praiseworthy.* (He had extremely sore

27

hands after an auto accident, but he still slapped the man in trying to do his duty as a doctor.)

(C) A large woman, who understood the situation perfectly, explains that she hit the much smaller doctor, because she knew it was the only way then and there to stop him from choking to death on a piece of steak. This was her reason and the doctor agrees that, though he has a nasty bruise, she was thoroughly justified in so acting for such a reason in such a context.

In philosophy of religion we are primarily interested in reasons like that in case (B), although reasons like that in (C) can be relevant also. We *try* to find reasons which really will justify us as reasonable people in moving from what we know or quite rationally believe to accepting new conclusions, thinking new thoughts, making new commitments and performing actions. We want reasons which are characteristic statements of careful, open-minded agents in cases of wise deliberation.

Many people have abandoned religious beliefs because they have been appalled by human suffering in the world (not least by their own suffering). Others have been so changed because of animal suffering. Then there are those who lose Faith because science is said to explain everything, or because science is said to offer the only way of establishing any truth of lasting importance. Some contrast "*natural evil*," like human and animal suffering, with cases of "*moral evil*," such as those offered by the multitude of morally depraved human beings who torture prisoners to death, beat and rape young children, pollute arable land for profit and in war. Certain people find moral evil too hard to square with Faith; others are put off by natural evil. Again, no few believers were glad to drop their Biblical ideas as soon as they were patronizingly assured that the theory of Evolution is incompatible with a rigidly Fundamentalist interpretation of the early books of the Old Testament. Then there are those who see falling attendance at churches on Sunday as proof that God has passed away. Furthermore, we find some who conclude that because not all the dietary and sexual laws mentioned in the Bible seem to fit the modern world, all theology is therefore pure mythology. (On the other side, some Fundamentalists conclude with similar sophistication that, because God exists, the theory of Evolution must be literally true, and we must not question the present relevance of any Biblical saying about ethics.)

I have been trying to bring out that many of the reasons which have propelled great multitudes into atheism (or into theism, for that matter) are mainly the province of psychologists, sociologists, historians, and anthropologists. They are reasons about which theists and atheists alike should be philosophically indifferent. Sheer numbers of

28

religious and atheist converts and trends of current conversion tend to impress us because we are social, highly excitable, and often sheeplike in our thinking. Consider two people who have abandoned a lifelong commitment to Judaism. Both say that their reason for changing is their present conviction that *science explains everything: Science has taken over the whole explaining business from religion.* In the case of Mr. X we find that he has never even thought carefully about the meanings of "explanation" and "explain." He now is led to agree that science explains a great deal by bringing events under testable laws which often facilitate prediction; that science explains still more by linking the behaviour of familiar macroscopic things like atolls and explosions to the behaviour of much less familiar, microscopic or theoretical entities like cells and positrons. We then point out to Mr. X that our present study of the diverse things which "reason" can be used to cover reveals that "explanation," as a related word, is likely to have many senses or typical uses—thus his soothing faith in science as the great explainer of all is likely to be based on confounding explanation in terms of scientific laws with explanation in terms of non-rational motives, of rational motives, of mitigating excuses, of justifications.

A sixteen-year-old girl is dying of leukemia and asks her nurse why she only has a few weeks at most of life. The nurse tells her patient about the state of her blood, the progress of the disease in almost all cases, the increase of leukemia since industrial wastes were allowed to pollute the local water, and a causal connexion has now been, etc., etc. The patient considers the well-meaning nurse, who rattles off more and more scientific explanations, to be unbelievably obtuse. What the patient is asking is whether there is some set of truths about her life and about all human history which can lend any consoling or justifying point to her loss. And so Mr. X can be made to see that his "knee-jerk" atheism is confused. Scientific laws are not justifying explanations at all. Science cannot explain everything in the way that religion was meant to do—or it would not be science. Science-worship is not the same as science.

On the other hand, Mr. Y may have lost his faith in Judaism and may offer us the reason that he no longer believes that a justifying explanation can be given for plentiful harvests, floods and famine, sexual pleasure and peace of mind, earthquakes, fatal diseases, and the rest. Mr. Y may tell us that after long reflection on the Bible, the sciences, human history, and his own experience he feels forced to conclude, as a matter of honesty, that such a world cannot be the work of a loving God. "Explanations," he adds, "in terms of intentions, purposes, emotions, excuses, and justifying reasons only seem to apply to men and any organisms very like men. Scientific explanations,

29

unconsoling as they are, remain the only ones that apply to most natural phenomena. And so I sadly conclude that the Biblical God, if He existed, could offer far more explanations of kinds we deeply want. But only explanations which make use of science and its laws are usually realistic."

The reasons which move Mr. Y belong to the kinds that primarily interest philosophers. One might say: It is philosophically interesting to analyze Mr. X's confusions, but it is philosophically important to evaluate Mr. Y's conclusions. The latter has reasons which deserve the most attention.

Part Two: Rational Responses to Arguments from Evil

Next we should turn to a familiar triad of claims:

(A) *God exists as the Creator and maintainer of the universe.*
(B) *There is a vast amount of moral and natural Evil in the universe.*
(C) *God is all-powerful, all-knowing, completely loving and perfect in every way.*

As they stand, these claims are logically consistent. I do not contradict myself, (as a matter of what words and sentences mean), by asserting them all at once. It is not as if I had been trapped by a clever prosecuting attorney into saying *first* that I have no unusual physical features, *but then* that I have no nipples, *and then* that the absence of nipples on a man is a very unusual physical feature. The so-called *sceptic*, however, has at least two interesting moves to try next. First, he may attempt to get me to admit to a new claim like this:

(D) *No loving, all-powerful, all-knowing and utterly perfect God would allow so much moral evil, let alone so much natural evil, since the latter attacks innocent children nearly as often as the most deplorable adults.*

Secondly, he may seek instead to exact a concession like this:

(E) *Although (A), (B) and (C) are logically compatible, it is as wildly improbable that an utterly perfect God should exist and allow us to encounter so much appalling Evil as it would be implausible for John King-Farlow to win a boxing match over fifteen rounds against Muhammad Ali at the champion's fiercest and best.*

The sceptic who pushes (D) wants us to admit that *either* some hidden implication of (A), (B) and (C) *or* some clearly undeniable addition to (A), (B) and (C) produces a fatal contradiction in the orthodox positions of Jews, Christians, and Muslims. (At least, the addition will be clearly undeniable for those who hold orthodox Judaeo-Christian positions.) The sceptic who advocates (E) is less dramatic, but has an easier case to make. Since words have different

30

meanings and varied shades of meaning, it is often hard to make a charge of clear contradiction clearly stick. Further, it is more in keeping with the traditional motion of a *sceptic*, one who doubts and withholds assents and says he does not know, to make (E) his option. But we also speak now of people as *sceptics* if they claim to *know* that what we think we know is either false or at least not possible to know. And so quite heterogeneous agnostics and atheists can be grouped together for some purposes in philosophy of religion.

In order to show that the believer need not be cowed by any appeal to a proposition like (D), one noted American philosopher of religion, Nelson Pike, has challenged the sceptic to prove the falsity of a supplementary claim like the following:

> (ABC-1)   *A good God could have a morally sufficient reason for allowing the actual amount of Evil in history to exist.*

Pike reasons that just as a child may not be old enough to understand why his mother causes him so much pain to cure him of a disease, and yet the mother has morally sufficient reason to do this, so a limited human being may not understand what a perfect God's morally sufficient reason could be for allowing so much Evil. Pike goes on to point out since the atheist has practically no chance, and probably none, of showing (ABC-1) to be false, he is almost certainly unable to produce a contradiction out of (A), (B) and (C) or out of these three claims and any further claim a Biblical theist should feel bound to admit.

Another interesting approach has recently been suggested by the distinguished Christian thinker Alvin Plantinga. Since Plantinga's important work is extremely difficult and technical—and sometimes unnecessarily so—I shall offer a partial analogue which should suffice here. Take first (A) and (C):

> (A)   *God exists as the Creator and maintainer of the whole universe.*
> (C)   *God is all-powerful, all-knowing, completely loving and perfect in every way.*

What is now needed is a claim in keeping with Biblical Revelation that generates a variant of (B). In contrast with

> (B)   *There is a vast amount of moral and natural Evil in the universe,*

Plantinga wants something like

> (BB)   *There is much moral evil in this world and in any possible world of free agents which a good God could be said to create.*

In other words, Plantinga wants to forestall the sceptic by finding an intelligible claim in the Biblical tradition which, when added to (A) and

31

(C) will imply (BB). This implication will explain/justify God's allow-ance of moral evil. He takes it that natural evil is usually accounted for in terms of God's permitting moral evil to exist. The natural conse-quence of moral evil first among Satan and his cohorts, then among fallen humans, will be a great deal of natural evil. If God were to prevent all natural evil, He would not really be giving created angels and humans a choice between moral good and moral evil. Cain must be free to kill Abel, if he chooses, not merely free to *intend* to kill *Abel*; otherwise intention, and so free choice, will soon be reduced to nothing. Moreover, if I understand Plantinga when he is especially obscure, a genuine testing of the worth of a created moral agent requires that there be an environment in which a limited creature cannot always remain perfectly flawless. Thus Plantinga is led to speak of *Transworld Depravity* as a property of every human being's very essence. Each human being, since he or she has the dignity of a truly free (but limited) moral agent, is bound to exhibit some moral failure in some situation that belongs to the history of any possible world which a perfect God could be consistently described as creating with humans in it. Thus Plantinga can offer us proposition (G):

(G) *In any possible world created by a perfect God and containing creatures that are free (but limited) moral agents, they will exhibit their Transworld Depravity by committing some moral evil.*

And (G) together with (A) will be sufficient to imply (BB). Moreover (A), (BB) and (G), together with a claim like (H),

(H) *There can be no great amount of moral evil without natural evil and God created this universe for vast numbers of free moral agents to inhabit it*

are sufficient to generate our original (B):

(B) *There is a vast amount of moral and natural evil in this universe.*

These tactics of Pike's and Plantinga's are meant to offer different ways of showing that the Biblical beliefs (A), (B), and (C) are logically consistent. They also seem to offer the rough beginnings of ways to argue that the main Biblical view of the universe might also be plausible as well as coherent. Before I turn to the question of plausibil-ity, however, I should offer some points for meditation on these moves by Pike and Plantinga. Pike's way of establishing the consistency of theism is, I think, relatively clear and effective. The charge of implausi-bility would be appallingly strong only if Pike were speaking about an abstract God in an historical vacuum. But Pike is writing for philoso-phers who know the Judaeo-Christian tradition, and who also know the theme of many world religions, Western and Eastern. One might call it the Testing Theme: *The point of this life is not to pile up a maximum of Joy Units and to avoid all discomfort; the point is to face harsh tests and to develop, then to increase, personal goodness through such tests.* The atheist does have some important replies, however: "Why is there so much pain and evil that some are bound to break completely and never excel? Why does so much pain fall to the lot of young children, animals, and fish who are not being tested or punished? How can Mongolian babies, or children with brains burned out by encephalitis, or virtuous old people who are now cancer-ridden and quite senile, be said to be tested or punished? There is too much evil for the Testing Theme to explain. The plausibility of Pike's additional premise is very weak. Possibly it must be false!" These complaints, I shall later hold, are far more easy to parry if we add belief in repeated incarnations to the Biblical tradition. I shall not be the first to say this, but in most current discussions such an obvious move is never seriously considered.

Plantinga's doctrine of man's Transworld Depravity is born of two very different intellectual parents. On the one hand we are offered the Libertarian picture of angels and men as beings ever gifted with Free Will for making choices between Good and Evil, whatever the causal antecedents of their deliberations. The Libertarian thinks of the choices as essentially unpredictable on the basis of scientific laws and knowledge of the relevant prior events. This may seem as extreme to the reader as the Hard Determinist view that all talk of Freedom, Free Will, and Free Choices is nonsensical. It may seem a no less wild conjecture than the Soft Determinist's pious guess that all human choices are, in principle, predictable by scientists; that man's Freedom can only lie in areas of *ability to do* what one necessarily chooses to do. On the other hand, Plantinga's doctrine of Transworld Depravity reflects the notion of Original Sin, Predestination, and Election in his Calvinist tradition. If a free moral agent is to be set difficult tests, why must he at least occasionally flunk those tests in any possible world? Surely we only need the thesis that *very probably*—(and NOT *necessarily-by-virtue-of-his-depraved-essence*)—such an agent will sometimes fail in any possible world? Another intriguing question is this: Must God really allow natural evil to result from moral evil? Why could He not be perfectly good and let Cain decide or intend to kill Abel, then trick Cain into killing a phantom Abel? To orchestrate such a vast divorce between moral and natural evil, without letting intenders discover their failures and gradually lose the concepts of choice, freedom, intention, action, etc., could be too great a task for Venus or even Zeus, perhaps. But why so for a Biblical God?

A final item of business in our Part Two is to consider the Limitation Strategy which not a few intellectually honest and humble

33

thinkers have adopted to meet Arguments from Evil for agnosticism and atheism. They would hold that the Biblical God has had no end of mysterious and possibly senseless properties attributed to Him by philosopher-theologians who care more for the abstractions of ancient Greek philosophy than for concrete descriptions in Scripture. Some of them would say that the Argument from Evil is the result of construing God as *almighty* in a way that is not appropriate: God is almighty because He *will ultimately triumph* over Evil, not because He is able at any time to do anything He likes. Similarly God is *all-knowing* because He knows which things will necessarily occur and He knows His own intentions: Whatever else in the future is not determined by natural necessity or by His own intentions cannot be known to Him. (What is not by now the case or necessarily going to be the case is not yet anything at all—"it" cannot be known now.) Others see the perfect goodness of God to lie in His unfailing compassion and concern for human beings, despite His freedom to ignore us. On this interpretation the perfect goodness of God arises from His willingness to *suffer* with the living beings of this world—a precious kind of goodness that unlimited power would make possible. Others who favour the Limitation Strategy (guided by which one eliminates (C) or alters its meaning to avoid possible incongruities) urge us to focus religious concern upon indefinitely many ongoing *processes* rather than a particular group of final *products*. God and every other individual must evolve through almost endless change and becoming towards perfection. Or God is an endless Divine Process of Self-Realization, while all else becomes, changes, and perishes. In either case, it can be pleaded, the argument from Evil only fits a world picture of God as a finished product with no new forms or degrees of perfection to attain.

If such accounts of God are developed from competent scholars' efforts devoted simply to understanding Biblical teachings, they may indeed begin to offer believers in a Biblical God nice grounds for rejecting certain versions of the argument from Evil. But what if they offer new descriptions of God's nature only or mainly in order to meet certain philosophical requirements? Then the believer who views God's nature as something not to be misconstrued may well prefer the moves of Pike to the Strategy of Limitation. One suspects very often, however, that the reinterpreters have had mixed motives. How to react is puzzling.

One option most worth noting at a time when different forms of "Satanism" are attracting more adherents is that of the Manichees' world view: Two equally powerful forces, one "good" and the other "evil" rule the world. One should serve one or the other, but be wary of too much commitment to both. Some who use arguments from Evil

34

would say that Manichees makes the best religious use of our knowledge of good and evil in the world. Others would retort: "But good and evil are too evenly distributed! Why believe in *two* when *one* would do? Why not believe in one almighty being who is perfectly good and perfectly evil?" But perhaps the price of such unity is a new contradiction!

Part Three: The Testing Theme and Original Sin

Let me rehearse briefly one Christian version of cosmic history. God, being perfectly good, wished to create several kinds of personal agents with whom He might have a loving relationship. Because He was truly good He did not want the illusion of being loved by helpless puppets or robots: He wanted His creatures to choose freely to love Him. Hence He gave them the choice of loving or rejecting their own devoted Creator. For them to receive the very possibility of such a choice in any meaningful way necessarily involved His making them agents quite frequently faced with choices between Good and Evil. So first He created angels, pure spirits like Himself, who could know Him far better than human creatures could know Him later on in their embodied state. The angels were soon divided between allegiance to God and service to Satan: Satan was the archangel who preferred to be the supremely evil being rather than next in goodness to God. The rebellious group of angels forfeited their relationship with God in their *madness*, for they realized that their natures required communion both with what is perfectly good and with what is good in limited ways. They had chosen eternal torment by choosing eternal rejection of God.

The story is now complicated by God's creating a physical universe which included embodied moral agents, the first man and the first woman. They lived in an earthly paradise, where temptation to do evil was kept very weak, yet where Satan and his followers could try to tempt them to break one simple, undemanding order from God. The man and woman showed such appalling ingratitude to God by refusing to obey so easy a request that God decided to expose them and all their descendants to appalling temptations and appalling cruelty from the fallen angels. Their descendants were blighted in nature, owing to the Original (First) Sin in Eden, making them helpless to choose good without special aid from God, and making them utterly unworthy of God's love. (Only Redemption by God Himself could make them worthy in the fullness of time.) Henceforward Satan's cohorts were free to unleash hurricanes, plagues, earthquakes, and natural evils of every kind on humans and the lower animals. Eventually through His mission to the Jews, the Incarnation and Crucifixion, the sending of the Holy Ghost, and other instances of His own goodness, God made it possible for largely virtuous men and women to be united with Him after death in Heaven. But those humans who still chose to be predominantly vicious were consigned like the fallen angels to eternity in Hell—to unending deprivation of the goodness and love without which all persons are in torment.

Some have tried to "demythologize" this account of history. The idea of unending and and unbearable punishment for a limited number of misdeeds by such very weak creatures seemed monstrous to them. The view that a child is guilty from birth because his parents or earlier ancestors had deliberately acted viciously (*long ago and at a mature age*) appeared abominable to them. The belief that an unbaptized baby will go to Hell because of Original Sin or that a hydrocephalic baby in great pain is getting its just dessert appalled them even more. Such types of revulsion from certain Churches' teachings encouraged even further the use of the argument from Evil. "*Ought*," said Kant, *implies* "*can*." How ought we not to have allowed what we could not prevent before our birth?

On the other hand, some "demythologizers" sought to find a deposit of ancient wisdom under the surface texture of Biblical stories and the Churches' interpretations. The phrase "the tree of the knowledge of good and evil" proved suggestive. The tale of Adam and Eve and their Fall in the Garden is that of every normal person's change from dreaming infancy to understanding, choice, and responsibility. The young, normal human infant is not only a potential swimmer and a potential lover, by virtue of his innate capacities to do many things that, say, a sponge or flea will never be able to do, but he is also a *potential person.* Just as he cannot fully actualize his natural capacity to swim at three days of age, so he cannot fully achieve the status of moral agent at three months or probably even three years of age. Sooner or later, however, the normal child must leave the paradise of freedom from responsibility and guilt. Sooner or later like Adam he must learn to work in order to have his desires satisfied. Nor can he ever cast off the menace of the open future: *Anxiety*, great or small, is always with him because the future is uncertain and demands even more decisions and commitments from him. And his final appointment in the future is *death.*The responsible adult, evolved from the infant, is doomed to be haunted by anxiety as the descendants of Adam are said to be dogged by Original Sin. The authentic Christian focusses on life after death. The authentic humanist focusses on death and on bringing some natural meaning to the time he has to live: Oneness with the universe and its persons, not union with a personal God beyond the universal, is the only honest goal.

36

This humanist reconstruction of such theist tenets represents an attempt to make parables that seem hopelessly unjust in their religious context sound fair and wise upon being "demythologized." And perhaps there are aspects of the baffling Genesis story, now known to be the patchwork of several hands across several centuries, which do not fit enough of our moral intuitions when they are given a Christian interpretation of the kind I have mentioned. Are there any religious alternatives? Is there no alternative? Doubtless there are many alternatives. What I propose to do next is to sketch an alternative which may well vex many Biblical theists *and* humanists *and* pure sceptics alike.

Part Four: Evil, Freedom and Reincarnation

One notable move by one particularly vocal atheist today is to pose the following question: *If a perfectly good God really had to test His creatures morally, why would He not confine them to making choices between* better *and* best, *or at least between* good *and* better? This atheist's obvious inference is that, since we are not confined to such choices, but live instead in a swamp of moral (and also natural) evil, there is no loving Creator. For purposes of argument I am going to assume that it does make clear sense to speak of souls being reincarnated in new bodies after death. Those who are interested in most of the argument, but who cannot tolerate the idea of souls or minds being disembodied and later carnally rehoused, may prefer certain analogues. We can think of the material components of a human at death being reassembled to resemble him and share some of his old brain traces on another planet. Or we can believe, rather like Homer, that when a man dies a gaseous or astral substance, which is a small replica of his body, having the same traits of personality and many shared memories, passes out of him and flies on to another place. Finding that talk of reincarnation seems so easily intelligible to Plato, to a powerful group of Buddhists, and to hundreds of millions of Hindus, as well as to myself, I shall talk in terms of old souls and new bodies.

One reply made to the atheist, who wanted God to allow no evil choices, has been that persons would not be truly moral agents if they could only choose between better and best, etc. I count it better to allow for something like what this atheist proposes. Another useful concession to the atheist is first to construct a parable where we speak of reincarnation, human choice and moral intuitions *without religion's being involved.*

Parable: Once upon a time a complete universe came into being, graced by a highly idealistic group of men and women, all appearing to be about thirty years of age and very well read. After discussing what it would be to prove one's personal dignity, they decide that in their case it would be to make consistent choices of actions which are as good as humans can be expected to perform in such a world from a moral point of view. They decide that anyone who has very consistently chosen so well after thirty more years will have proven his personal worth and so deserves to live in a world without testing. Those who do fairly well, they decide, should have to strive for another thirty years in the same sort of world. Those who do very poorly, they add, should take stock of themselves autonomously as moral agents and decide what worse sort of world they deserve to enter—either for punishment, or for harder tests, or both. After thirty years the physical universe disappears leaving only the souls. After reflecting on his or her performance each soul chooses what sort of area in a new universe it would be appropriate for him or her to face next. A new universe promptly appears with areas which fit each person's (unfailingly honest and sound) evaluation of the previous life. Those who repeatedly fail badly and are convinced it is through their own fault yet again eventually find themselves on our planet Earth. Some are born here only to be punished; some to be punished and also to prove themselves. Some of the worst are "plugged in" to the consciousness of suffering animals or radically defective human babies: The distress will purge them and ready them for a chance in the next incarnation to achieve a higher moral stature, more worthy of *themselves* as persons.

The Parable with God Returned: Let us suppose instead that God creates such a first physical universe with such mature and idealistic humans in it. The humans ask God to help them affirm their own dignity as persons by allowing them to be tested in a series of ways very similar to those of the first parable. After their deaths they examine their modes of life and each asks God to put him or her in an area of the new physical universe which will be most conducive to personal development for someone with such a past. God offers each a choice of possible areas and incarnation-bodies: Each chooses the area most in keeping with the pursuit of his or her own moral ideals. Those who come after many incarnations to be associated with our planet Earth in its present state are reincarnated here because of their own decisions about what they owe to their dignity as persons. *Heaven* is the state they speak of as that where no further testing or suffering is needed. By *Hell* they mean an apparently unending descent to more and more dismal reincarnations, although it is a descent that can be changed. *Purgatory* is upward progress through lives in better and better areas, where testing is less and less difficult, until the souls reach Heaven.

These two parables, I submit, offer means to make much better sense both of Evil in a good God's Creation and of the idea that we suffer here on this earth from Original Sin. I do not wish to suggest that the priggish second parable is true, still less that it cannot be improved upon. But if each human has inherited from his or her own misdeeds the sufferings and ugliness that each now encounters, then each is his own Adam or her own Eve; each suffers as each has personally *chosen* to suffer after reflection on failures and the demands of personal dignity. For a rational person realizes that he owes it to himself and all persons, not just to God (if there be a God) to become good, honest, strong, authentic, loving, and much else by virtue of being a person.

What the second parable crudely begins to offer is one cosmic model in which Pike's *morally sufficient reason* is realized. Again, it offers a model for interpreting the Genesis story of the Fall without violating our apparently useful intuition that *ought* implies *can*. With more sophisticated additions one can place Satan and his followers in the cosmic model, making it clear that the relevant humans have *chosen* to inhabit a terrifying area over which they know that evil angels would have so much power. If one or two cosmic models can be constructed which make consistent moral sense of the Bible and the world we know, but which do not tamper with Biblical teachings about the nature and perfections of God, then we can reply to the sceptic that probably there are many possible cosmic models which can integrate Biblical teaching, human experience of Good and Evil, and also our safest-looking moral intuitions.

Part Five: Wagers on God in Spite of Evil

Suppose that I give a greedy man a drink in my Edmonton apartment, then lead him out to my balcony which hangs from the twenty-sixth floor. I offer this fellow, Fergus, a hundred dollars to do me a quick favour. The greedy Fergus promises at once to do it for such a handsome sum, then takes back his word when I tell him the favour is to jump off my balcony: He must jump with no artificial aid like a parachute or a trampoline *and survive*. Knowing Fergus' avarice I continue to "up the ante": Will he not jump for a thousand dollars, ten thousand, a million, and so on up to the whole of Canada's cash reserves? I add fringe benefits like free dental care, acupuncture, photographs each wedding anniversary, and a new diamond ring every Labour Day. Any one of these offers would normally suffice to make Fergus run a hundred miles in a week, or eat thirteen pounds of Irish stew in an hour. Why am I failing to interest him?

Sometimes we are told that we should believe in God and obey certain Biblical commandments, because we stand to gain an infinitely long existence in pure bliss if we so believe and if we turn out to have believed correctly. Sometimes we are warned, especially on what are thought to be our deathbeds, that we should believe and obey, because we stand to plunge into the eternal misery of Hell if we do not believe and if it turns out that God exists. Some people are moved by such variations on what is often called *Pascal's Wager*. But many are not moved at all. How can this be? They would love to be sure of being happy forever. They dread the very thought of being unhappy forever. Yet, rather like Fergus, they show no inclination to gamble.

Why are they so indifferent? Suppose that I am giving an engagement party for my fiancée. I find that I have invited more women than men and realize that *these* women will be very dissatisfied. On my way home from work I stop at a tavern to buy more cases of beer and become acquainted with three extremely handsome, already half-intoxicated sailors, who are obviously dying to attend a party involving a generous number of women. I am in a great hurry and must think fast. My options (acts) are *A* to invite them and *B* to forget about them: They are most unlikely to remain retrievable from the tavern for very long. The two possibilities (events) which really concern me in this context are: I) that they will offer agreeably more male company to my lady guests without disturbing anyone; II) that their rapid drinking will make them so violent an addition that the party will be a disaster and my fiancée will break off the engagement. Looked at in cold print, the situation stands as follows:

Utility of Outcome

	Act A: *Invite the sailors*	Act B: *Forget the sailors*
Event I* *The sailors will be fun for the women.*	Act A + Event I = 500 Joy Units (Ladies delighted; fiancée thrilled; everybody happy.)	Act B + Event I = −500 Joy Units (Ladies and fiancée dissatisfied; male guests overtaxed, etc.)
Event II* *The sailors will be appalling.*	Act A + Event II = −15,000 Joy Units (Everyone upset; crockery smashed, police intervene; fiancée breaks off the engagement.)	Act B + Event II = −500 Joy Units (Ladies and fiancée dissatisfied; male guests overtaxed, etc.)

* Probability of event = .5

Rapid calculation tells me that Act A, inviting the sailors, stands to lose me 14,500 Joy Units while Act B stands to lose me only 1,000 Joy Units. The probability of Event I is the same as the probability of

Event II. So probability need play no significant role in my calculations. In Fergus' calculations, however, probability does and should play a major role! For it is extremely improbable, as he knows, that he will survive to collect the reward offered to him if he *both* jumps off my balcony without taking any precautions *and survives*. In the case of the person urged to believe in a God of type T_1, George Santayana once commented, the person may well not agree that the only metaphysical or religious alternatives (*events*) are either that a God of type T_1 exists *or* that life has no meaning at all. Perhaps, says Santayana, we would be wiser not to gamble on a God of type T_1 lest there turn out to be instead a God of type T_2 who is exceedingly jealous and vindictive. It would be found, then, to have been far wiser to not to have gambled on any God at all or to have done something to placate possible deities of many different types that appear in human writings.

For Fergus the probability of his jumping and surviving is for all *practical* purposes *nil*. But it is "theoretically" or "logically" possible. It would not be courting a contradiction in terms for him to be thought of as jumping and surviving. A sudden and fantastically strong prairie wind might carry him off to a soft repository in a mountain of fluffy snowflakes and eiderdown stuffing. If, however, there is a radical contradiction in the most central parts of the Biblical accounts of God, then there is no possibility that the Biblical God exists. Not even infinite amounts of hoped for celestial pie will tempt the rational person, if he realizes the contradiction, to wager his soul on such a God's existence. It seems to be a crucial part of the Judaeo-Christian Testing Theme that in this life most of us can only see "through a cloud darkly"; that God is largely hidden from us (*Deus est absconditus*). Hence we are being challenged to develop and maintain our Faith in the face of difficulties about feeling sure of God's existence. But the Biblical writers do not admit that there is anything contradictory in their account of God as the Creator Who allows evil to exist for now but will triumph over it. For them it is very far indeed from being utterly improbable that God exists: Despite the difficulties, they hold, there is persistently good reason for us to believe that God reveals His concern for men and women. Given such a positive measure of probability that God exists, even if the measures seem small, the infinite utility of keeping the Faith honestly and being right makes it rational to gamble one's all on His existence and love. A tiny number multiplied by an infinite number becomes "very large" indeed! If the probability of God's non-existence sometimes seems much greater, the utility of the outcome of successful atheism, even multiplied by such a high fraction of probability, is not so great a number. (For the truly religious gambler the utility will not merely be pleasure, but will include love, wisdom, etc.)

41

The great American philosopher-psychologist William James commented on Pascal's Wager in a very Biblical spirit that such a gamble only makes sense for those to whom belief in a Judaeo-Christian God has become a *live option* from their own experience. It is only if life has drawn one at least slightly to live interest in the idea of such a Creator's existence and love for man, that one can sanely wager. If life has really narrowed down a sensitive person's live options to choosing between Faith and acceptance of the universe as a place devoid of higher purpose, then the wager can be legitimately on. Again, if one believes that the Biblical account of God is profoundly incoherent, one cannot very reasonably choose to wager. That is why it is so important to dwell upon attempts like Pike's and Plantinga's to show there is no inconsistency about a perfect God's being said to allow so much evil. The story of the Fall in the Garden of Eden seems to some believers to suffice for showing the Bible's consistency. The *Free Will Defence* is said to emerge from the first chapter of the Book of Genesis and to make Evil in a God's universe fully intelligible. Others who would like to dare to believe find the story of the Fall a greater stumbling block than ever: It would be better to be told like Job that God can have a morally sufficient reason to allow Evil which puny human minds should not dare to ask. I have devoted the third part of this essay to trying to show how open the story of the Fall can be made to interpretations that need not outrage our sense of what is moral and of what is just to persons as free moral agents.

The answers of the Jew, the Christian, and the Muslim to problems about God and Evil are not purely philosophical. They are not mere appeals to logic. But if logic can show them a little daylight and if life can provide some personal inspiration, then the believer's gamble is on. His wager can be highly reasonable. The sceptic's mockery can be based on hideous dogmatism.

Bibliography

King-Farlow, John. *Reason and Religion*, London, 1969.

King-Farlow, John and William N. Christensen. *Faith and the Life of Reason*, Dordrecht, 1972.

Pike, Nelson (Editor). *God and Evil*, Englewood Cliffs, N.J., 1964.

Pike, Nelson. "Hume on Evil," *Philosophical Review*, LXXII, 2, 1963.

Plantinga, Alvin. *God and Other Minds*, Ithaca, 1967.

Plantinga, Alvin. *The Nature of Necessity*, Oxford, 1975.

Plato. *Republic*, Book X. (See Plato's *Myth of Er* for a superb introduction to problems of evil, religion, justice and reincarnation.)

The Best World Possible

JOHN LESLIE

Men have argued for God's reality by pointing to the beauty of the world and the intricate ways in which Nature's laws cooperate to make life possible. But their argument appears to run into a fatal difficulty. Though we may sometimes bless the laws which produce life, we are often more inclined to curse them because being alive can seem worse than being dead. If we are wrong here, that scarcely helps matters. For if life is a blessing, then the death which so constantly threatens us, and which practically nobody escapes for longer than a hundred years, is all the more terrible. The Himalayas, while no doubt beautiful, are awe inspiring in their capacity to smash or freeze or smother whoever moves among them. In any case they are virtually uninhabited. It is the unlovely mud-flats of the Ganges Delta which carry a teeming population, millions who can expect to be wiped out by floods if war or famine, snake-bite or cholera, do not destroy them first. How could a world with so much evil in it, a world whose value can even be thought negative, be the creation of God as he is traditionally conceived? How could omnipotent benevolence permit napalm bombs, plague, volcanic disasters, the torture of religious dissenters, cancer, paralysis, loss of limbs in accidents?

"So you get paid for teaching philosophy! Me, I've never managed to persuade myself to accept things philosophically. Let's do something to improve the world, that's what I say!" Cocktail-party conversations of this type are the curse of the modern philosopher's existence, making him detest the kind of optimist for whom he is so frequently mistaken. Typically, he sees his job as clarifying our ideas about the world or about the words which we use when describing it. If ever he bothers to consider the doctrine that it is a world of which a Creator could be proud, his thoughts will probably take a hostile form. For the arguments supporting this doctrine include some of the weakest and most sickening in philosophy's history. For example:

That floods and fires, pestilences and massacres, bring benefits because they make the world less crowded.

That without starvation (at about the rate of one person every ten seconds!) you could not have all the good which lies in being generous to starving men.

That each year the Mississippi alone carries 140 million tons of mud and pebble into the sea. We need a volcanic eruption now and then, to help build up the land again.

43

That death's approach is in no way to be regretted because when we are dead we shall not be there to regret anything.

That horrible experiences help us to appreciate pleasant ones.

That Natural Man, in contrast to modern weaklings, has a healthy disregard for pain and mutilation.

That people who are murdered really deserve their fate because they were themselves murderers in previous incarnations.

That world peace is an evil dream because war embodies the noblest characteristics of mankind: courage, self-sacrifice, standing loyal even unto the grave.

I do not say that all such arguments are worthless for defending the world's goodness. Some of them might help us to see silver linings on clouds which at first appeared entirely dark. But it is despicable to suggest that they could be enough for the task in hand. By themselves, they certainly could not show that God's reality can be reconciled with the world which we see.

Ought not God to have produced the best possible universe? Well, some have maintained that a superlatively good universe is not in fact a possibility. Perhaps the realm of what is possible contains an unending series of universes, each better than the one before. In this case we could not blame God for not creating the best, because there could be no best. "Best universe" would be an absurdity like "highest number." Surely we can object to this: that God should at least have created a universe which was, unlike ours, very obviously better than a blank.

But if "the universe" means "everything which exists," and if God is himself an infinitely good existent, then the universe would be infinitely good whether or not anything existed in it besides God. So cannot it be argued that God could serve no good purpose in creating a world more excellent than ours? *God plus a very good world* would be no better than *God alone*, just as *infinity plus ten* is a number no higher than *infinity*. And if so, then how could God have a duty to create a very good world? How could we fairly blame him for failure to create one?

In combination with this it may be urged that God cannot be accused of creating a world worse than a blank, worse than nothingness, because "being worse than nothing" is an impossibility. Here the Privation Theory of Evil comes into play. According to this theory, fairly popular among theologians, evil—even the evil of, say a state of mind dominated by agonizing pain—is just a comparative lack of goodness. It is real, but only as a shadow is like a real absence of light. The evil of being blind, for example, is simply that of lacking the good of sight, rather than of being cursed with something positively bad, something whose value is actually negative.

44

It is tempting to object that those holding the Privation Theory, though they may hate evils as a man might hate a low salary (while still thinking it better than nothing), cannot hate them properly. But this is question-begging. "Hating them properly" would have to mean "hating them in a way which would be proper, were the Privation Theory wrong." And it can look equally question-begging to say that we all do know that pain is positively bad. Agreed, men have a firm dislike of pain, but this may be because organisms which lacked it would fail in the struggle for survival. It may be Natural Selection, working as outlined by Darwin, which builds the dislike into us. But presumably dislikes built into us in this way would not be trustworthy guides to philosophically complex issues. They could not tell us whether the Privation Theory was mistaken.

A far more powerful objection suggests itself, however: Even if evil is only an absence of good, much as cold is only an absence of heat, God could be blamed for permitting it. Omnipotence could be as responsible for all the good which the world lacked, as for the good which it contained. And here it is not enough to fall back on the defence that God's own infinite value makes it morally inessential for him to create anything. For this defence lends itself to atrocious uses. Consider: "I did no wrong in killing John Smith. For God's existence has infinite value, so the sum of all existence remains infinitely good even though John Smith no longer forms part of it."

The value, even the infinite value, of one existent, cannot remove the value of others. The need for John Smith to live remains as great, whether or not God has immeasurable worth.

But perhaps Natural Selection has made us very poor judges of good and bad. May it not even be, then, that the world is perfect without our knowing it? It does seem to me that we cannot claim sure knowledge of good and evil. If, for instance, we conducted a social survey, discovering that almost everyone agreed that pleasure was good, we could not then say that the ordinary use of the words "pleasure" and "good" made the goodness of pleasure as certain as the wifelessness of bachelors. Whether ordinary people call something red is an adequate test of whether it really is red. Real goodness, however, could never be determined by any similar test, since beliefs about goodness inspire us as no sociological survey could. Yet should any inability to be certain about goodness encourage the belief that God has made our world perfect? Surely not; for if God has guaranteed our world's perfection, then there is no point in being encouraged to believe anything. There is no point in being right rather than wrong about whether the world is a good one. There is in fact no point, no added good, in thinking or doing any one thing in preference to any

45

other. Because, whatever we think or do, God has seen to it that our world is perfect. Even if we go through life torturing and cutting throats we shall not lessen its perfection.

We seem to face a dilemma: Either we admit that the world is as imperfect as men ordinarily think—in which case we seem forced to deny that God combines omnipotence with benevolence. Or else we regard it as really perfect, despite all the badness which it appears to contain—in which case we can have no reason for fighting against evils or for doing anything in particular.

The second of these alternatives is monstrous. It is wicked to preach the pointlessness of effort, the passive acceptance of whatever disasters befall our fellow men. In view of this it can seem only natural that so many philosophers have turned their backs on optimism, the theory that our world is the best possible. What may be surprising, however, is that some of them have seen fit to remain believers in God. For a deity partly wicked in his aims, or alternatively, one whose power is so limited that he can produce no world better than ours, although better worlds are possible, could be considered a demigod and not God at all. If even partly wicked, he scarcely deserves worship. If of severely limited power, he seemingly fails to tally with the dominant traditions of Judaeo-Christian thought. One very important school maintains that anyone seeing problems in the sheer existence of a finite world, or in the fact that its events obey laws which cooperate in making life possible, could find no intellectual stopping place in a divinity who was himself only a finite being, a being whose power was itself limited by laws which stood in need of explanation. The problems set by the finite can, it is said, be solved only by postulating something infinite and of infinite power.

A second school suggests that any genuine ground for the existence of a thing could stand a respectable chance of producing its existence. It may even be that God's reality is intimately associated with a principle that the ethical need for certain things to exist is strong enough to bring them into being. There is thus no question of there being any Nihilistic Factor acting to exclude good things from existence, a Factor with which God would have to struggle, perhaps with only partial success.

Whichever school you follow, one point is clear: The Problem of Evil, of reconciling God's reality with the need for efforts to improve the world, presents difficulties so massive that they threaten to reduce religion to a blind acceptance of contradictions.

Yet despair in the face of the problem may be unjustified. There are two main defences against it, defences which can look effective when acting together. The first is to suggest that the world, when taken

46

in its totality, can be pictured as immensely good without any severe testing of our credulity. The second is to point out that the need for one thing may conflict with the need for another. The need for world peace, say, is a very strong need, but it may be overruled by others which are still stronger, as for example, by the need for men to have the kind of freedom which leads to wars when misused.

In considering the first of these defences we should appreciate that those who have called our world "the best possible" have never intended to suggest that it was as good as possible in any one place or at the moment at which they spoke. By "world" they meant the sum of all things throughout space and throughout history. Now, in our galaxy alone there are about two-hundred-thousand-million sun-like stars, of which a fair proportion can be expected to have planetary systems capable of supporting life. And even inside the limits probed by modern telescopes, there are around one-hundred-thousand-million further galaxies. There is, moreover, no reason to suppose that ours is the only cosmos, if by a "cosmos" you mean a system of causally interacting things; for there can be no evidence disproving the existence of further systems which have no causal contact with ours. We could not say that, if they were there, they would be influencing us in ways in which we are not in fact being influenced. Hence the world of life may be inconceivably rich in its totality. Nor is it yet clear that life on earth cannot be followed by an afterlife of the sort to which religious men so typically look forward.

"But what is speculation about an afterlife but a foolish argument that, since the apples at the top of the barrel are rotten, there are probably ones underneath which are better? And how is the reference to billions upon billions of planetary systems of any help? How is it a defence against any theological problems raised by the shortness and unsatisfactoriness of our lives? Compare the suggestion that the poverty of the average Briton does not matter, since the British Nation, taken as a whole, still has very considerable wealth!" Well, optimists do appear open to objections on these lines, particularly when they talk as if the world's goodness were entirely obvious. But so long as they limit themselves to the humbler claim that its lack of goodness is unobvious, they may stand on firmer ground. Even if I abandon all hope of a life after earthly death, so that my life must be seen as of severely limited value, it is unclear that anything but selfishness could lead me to see this as a reason for condemning Reality as a whole.

After all, contemporaries so often argue that an afterlife is impossible because they view the cells of a man's mortal body, and of his brain in particular, as the carriers of his personality and experiences. Now, they would agree that the activity of any individual cell in a man's body or brain, when considered in isolation, has no intrinsic value. Yet they would not dream of concluding that the man's living experience could therefore have no such value. So it seems that even they accept the principle that a whole can possess a value greater than any suggested when its parts are each examined separately from the others. By setting such a principle to work, optimists can perhaps avoid the kind of strain placed on our credulity by any claim that the apples are bigger and better elsewhere in the barrel than they are just here and now. For if a barrel is sufficiently large, and if it is the amount of food in the barrel as a whole which is ultimately important, then perhaps the strictly limited food value of each individual apple is not as disastrous as might at first be thought.

We must however avoid the temptation to step from, "It does not matter very much if the individual apples are small and partially rotten," to, "It doesn't matter much or at all how small and rotten they are."

Let us move on to the second main defence. According to this, it is absolutely impossible for God to guarantee, through his creative commands, a situation in which all goods are present simultaneously, since the need for some things conflicts with the need for others. Although emphasizing how much good there may be in Reality, optimists have always given considerable time to pressing this second defence, an insistence of how little good there is in Possibility. Thus their claim that the world is the best possible is much less startling than it looks. As already hinted, the defence may be essential to any rational religion. For: (a) A diety who did not create as much good as possible would be hard hit by Abelard's question: "If he does not produce some things fit to be produced, who would not infer that he is jealous or unjust?" (b) But suppose that "creating as much good as possible" meant creating a world in which all goods were guaranteed to exist simultaneously: the kind of world, in fact, which people have in mind when they claim that Reality, despite appearances, is not just "best possible" but "utterly perfect." It would follow that no room would remain for moral effort. Instead of aiding the sick, we could equally well steal their blankets while they lay helpless. The wickedness of such action, its ability to make the universe worse, could be concluded to be only apparent. But such a conclusion is monstrous. (c) Hence if believers in God are not to claim, against tradition, that God cannot do many things which a stronger being would find possible, there is only one way of escape for them. They must insist that a world in which all goods are guaranteed to exist simultaneously is an impossibility.

This analysis seems confirmed when we read those Hegelian Idealists who claim that the world is indeed utterly perfect—such

48

writers as F.H. Bradley, J.M.E. McTaggart, A.E. Taylor and B. Bosanquet. They interpret Hegel, I believe rightly, as having taught that Reality is a timeless or eternal unity in which all evil is successfully digested by good. Any conflict between ethical needs is dismissed as mere Appearance. Now, they appreciate that this causes problems for morality and evolve four main defences against these problems. But all four turn out to be inadequate. (i) The first is that our moral struggles may bring a perfect situation closer in time. This defence cannot work because to them Time is ultimately illusory. The Ultimately Real is, they say, in some sense "already perfect." (ii) The second is that moral struggles form an essential part of the reality which is already perfect. This again cannot work, because they think that Reality's perfection is absolutely inevitable, regardless of whether you or I personally engage in such struggles. Hence you and I have no good reason to engage in them. (iii) They do advance a bad reason for engaging in them: By doing so a man obtains a bigger share in Reality's value. Plainly there is nothing moral in this. Grabbing a bigger share of a cake is an act of selfishness. (iv) In final desperation they agree that Morality is incoherent, telling us to turn to Religion instead—Religion which "knows nothing of merit or demerit," which teaches "a final identity of God and Devil," and which declares that "Heaven's design can realize itself as effectively in Catiline or Borgia as in the scrupulous." These words can be left to speak for themselves!

But is it truly open to us to suppose some things which even omnipotence could not do? Not if by "omnipotence" we mean "ability to do absolutely anything"; yet this is not a reading of "omnipotence" standard among theologians. The objections against reading it like that are all too evident. Omnipotence, so understood, could create weights too heavy for itself to raise, puzzles too hard for itself to solve. It could bring it about that someone who had existed, had never existed. It could produce spherical cubes, objects longer than themselves, married bachelors. But of course there could not possibly be, for example, anything corresponding to the phrase "bachelor who is married." The words "who is married" snatch away the description which "bachelor" tried to give, so that the phrase as a whole gives no description at all. And naturally nothing can correspond to a description when no description has been given.

More often overlooked is the fact that there may be many absolute impossibilities of a very different type. I argued earlier that the goodness of pleasure was not in the same trivial class as the wifelessness of bachelors; and similarly, it would seem, with the badness of pain. A social survey could show that pain was disliked and called bad. Yet there are many things which people have disliked and called bad, but which we might describe as good without using language contradictorily. But does this imply that a deity could make all pain good and all pleasure bad, just through his arbitrary decree? It seems not, since there appear to be many necessary facts, facts which even God would find it impossible to overthrow, which could be doubted without linguistic contradiction. Suppose we have two objects in front of us and attempt to doubt their colour similarity. It is no good anyone's telling us that both objects are red and that therefore we have a logical proof that they must be similar in colour, a proof deniable only at the cost of contradictions. For describing both with the same colour word, "red," simply begs the question of whether they are colour-similar! Nonetheless it can seem clear that the two objects are colour-similar, by virtue of how each is what it is, and necessarily must remain so for as long as neither undergoes alteration. Their colour similarity is not something which a deity could take away by arbitrary proclamation. Likewise, I suggest, with the goodness and badness of pleasures and pains, even though this goodness and this badness cannot be known in the way in which colours can. Given that a case of pleasure is what it is, and that a case of pain is what it is, it can follow necessarily that this case of pleasure is better than this case of pain, even though the necessity met with here is not one which logicians could prove by examining the meanings of words. To suppose that God, having created a case of pain and one of pleasure, could settle by his mere decree that the case of pain was the better of the two, seems to me like supposing that, having created Greenland and Elba, he could arbitrarily decree that Elba was the bigger.

Were God able to do absolutely anything, then no Problem of Evil would arise. For how could he, as a benevolent being, create a seemingly terrible world, a world filled with misery? "Simple!" the answer would come. "He can do what is logically contradictory!" Or else: "Simple, for he has only to decree that misery is the supreme good."

No one in his right mind would accept such defences of God. Correspondingly, God could not be blamed, nor his power diminished, if absolute necessities made it impossible for him to allow all goods to be realized simultaneously.

But when he believes that God has made the best world which he could make, how exactly can the optimist cash the vague suggestion that the need for some things is in conflict with the need for others?

Perhaps the move most popular among optimists is acceptance of libertarianism's version of the Free Will Defence. By the "Free Will Defence" is meant the view that freedom is a great good, and that God could not give it to men while at the same time guaranteeing that

50

they would always use it well. On this view it is up to us to ensure, by freely acting well, that the need for us to have freedom does not enter into conflict with the need for us to act well. God could not guarantee the correct use of our freedom by constant interference with our decisions and actions, because such interference would mean that we were not free at all. How bizarre to suppose that divine power could frustrate all attempts to act evilly while leaving us just as free as ever to choose good actions! For how could you choose to do *A* rather than *B* in a world in which it had swiftly become plain that *B* could never be done?

"Libertarianism" is a term used in several ways by philosophers. I shall take it to mean the doctrine that men have a freedom which is incompatible with determinism. And while "determinism," in turn, has had many uses, I shall take "determinists" to say that any world which started off exactly like ours would develop in exactly the same way, with every man in it selecting just the same path as the corresponding man in our world. Another way of expressing the position is that according to the determinist, our world, were it returned to one of its earlier states, would follow again precisely the same course, like a clock which has been rewound. The chain of causes and effects would repeat itself, precisely as before. The libertarian thinks that we have freedom of a kind which would make such a repetition extremely unlikely.

Clearly, a libertarian must set strong restrictions on the sense in which the world could be "the best possible," even when he thinks, as libertarians frequently do, that libertarian freedom is a gift from God and that its presence is for the best. By calling our world "the best possible," libertarians can only mean that it is absolutely as good a theatre as God could have provided for us, granted that he could not himself settle exactly which drama men would choose to act in it. Libertarianism insists that God could not guarantee that the actual course of events would be the best possible. The presence of libertarian freedom involves the logical absurdity of any such guarantee. At the world's beginning, it would be just conceivable that human free choices would later give rise to a best possible series of events; but in practice men would be virtually certain to choose in ways which led to wide departures from this ideal.

Now, there is much room for disagreement over whether freedom as a good is great enough to compensate for all the evils attendant upon freedom used badly. But all that believers in God need show is that they are not absurd in thinking the price worth paying. Freedom, the capacity to make our own road through the world, instead of having it made for us, can well seem life's most important feature. True, one man's having freedom can lead to another's losing life

51

altogether, as when murder is freely performed. But one feels tempted to say that in a world in which there was no freedom, there would be no lives to be lost, or at any rate no lives which were much worth having. The life of a typical man can well seem to have far more value than the "life" of any puppet whose movements were forced on him by a divine master.

Less clear, however, is whether escape from puppetry could be achieved only through the gift of libertarian freedom. For many philosophers doubt whether freedom of this kind would be specially worth having, or even whether it would be freedom at all. What could inspire such doubts? Imagine a future time when our world has pursued the kind of course which libertarians envisage and is then succeeded by a heavenly state of affairs from which those who used their freedom badly are excluded. Consider the feelings of someone whose life after earthly death involves exclusion from heaven, perhaps even imprisonment in the flames with which we are sometimes threatened. Could he not protest that he had suffered bad luck? For libertarianism's suggestion is that, were the world returned to its situation at the moment of his birth, then it would be extremely unlikely to pursue the same course as before. Souls which, on the first occasion, had taken the road towards heaven, might well this time take the path to hell, and vice versa. An earthly career could thus perhaps be likened to taking part in a gigantic lottery.

It might even be argued that someone whose choices followed a libertarian pattern would be in no way responsible for them. For the choices would not follow from the nature of the mental states leading up to them. At the moment before any decision, it would remain uncertain which form the decision would take. So might we not have to say that its taking one form rather than another was something which simply happened—that it was, in effect, no more chosen than if it had resulted from a penny's falling "tails" rather than "heads"?

What is startling here is that many libertarians look to quantum physics for support. On one widely accepted interpretation of quantum phenomena, many or all laws of nature are ultimately only statistical. That is to say, they are rather like the law which states that when you throw sixty tons of dice, you will get pretty well exactly ten tons which land as *sixes*. They do not settle all the details of how each individual atomic particle behaves. Yet, although this would no doubt ensure that worlds which started off exactly like ours would not all follow precisely the same course, it is hard to see how it could represent any gain to freedom. If our lives are to any degree governed by physical laws which are only statistical, then to just that degree, so it seems, we are at the mercy of chance and not free.

52

In short, quantum physics appears unlikely to help the libertarian —quite the reverse. He must say that freedom is *neither* being at the mercy of chance *nor* a matter of arriving at decisions through deterministic decision-making processes. In the field of what is logically possible, can there be anything fitting this double negative? Or is it like "number exactly divisible by seven which is neither below 36 nor above 41"? I have little idea of how to begin to answer this.

"But isn't the answer plain? Do we not all know in our hearts that we are not tyrannized by laws of nature in the way which determinists suppose?" Well, I shall next attempt a sketch of Compatibilism (otherwise known as Soft Determinism). This theory, very popular among modern philosophers, holds that there is no incompatibility whatsoever between *being free* and *being causally determined.* The case is viewed as on a par with that of *being a man* and *being alive.* Admittedly some ways of being causally determined are incompatible with being free, just as some ways of being alive, for example, being a porcupine, are incompatible with being a man. The person whose movements are caused by an epileptic discharge in his brain, or by how he has just been thrown over a precipice, is definitely not acting freely. But people are ordinarily not in these situations. They plan their actions, weigh alternatives carefully, are influenced by moral considerations, and by complexly competing desires. Perhaps the planning, the weighing, the being influenced, are matters of which a deterministic account could be given. Perhaps what is ultimately involved here is the operation of brains whose cells work in accordance with fixed laws of nature. But to say that this amounts to "tyranny by the laws of nature" is, says the compatibilist, an odd forgetting of what "tyranny" really means.

Many have a difficulty in coming to see that the compatibilist means precisely what he says. He is not claiming that men are free "despite the world outside them being governed by natural laws." Again, he does not say that their acts are free "despite being partially determined." Instead, he says that many acts are free and at the same time wholly determined. He contrasts determined actions, which he says are often free, with undetermined ones, which he says are probably at the mercy of chance and not free at all. One of the most influential modern papers in this field claims that they *must be* at the mercy of chance. It is entitled: "Freewill as Involving Determinism and Inconceivable without It".

Imagine that a libertarian of the year 5000 becomes involved in an argument with a computer much cleverer than himself. He claims that despite the machine's ability to pass for a human being when interviewed by telephone, it is not "really free" as humans are. "For," says he, "you are tyrannized by the laws of physics which control the transistors with which you think. You are enslaved by the electricity which flows through you, forcing those transistors to operate as they do." The computer could reply that without the electricity flowing through him he would be, not a thinking, decision-making machine, but something little better than a mass of scrap metal. How, then, could he be the hapless slave of this electricity? As well say that he was enslaved by being made up of transistors, not of pebbles! And similarly by the physical laws which this electricity and these transistors obeyed: Were the laws to change through some freak, his mental identity would be destroyed; he could no longer think or decide anything. "These laws," he could say, "are essential to my being *me*. And, seeing that their operation inside me is in this way *part of me*, why say that they stand outside me, interfering with me as a tyrant would?" Nobody protests that his walking is "restricted" or "not free" because he can walk only with his feet. Why then protest that thoughts and choices would not be free if one could think and choose only with a brain whose cells operated in accordance with natural laws?

Sure enough, determinism seems not to allow for any freedom which might, for instance, justify God's sending men into eternal flames when they had acted badly. Yet it would appear to leave room for encouraging them to act well, for example by praise and blame. For our world's being deterministic would not imply that our acts of praise and blame could have no effects. When billiard ball 1 starts to move, its movement may have determined the future movements of billiard ball 3. Does this then mean that billiard ball 2 can play no part in causing 3 to move? No, for 1 may cause 3's movement by knocking 2 against it. Events which are parts of a causal process can have results even when how that process will develop is determined from its very beginnings. Determinism, the doctrine that our actions are links in an intricate cosmic chain of causes and effects, is in flat contradiction to fatalism, the doctrine that our actions are not caused by our deliberations, are not influenced by praise and blame, and have no effects whatever.

But would not determinism's correctness make possible many things which we see to be impossible? Would it not involve the possibility of our predicting to each man exactly how he will act? Not at all. Even in the case of billiard balls, accurate predictions are none too easy to make. And a man is not as simple as a billiard ball. He can take offence at and resist our predictions. It is even quite an easy matter to produce machines which mimic this, machines which do the reverse of what you predict if you predict it *to them*. Any device which can detect the difference between the words RED and GREEN can be used to illustrate the point. "Your RED light will flash" can be made a message which causes a green light to do so instead, and vice versa.

Yes, introspection fails to reveal those brain cells which are featured so largely in the typical determinist's story about mental workings. But there is no reason to suppose that a brain which could report on its own workings would be able to report that they were carried out by millions of brain cells, or even that they occurred in a brain and not in a heart or a liver. Computers regularly report on their workings, printing out the various steps which they go through in reaching solutions to problems, without being able to say whether these workings occur in Africa or in New Zealand or to describe the transistors which are involved. They do not come equipped with vast sets of microscopes through which they could observe all the details of their activities. And neither do brains.

I shall not go further into this affair, since arguments for and against compatibilism can be found in almost any textbook introducing philosophy. What can seem fairly clear today is that no introspective reports, no laboratory experiments, no reasoning carried out in an armchair could show that libertarianism was right and compatibilism wrong. More controversial, however, is whether the compatibilist describes a kind of freedom which optimists should welcome; for the grounds most frequently given for rejecting his position are ethical grounds. It is felt (particularly by those who dislike justifying praise and blame, reward and punishment, by their effects in reducing crime and spreading happiness) that compatibilism attacks the dignity of human freedom. Now, it seems to me that the blow to our dignity would not be very serious if neither introspection nor laboratory experiment could give us any sure knowledge of it. But I may well be wrong in this, for there are many affairs which I myself think important although I view them as beyond verification. We cannot prove experimentally that pain is truly worse than pleasure (and not just more disliked), or even that "good" and "bad" are words which correspond to realities. Nor, I believe, can armchair reasoning settle these matters. They are nonetheless, important.

Developing the Free Will Defence in terms of the compatibilist's account of freedom has one decidedly odd result. Any optimist who accepts compatibilism cannot use the words "best possible" in the highly qualified sense in which a libertarian could use them. Yet if the world is "the best possible" in any stronger sense, then we may be in difficulties when we recommend moral efforts.

In fact, I suggest, the difficulties are only apparent. The oddity which confronts us here is only a variant on the paradox which compatibilists swallow cheerfully: that free moral efforts are to be recommended even if our world is one whose every event is completely determined. As already outlined, the path through this paradox is that such moral efforts can themselves be parts of, and so can have good effects inside, a fully deterministic system of causes and effects. If we could influence a deterministic stream of events from within itself, we should be in a position to influence it well or badly. Now, the situation is little changed by belief that the best of all possible worlds would be deterministic. That a deterministic world could be "the best possible" in a strong sense seems in no way disastrous to any moral struggles which took place inside it. "Best possible" would still not mean "having a perfection in which all goods are realized simultaneously, the need for one never entering into conflict with the need for another." The need to struggle morally, to use freedom well, so that other needs would be satisfied at the same time as the need for people to have freedom, would remain in all its force. Whenever people acted badly it could be said that they had wrongly allowed the good of freedom to come into conflict with other goods, so that it overruled them.

It may be protested: "If freedom and determinism are fully compatible, then how could any misuse of freedom be permitted in a best possible world? According to the compatibilist, the free man is, roughly, he whose actions are unrestrained expressions of his character. The belief that this character is itself a product of deterministic processes is not regarded an a stumbling block. So would not God, when creating a world, have created it in such a way that the deterministic unfolding of its processes led to ideally virtuous characters in all its inhabitants?" In many card tricks a cunningly prepared pack can be "developed" according to complex laws, passing through one arrangement after another, and yet manage in the end to display whatever startling pattern the conjuror has planned. So could not a divine conjuror, if able to create any world which was logically possible, make one whose parts started off so cleverly arranged, and moved in obedience to laws contrived so brilliantly, that the outcome was millions upon millions of people whose characters were entirely saintly?

It can seem that No is here an answer every bit as plausible as Yes. Granted, I can discover no plain and immediate contradiction in the world envisaged. Compare how there is no plain and immediate contradiction in a world much like ours, obeying just the physical laws which ours does, in which ordinary dice always land *six* when thrown, because of God's cunning in his initial positioning of every atomic particle. But nor do I discover a plain and immediate contradiction in a prime number lying between 1,951 and 1,973. Is it logically possible to find such a prime number? We cannot answer without a careful search among the numbers falling inside those limits. And who has seen in a vision all logically possible worlds, so as to be able to make a careful search among them?

If what really is logically possible were always clear at first glance, then logic and mathematics would be simple disciplines.

Yet suppose for the sake of argument that, thanks to God's cunning use of determinism, or perhaps owing to a supremely fortunate way in which libertarian freedom came to be used, a world much like ours came to be one in which absolutely every action was ideally virtuous. Would all distinction then have vanished between "best possible" and "utterly perfect"? It seems not. For many evils are not due to misuse of freedom. People cannot be held responsible for every drought or flood, every tidal wave or tornado, every earthquake or galactic cataclysm caused by an exploding star. They did not create cobras or cholera or even thorns. They are not always culpably clumsy when they break their necks falling downstairs. Yet this is no sufficient disproof of a benevolent God. For worlds in which "natural evils" were impossible, worlds obeying the magical principle that suffering was never to result from anything which free beings could not control, might well not be worlds containing life and freedom of any very worthwhile sort.

But why not? We could scarcely act freely if the consequences of our attempts to act were totally unpredictable, as in a world which followed no causal laws at all; but what limits can we set to what might count as a causal law? Why not have it as such a law that meals are to appear before us whenever we say "Hungry!" or that we are to know absolutely anything which we express a wish to know, or that our every caprice is to be gratified immediately, an endless succession of new caprices also entering our minds without our having any of the bother of dreaming them up? A possible reply to such questions is that the good of freedom merges with another good: that of being able to use freedom in a world which is other than utterly trivial. There would be little point in having a freedom which involved being imprisoned in a milk-and-water paradise where all that is admirable in man's use of freedom was lost.

"Trivial" and "milk-and-water" are evaluative rather than just descriptive words. And, for all I know, they may be unjustifiable here. The paradise which I should like to dismiss contemptuously might be the best of all possible worlds, since I make no claim to infallibility in ethical matters. But it can be persuasive to point out that anyone attracted by such a paradise may have a practical strategy for producing something like it. Writers have often suggested that dream-experiences either just *are*, or are determined by, the patterns of activity in brains, and that these patterns could be controlled with the help of implanted electrodes. Let an advanced computer be set to generate patterns corresponding to the experiences of a being who, blessed with an endless succession of new caprices, lives in a dreamlike "world" where these caprices are at once satisfied. Let the computer-generated patterns be fed into brains taken from babies and kept alive in bottles. Perhaps the "lives" of these brains would be of immense worth. Perhaps they would at any rate be better than the lives which men actually experience. But to think the opposite is far from silly. When a man has to face the fact that his wife or daughter is dead, then conceivably he should at least be thankful that she was once in living interaction with him, instead of being an isolated island of consciousness enjoying patterns of experience planned by some computer program.

But might it not be logically possible for there to be a world much like the one we know, a world governed by causal laws little different from those controlling ours, in which God had so cunningly arranged all the particles at the beginning of time, so cleverly chosen the precise nature of the laws which these particles would obey, that people never (or at least hardly ever) fell downstairs, or were scratched by thorns, or suffered droughts or floods or tornadoes or any equivalent evils?

Enough has already been said on how to react to such wildly speculative questions.

In practice, no doubt, the optimist will have great psychological difficulty in viewing actual events through the spectacles of his principles. Suppose he sees someone tortured. His theory does not discourage him from intervening. As discussion of the Free Will Defence should have shown, it is unfair to picture him as teaching that there is no need for moral effort. He thinks that God allows, however, perhaps even perpetually acts to sustain, the operation of those natural laws which are involved in the heating of branding irons, the application of pressure by thumbscrews, the transmission of nervous impulses from limbs which have been broken on a wheel. Does not all this make God some kind of accomplice in the torture? In answering this the Free Will Defence is put to a severe test. But others more severe are still to come. When a rotten tree falls and crushes the only person to pass that way for hours, was it not God who permitted or encouraged the tree to fall at just that instant, in accordance with the natural laws which he had established? And when, at the end of the First World War, a new variety of influenza brought death to as many millions as that war itself, did not God bear a similar responsibility for the slight change in the single large molecule which initiated the disease? And how would it have been any great loss to human freedom, or to the dignity in actually living (instead of experiencing something as "trivial" as a computer-generated dream), if God had, just for once, permitted the

58

laws of nature to break down, so as to prevent the molecular change in question?

Probably the optimist's strongest counter lies in asking: "Just where is any limit to be set to the miraculous exceptions which God is being called on to make?" A deity who could have blocked a change in a single molecule, so preventing the many million deaths of an influenza pandemic, would presumably have found no greater difficulty in saving the same lives through millions of imperceptible acts of interference with the descendants of that molecule. He could save lives individually or in thousands, day after day, through countless similarly minor acts of interference. Again, he could so meddle with the workings of our minds that even gross acts of interference with Nature's normal operations passed undetected by us. But when we contrast life with the triviality of dreamlike states, other issues may be important besides how many kinds of interference, or how many instances of it, could pass undetected.

Here, perhaps more than anywhere else, the optimist can be thought to be on very shaky ground. But I feel that his position remains defensible.

I should not myself want to defend it, however, if matters were left at this point. Let the optimist be as eloquent as he pleases about the good of actual living interaction with those we love—as distinct from the mere illusion   such interaction in any "world" of identical experiences, the wish to feel loving, and to feel loved in return, being just one among countless caprices which were automatically arrived at and equally satisfied. Let him use all his rhetoric to describe the nobility of struggling with fixed natural laws—as distinct from the triviality of mastering whatever problems a deity allowed, or intervened to prevent, or even supplied new ones where Nature's normal uncooperativeness failed to provide challenges sufficiently dramatic. Even were the optimist right in thinking various aspects of our lives very good, the price which he asks us to pay, the unsatisfactoriness and briefness of even the happiest lives, let alone all the misery in the others, can appear altogether too high. When he protests that the universe as a whole may possess immense goodness, even if its individual parts look very unsatisfactory when viewed each on its own, it can still (despite the arguments mentioned above) seem that this defence is inadequate. For there can appear to us no sufficient reason why the parts could not have been much better, without detriment to the glory of the whole. It would have been only too easy for God to have prevented that influenza pandemic, for instance, without markedly reducing the lustre of man's struggle with Nature. Nor is it clear that a much greater injection of miracles into our lives would be anything but good. A world from which death was absent, so that each individual could look forward to an eternity of varied experiences, might well be considered worth almost any cost in destroying the "elegance" and "challenge" of fixed natural laws.

Confronted with such reasoning, optimists may decide that their best refuge lies in the traditional theory that the death of a person's body never ends that person's life, since he always reappears in a heavenly realm, or else in another body on earth or on some other inhabited planet. Now, though I am much against theories of this dramatic type, I feel that they probably escape any logical contradictions. It is pointless to argue that, in the context of a railway disaster, the two categories "dead passenger" and "survivor" are universally recognized to be separate, and that therefore life after bodily death is a logical absurdity. For in this context all that is being considered is whether a person has ceased to live in association with a particular body. That a passenger is classified as dead does not preclude the logical possibility that his personal identity is manifested elsewhere, for instance in a Christian heaven.

True, there may be more serious difficulties to be overcome. For example spatio-temporal continuity, the fact that a person's history does not include any instantaneous spatial jumps (say, from America to Australia), is often viewed as essential to personal identity. How could such continuity be maintained between a person on earth and the allegedly identical person who appeared later in a heaven? Well, perhaps those who picture God as an omnipotent creator can fairly plausibly suppose, for example, that he has created immaterial souls which are not subject to normal physical restrictions; that a soul on earth can be in some important ways continuous with a soul in heaven, even if the continuity is not spatio-temporal; and that it is the soul which forms the core of a person's identity. While I like none of this, those who do like it are by no means logically blind. Just how philosophers could best treat personal identity has not yet become obvious. Even less obvious is that there could be only one reasonable way of treating it.

Speculations on the above lines, however, can still be thought insufficient to supply the kind of solution to all problems which optimists have been ever too ready to adopt: that life on earth should not be judged on its own merits, because its sole function is to provide preparation for a heavenly afterlife. On this view it matters scarcely at all if earthly life has an intrinsic negative value. Our vale of tears is to be seen as a "vale of Soul making" in which morally beautiful characters are built up through free struggle against evils. Only people with such characters, it is said, could truly appreciate companionship with God, and only through free struggles could they be built up. Even God could not create a full-fledged saint.

But why not, when God can do anything which is logically possible? If by a "saint" you mean not just someone with a morally beautiful character but someone who in fact built up this character during earthly struggles, then to create a full-fledged saint is logically preposterous. "Creating someone who has a past at the instant of his creation" is nothing like "creating someone complete with white hairs and rheumatism." Having-existed-in-the-past could not be a part of anyone's present state, as capable as any other part of having been created at this very instant! But unfortunately none of this is of any clear help to us. If having a past is not *part of* the morally beautiful character of a person appearing at heaven's gate, then how could having a past be *a logically essential element in* his having this morally beautiful character?—that is to say, in his being built in a way which would give him a strong tendency to choose good rather than evil, if ever heaven offered him the choice. Why should not such a character be given to him in just the same instantaneous fashion as impressively silvery hair, by God's creative command?

We cannot have things both ways. Either earlier states really are parts of later ones, in which case a person can be created complete with a past of an appropriate type, or else they are not.

Appeals to libertarian freedom are of no obvious assistance here. For the problem remains: Just how would a situation which exists *now*, even a situation containing libertarian freedom, be a logically necessary preparation for any situation which *will exist* later, for instance in a heaven?

Making no claim to have dismissed competing solutions in any conclusive way, let me now work towards the solution to the Problem of Evil which I consider strongest. The central difficulty is, as we have seen, this: that the briefness and unsatisfactoriness of each individual life can seem to make nonsense of any claim that our universe is the best possible. Solutions which postulate reincarnation on earth, or a heavenly afterlife, I find unpersuasive because of my scientific prejudices. And to the claim that the universe as a whole has immense goodness, despite the unsatisfactoriness of each life in it, I feel impelled to reply that what one would like to see would be a universe consisting of infinitely many existents, each one of which had immense goodness. But how could what we actually see be reconciled with this fantastic ideal? For surely one would like it to be *true now* that such a universe existed. Those who oppose this, perhaps on the grounds that it is more exciting to have a universe "like ours" in how it gets constantly better and better, can appear to be involved not just in a naive view of history, but in a logical contradiction. For how could it ever be truly "better" for the best not to exist?

As a start towards dealing with the difficulty, let me introduce what is today named "the B-theory of Time." This was vividly summed up by Einstein when he wrote, "It appears more natural to think of a four-dimensional existence, instead of, as hitherto, the evolution of a three-dimensional existence." B-theorists propose that in some acceptable sense it is *true now* that past and future events are real or are in existence. All that we need recognize is that they *do not exist now.* For "what exists now" means, or ought to mean, "what has nowness relative to me as I say this." And this corresponds only to an abstraction, a three-dimensional cross-section of a universe which really exists four-dimensionally.

Luckily there are other less potentially confusing ways of expressing what a B-theorist believes. One of them is that pastness, presentness, and futurity are strictly relational characteristics. No event is ever, no matter how temporarily, intrinsically past or present or future. At no second in historical time does it become any of these things in itself. It has pastness only in relation to other events bearing dates later than its own, presentness only in relation to those whose dates are identical, futurity only in relation to those whose dates are earlier. Compare how no castle is ever intrinsically possessed of leftness or rightness, aboveness or belowness. To the left in relation to one observer, it is also to the right in relation to another. It is above a cliff, but also below a passing eagle.

There is seemingly no way in which the B-theory can be refuted by an appeal to what we actually experience. For let us suppose that the theory is wrong and that existence is truly three-dimensional. Let us suppose, in other words, that the gift of existence is constantly being passed from one state of affairs to another, like the baton in a relay-race. There is thus no sense in which it is true now that past situations are in existence. The stuff which once formed those situations has been commandeered to form new situations instead. Very well; we shall assume all this about our world, for argument's sake. But may there not conceivably be another world, a four-dimensional world, to whose successive cross-sections a playful deity has given patterns mirroring those which existed in our world at successive instants in our pasts? In which case, might not this other world be said to contain thoughts and experiences which were very much like those existing in our world? Admittedly these thoughts and experiences would not succeed one another in exactly the way in which (for argument's sake) our own thoughts and experiences do. But could they not be, in other respects, thoughts and experiences very much like ours? If so, then many would

62

concern time's flow: the ticking of clocks, the whizz and rush of a fast descent on skis, the difficulty of remembering the distant past or of seeing into the future. So would not these thoughts and experiences include all the grounds which we have for believing in a world which exists only three-dimensionally?

A possible reply is that, because the B-theory is wrong, any "thoughts and experiences" of "people" in the four-dimensional world could only be the quasi-thoughts, the quasi-experiences, of quasi-people. But who has said, except for argument's sake, that the B-theory is wrong? And exactly what characteristics would the "imitation" thoughts and experiences necessarily lack, which our "genuine" thoughts and experiences are definitely known to have?

Were the B-theory correct, just how could its correctness be of help to optimists? The benefits to them would, I think, be two. First: What troubles us about Time is often not so much the fact that no lives extend very far in it (though this is of course important, especially in the case of a child dying when his life has scarcely begun), but is rather the fact that lives which are in the past are viewed as "completely annihilated" in some readily understandable sense. It is quite typically felt that being in the past is radically different from being distant in space, and different in a disastrous way. A young man will feel some kind of pity for those who are dead, even when the lives which they led were long and very much richer than his own. Or alternatively, if his own life is miserable, he will envy them; he will envy even those whose lives were much more filled with misery; "because for them," he will say, "it's all over." But attitudes of this type make no sense whatever if the B-theorist's picture of time is correct. Compare: "John Smith is to be envied because his sufferings are all elsewhere. They are all in France, where he lives, and not in Canada, where I suffer. In relation to me, they have in-the-distance-ness."

Any benefit which optimism derives from the B-theory may be won at a heavy cost. The optimist who finds the theory comforting, when he considers all the richly varied lives which historians record, may well find it less so when he contemplates some particularly horrible past event such as the burning of Joan of Arc. For though he could say, "Thank goodness that was soon over," he could only take this to mean that the event was of strictly limited temporal extent. It is as if he were to reflect that at least Joan's agonies were not infinitely great. Compare how a man might take comfort in how a facial rash was of limited spatial extent, not having spread to his neck as well. (But it is not here being suggested that all experiences which are in the past "are being experienced today" according to B-theorists. Thinking of his toothache of yesterday, a B-theorist may not even be able to say which tooth had hurt, nor does his theory deny facts as obvious as this. He does not say that all the pains and pleasures of his babyhood continue into his old age.)

The optimist's second reason for welcoming the B-theory is that it undermines an argument for optimism's wrongness which would otherwise threaten to be overwhelming. As previously discussed, there might seen to be a logical contradiction in the idea of a best possible world which developed historically. If God wished an ideal situation, why did he not create one, then maintain it in existence unchanged? Why should he be, so to speak, continually altering his mind about just which possible situation was the best? By viewing the universe as existing four-dimensionally, we destroy the force of such questions.

Although B-theorists deny that events throughout history "all exist today," may there not still be some acceptable way of understanding "at the same time" or "together" which would allow them to say that they exist all at the same time, or all together? Well, perhaps there may, but to discuss the point here would take too long.

The next major ingredient in my defence of optimism is a position often named "monism," although it is not the only position answering to that name. It is a position suggested by prayer to "God in whom we live and move and have our being": the position of Spinoza for whom "God" and "Nature" referred to one and the same reality. By no means do all monists, however, wish to put the word "God" to this use. What is essential to monism is not that the natural world *is* God, but rather that it has one of the features usually attributed to him, viz. that of being a single unity, a single existent. What this means is that its elements are logically incapable of existing each in isolation from the others—somewhat as the roundness or the grayness of a stone, or its size, its temperature, its weight, are not capable of independent existence, because each is only an abstraction, an aspect of the larger reality to which the others contribute.

What help could monism offer to the optimist? To begin with, it might form a basis for the principle, let us call it a Principle of Ethical Unity, to which we previously drew attention: The intrinsic value of a whole can exceed the sum of whatever intrinsic values its isolated elements would have. Acceptance of this principle is presumably essential if we are to see much value in any mental states; and if we cannot see value there, then we are unlikely to see it anywhere, since other things—television sets for instance—are usually valued only for their ability to produce mental states of certain sorts. The mental state of a man at any given point in time is usually very complicated, and so might be said to be compounded of many elements. Just what are these? Individual basic sensations of colour or of sound? Particles of pleasure? Nerve cell firings in the brain? For present purposes, the answer does not matter. The central point is that each element considered in isolation would be judged worthless by almost everyone. It is the whole formed by them, in all their complex relationships with one another, which takes on ethical significance in our eyes. As the monist may be eager to point out, it could even be that the entire program of identifying separate "parts" of a state of mind will lead to crudities if taken too seriously.

Must our Principle of Ethical Unity be given a basis in monism or in something closely approaching it? I should myself argue that it must, but my argument would be a lengthy one. Now, the more links there are in a chain of reasoning, the more it is open to doubt, so I shall not insist on the point here. Besides, so long as the Principle is accepted it may not matter very much whether monism is accepted also. For any help which monism offered might be brought by the Principle on its own, if it really could operate without the kind of support which monism might give to it. And even if it could not, we might not have to move at once to a full-blooded acceptance of the theory. We might begin hesitantly, seeing existential unity—I mean, the unity of any whole whose elements are mere abstractions incapable of separate existence—as present only in the states of mind of particular people at particular instants in time. In fact, philosophers commonly make this sort of very hesitant commitment to monistic thought, believing that immaterial souls each have a unity which could not possibly be enjoyed by a material brain, let alone by the material world as a whole.

Once, however, the first hesitant move has been made, it is tempting to become more bold. For typically people feel that no single state of mind, existing at one point in time, could have much ethical significance when taken in isolation. The value of living comes from how successive states of mind combine to form an entire life in all its rich variety. Yet how could this be so? Does not the value which Existence *has now* depend solely on what it is like *now*, and not on what existed previously or on what will exist in the future? Well, such questions lose their force if the B-theory of time is accepted and combined with monistic reasoning. For it then becomes possible to view a man's entire conscious life as forming an existentially unified whole. The elements of such a whole, the mental states existing at successive dates, would be abstractions which could only very artificially be evaluated each in isolation from the others. When this point has been reached there seems to be every excuse for pressing further. We then come to view all Nature, throughout space and throughout history, as unified in its existence.

But cannot everyday experience assure us that a full-blooded monism is nonsensical? I believe not; no more than it can assure us that the B-theory of time is wrong. Just as the B-theorist need not expect to see into the past and the future as clearly as into his neighbour's back yard, so the monist need not claim that his experiences of today give him knowledge of all his experiences in years past and to come, let alone of the experiences of all living beings throughout space and time. No monist in his senses would make the universe into some kind of large sea-side boarding house, with no private bedroom in which to take refuge from the curiosity of one's fellows. After all, to say that the colour and the weight of a stone are abstractions, unable to exist each on its own, is not to declare that anyone who has knowledge of the colour therefore has knowledge of the weight!

Though modern critics of monism often fail to appreciate such points, they were made by Plotinus seventeen centuries ago. In arguing that "there is nothing strange in the reduction of all souls to one," he insists that "the unity of soul, mine and another's, is not enough to make the two souls identical." He is not, he says, "asserting a complete negation of multiplicity." And here he uses a persuasive analogy: "Many things which happen even in one and the same body, escape the notice of the entire being." People who wear spectacles tell of the oddity of first becoming completely accustomed to them; the user finds himself searching for them when they are perched on his face.

There are, however, philosophers who attack monism on what they consider conclusive grounds of pure logic. This doctrine, they allege, cannot allow for the plain truth that the world contains many "asymmetrical" relationships. When a girl is taller than a boy, the boy must be shorter than the girl. We could not account for this, they say, were we forced to resort to some such prodigious formula as, "A monistic boy-girl unity in charactarized by diversity of size." For this would leave it quite undecided whether the boy or the girl was the taller.

Yet is this a serious problem? The colour purple might be viewed as a unity compounded from the two abstractions, reddishness and bluishness. Now, there can be asymmetrical relationships between these abstractions. For instance, the reddishness stands to the bluishness in the relation being-nearer-to-orange-than. Or, when the colour is very bluish purple, its blue element stands to its red element in the relation being-more-dominant-than.

It may be that monists, in turn, exaggerate Logic's power to establish anything here. A suggestion often made, notably by the Hegelian Idealists, is that absolutely any relationship between things points to an underlying existential unity. From this it would follow

66

that all things would have to form just one monistic whole. For no matter how insistently it was declared that there existed a cosmos truly separate from ours, this other cosmos could hardly fail to be related to ours either by similarity or by dissimilarity. Again, being-separate-from is itself a relationship.

All this can be unpersuasive. No doubt it is fairly plausible to suppose that the "separate things" of everyday life are less separate than common sense tends to assume. Redness and hardness are usually taken to be essential characteristics of, say, a ruby. Could the ruby be hard if there were no other things, such as fingernails, which would find it difficult to scratch? Could it be red if it were all alone in the universe, so that there were no light rays with which it could interact? Perhaps not. But I see in this no reason for saying that we should necessarily fall into the same existential unity as another cosmos, even were that other cosmos to separate from ours that the two in no way interacted.

The optimist who is attracted by monism may, however, find it helpful to suppose that many another cosmos is, as a matter of fact, existentially unified with ours. For in this way the monistic whole which he postulates can be increased immensely in its value. Any number of worlds, non-interacting causal systems, can be packed into it. At the same time, he can insist that logic allows any number of separately existing monistic wholes, each bearing the pattern of more than one cosmos.

In short, the "fantastic ideal" mentioned previously, the universe consisting of infinitely many existents, each one of which is immensely good, now looks less fantastic. As was seen, Experience cannot stand against it, since the monist need not claim that elements which form an existentially unified whole must be experienced as a whole. Nor do I see why Logic should oppose monism's guiding principle that a thing, when so unified that any elements which it had would be abstractions incapable of separate existence, could yet be in some way complex, so that it really could have many elements.

But why on earth believe in a situation as good as the one envisaged, even if Logic and Experience could not disprove its existence? Well, this reduces itself to the question, Why be an optimist? Even when our world strikes a man as impressively beautiful, it would prove his madness if he were simply to gaze around him and then say, "I am obviously in the best of all possible universes." For one thing, it would show an insane callousness in the presence of human and animal suffering. But the optimist does not adopt these tactics. His starting point is typically a conviction that the world could reasonably be viewed as much better than a blank, despite all the suffering in it.

Although she was burned alive; although she was perhaps a schizophrenic; although there may have been no afterlife waiting for her; still, he may say, the life of Joan of Arc was something great and glorious. Although so many lead lives of appalling poverty or remarkable dullness in the midst of wealth, still each man's first adventure of being born into space and time, into a world of animal and vegetable and air and water and stone, is far more exciting than that of visiting the moon. But how do there come to be any lives at all? Through Natural Selection, you explain? But Darwin certainly never maintained that Natural Selection was responsible for those physical laws which make life possible. His theory of evolution made no attempt to say why the world obeys such laws, or why there is any world and not sheer emptiness. There is no contradiction in being a good Darwinian and also a firm believer in God. Where contradiction may well be found is in a belief in a God who created an ethically second-rate world. Anything less good than the best possible could seem not to fit theology's bill. Let us see, therefore, whether Logic or Experience can prove that our world cannot fit it.

Are optimists involved in mere wishful thinking? Well, how could this be so, if their belief in God forces their optimism on them? You attack them on the grounds that God can allegedly do anything which is truly possible, and so should have made an immensely good universe. Well then, when they dare to defend themselves by supposing that God has indeed done many logically possible things, all compatible with our experience, you cannot reasonably cry at them that by insisting on what is logically possible they overlook Plausibility's claims. Once given the belief that God is in charge, precisely what is implausible in the suggestion, say, that Reality consists of an infinite number of monistic unities, each one carrying the pattern not just of a single cosmos, a single system of causally interacting things, but of indefinitely many? Or what is implausible is a heavenly afterlife, or in our having libertarian free will? Attacks on grounds of logic or of experience might succeed here, but confident accusations of wishful thinking will not.

Yet even granted that we found anything puzzling in such matters as the sheer existence of a world, how could belief in God help us to solve our problem? The child's question "And who created God?" can appear one of the most forceful in philosophy.

Any full-scale treatment of this issue would take us very far afield, but even something more brief may be helpful. (1) Most philosophers nowadays agree that God's existence could not be logically necessary. Logical necessity would govern only the fact that *if* there were something which fitted a particular description, for example "a Perfect

Being," *then* this something would be an existent. No such "if . . . then
. . ." could carry us beyond the realm of possibilities to an actual divine
person. (2) Admittedly some competent thinkers argue that the
description "a Necessary Being" could not be applied to something
whose existence was no more than possible. "God is a Necessary Being
who is only a possible being" is a flat contradiction. This argument fails
however, to show that "a Necessary Being" is a description applying to
something which is at least possible. And that it applies to such a
something is just what most philosophers nowadays deny. They insist
that "a Logically Necessary Being" is like "a bachelor who is a
bigamist." (3) But what if God's necessity of existence is not a logical
necessity of existence? Well, it is not clear whether there could be any
other kind of necessity of existence. This matter is still in doubt, but
that is hardly enough to make a necessity of existence into something
which is "at least possible" in any sense which would set up a Proof of
God. Nonetheless this aspect of the situation may be worth investiga-
tion. (4) One writer who has investigated it, A.C. Ewing, suggests that
it is necessary that God should exist is associated with that it is
extremely good that God should exist.

I have been looking into this. Some results, nutshelled: (a) The
existence of a good thing could helpfully be said to answer or satisfy an
ethical requirement, somewhat as the occurrence of an explosion when
nitroglycerine is heated might be said to satisfy a causal requirement.
(b) It can be attractive to suppose that ethical requirements are not just
matters of what social custom requires of us. (c) It can even be argued
that, in an absence of all living people and other existents, there would
be an ethical requirement which was unanswered: that there should
exist a good world of living people. Imagine an Annihilation Machine,
a doomsday device able to replace all existence by nothingness at the
touch of a button. Few would try to justify using this machine by
saying that once it had been used there would be nobody there to lack
anything, and that therefore no ethical needs would be unsatisfied! (d)
Merely that something is ethically required does not, of course,
logically guarantee its existence. As far as logic can prove, ethical
requirements might very well be creatively powerless. But similarly, so
far as logic is concerned, all cows might fail to be brown. Despite this,
brown cows are not impossible realities. So may there not possibly be
such realities as ethical requirements which are creatively effective? To
suppose that the ethical need for something supremely good could
manage to be sufficient to produce that thing—this can look every bit
as plausible as supposing that some things pop into existence, or have
existed always, for no reason whatever. (e) So perhaps Ewing has a
viable theory when he suggests that the reason for God's existence lies

69

in how it answers a supremely weighty ethical requirement. It seems no compliment to God when we deny this, saying that his existence is instead utterly reasonless, or that it somehow follows from the truth that he is infinite, or that anything eternal needs no explanation.

This discussion of Ewing's suggestion has been much too brief to be really convincing. The reasoning needs to be expanded at many points: for instance, by a confession that in some sense ethical needs, "simply as such," could never be creatively powerful, just as cows "simply as such" are female but never brown. But even if you are attracted by such reasoning, you may well not accept God-as-an-existing-person, the God whom Ewing pictures. For instead of saying that God-as-a-person owes his existence to the Principle that the need for a supremely good thing is sufficient to produce it, one could perhaps say that God simply was this Principle itself, a Principle bearing responsibility for the entire realm of existents. If I read them rightly, this is the picture of God which is favoured by such "new theologians" as Paul Tillich and John Robinson (known for his controversial writings when Bishop of Woolwich). They stress that their position is in fact anything but new: It stands firmly rooted in the long-established Platonic tradition of Christian theology, whose central claim is that God is not a being, but the Ground of all being.

"Yet if God is the principle that the need for a supremely good thing can produce its existence, then why isn't our universe supremely good? Why are we not in the best of all possible worlds?"—questions like that are what this paper is all about.

The best possible world which a philosopher prefers to defend will often not be that of traditional Christianity. Not everyone in a Platonic tradition is a Christian.

Admittedly, as the case of Tillich perhaps illustrates, it is extremely hard to be sure of what is to count as "inside the boundaries of Christian teaching." To the man in the street, God is a person if God is real at all; to deny such a person is to turn away from Christianity, perhaps substituting for it a belief in the kind of Life Force or Universal Purpose in which, so recent social surveys show, millions who "reject God" nonetheless firmly believe. If Tillich is correct, what has gone wrong here is that a very traditional picture of God is not passing from the theological libraries to the preacher's pulpit. But when, after joining with Tillich in denying God-as-a-person, I go on to reject an afterlife in favour of comforts drawn from the B-theory of time and from a monistic view of our cosmos, also throwing in strong doubts about libertarian freedom, then it may well be impossible to reconcile this package with the attractions of belonging to an established religious movement—though it is not easy to feel sure even of that, in the turmoil of modern theological discussion.

70

It is even less easy to feel sure—let alone to have a right to feel sure—that one's own ethical intuitions are correct. Even the claim that the world is better than a blank has no very obvious correctness. Schopenhauer is not being absurdly gloomy when he regrets that the earth did not remain, like the moon, a lifeless mass. He may simply be drawing a harsh but justifiable conclusion from the sight of all the misery of our existence, misery perhaps too quickly glossed over by Tillich's remark that "creation is the creation of life, with all its greatness and its danger." And when even this matter is uncertain, it can look odd for an optimist to make confident claims about just which possible universe would be the best, then rejecting any religion which failed to square with those claims.

One final point: Those who accept that the universe is the best of all possible are not thereby committed to liking it. An optimist can declare that he would prefer one much less good if only he personally had a greater share in its goodness; for selfishness is not logically contradictory. And in any case "selfish" is not quite the word for someone who would like a better life for his family or his friends, for the blind man whom he happens to meet, or for the dog which he sees kicked, even if it had to be at the expense of reducing the goodness of the universe. Love, or at any rate human love, may be largely incompatible with caring very much about Reality-as-a-whole. The man who curses the world's plan when he sees misery may be better than those who do not, regardless of whether optimism is correct, or even of whether he personally believes it to be correct. And if a man thinks that optimism preaches the pointlessness of helping the blind, or of trying to save dogs from kickings, then although he may be committing a philosophical howler, this in no reflection on his moral health.

Optimism is so open to misunderstanding, so prone to be taken as an excuse for complacency, that it might even be best if all philosophers taught that it was obviously wrong. But in what maneuvers would they then be involved if continuing to defend belief in God?

Bibliographical notes: The *Enneads* of Plotinus are an important source of optimistic arguments, some alarmingly poor. The most famous optimist is Leibniz, whose *Theodicy* contains a strong statement of the Free Will Defence: he thinks freedom compatible with complete determinism. Optimism's history up to its golden age, the seventeenth and eighteenth centuries, is fascinatingly outlined in A.O. Lovejoy's *The Great Chain of Being.* Among accounts of the later, very complex Hegelian doctrine that Absolute Reality is utterly perfect, A.E. Taylor's *Elements of Metaphysics* (which actually defends this doctrine) is perhaps the most readable. A.C. Ewing's *Value and Reality* is one of the most impressive of the modern works which place optimism in a wider philosophical setting. P. Tillich's *Systematic Theology* may also be found helpful, though less easy to understand. Opponents of optimism include Voltaire, whose novel *Candide* is an entertaining but often unfair satire on Leibnizian praise of the world; Hume, whose witty and influential *Dialogues Concerning Natural Religion* suggest that theologians can give no plausible account of evils, so that their Argument from Design falls flat; and Schopenhauer, whose bad-tempered *The World as Will and Idea* portrays optimists as wicked mockers of mankind's suffering.

Letters Concerning Naturalist Religion

RICHARD BOSLEY and JOHN KING-FARLOW

Majorca
Palm Sunday, 2076

My dear Ricardo,

So we shall not meet at all—I find it hard to believe! My daydreams of conducting a *Dialogue Concerning Naturalist Religion* with you and my pachydermous dogmatist of a neighbour, Phewlesse, had come to feel like the substance of real life. It seemed that childhood memories of us three in argument were but coins whose other sides were philosophically brighter prophecies of three middle aged debaters' battles in this Spanish sun. The sun has bred delusions once again. It's so long since you visited me last, Ricardo. And yet the opportunity that draws you away is one which no reasonable man could resist. We are both, I hope, still reasonable when we talk to each other, however crazed each might become after talking alone to Phewlesse. (Why must he be my neighbour, rather than you?)

Those debates of our adolescence about the nature of religion and the possibility of faith may never be renewed in convention between us, face to face. Mankind is still too fond of the wrong kind of war, I dare say—Samson's kind requires less effort than Socrates' alternative.

Although we have lost our chance of Dialogue, let us try our writing fingers (and thinking knuckles) at *Letters Concerning Naturalist Religion*. Our letters could never rival the literary genius of Hume's *Dialogues Concerning Natural Religion*. But that is not the point. For we may yet bring the ideals of *Reason* and *Religion* into better balance than Hume's characters could manage to achieve. We have not let each other know for many years how our thoughts on such matters have gradually evolved in response to painful and joyful experience and to patient reflection. (Usually that will be the only reasonable way to think such things through, to wherever one arrives.) So please sketch for me the landscape of earth under heaven as you now see it. You'll find me overjoyed to try responding in kind.

Your devoted cousin,

Jonah

73

Dear Cousin Jonah,

Thank you for your letter of a week ago. I, too, am sorry that we will not see one another in the near future. I am excited by your suggestion of serious correspondence. You ask me to set forth the principal tenets of my view so that we can discuss them in a critical way. I am happy to do that. For I would like to make clear, not only to you, but also to myself what those principles are in accord with which we can guide an inquiry regarding religion. Although both of us— particularly you—have written about religion and other related matters, let us use the personal and informal nature of writing a letter to come to basic canons regarding the adequacy and completeness of religious form. Let us see to what extent we can agree and try to understand the reasons for our disagreement, should there be such. Let us by all means make common cause against the irrational dogmatism of our mutual friend Phewlesse. Perhaps we can even do that without turning a friend into an enemy. Let us then begin!

We are accustomed to dividing our views between those that are critical and those that are constructive. It is not enough to destroy and to tear down; let us also try to construct and to build up. I will therefore follow our custom in stating two critical views and then several constructive views.

The first critical view is that Western religions sometimes *mislocate* our religious tasks: For example, they mislead us into talking about the universe rather than about human community and the lives of its members. The second critical view has not changed since we last talked together many years ago: Our Western religions have been subject to *rationalizing*. The agent of this wearing process is largely ancient Greek philosophy. It has worked against religion as the elements do against the face of a mountain, changing it into shapes and forms which the mountain was never meant to wear.

My positive views are adopted in an effort both to stand against the fault of mislocation and the process of rationalization and also to restore us to the possibility of pure religious language and experience. Towards taking our stand and making the restoration possible I lay down an elementary premise, namely that there are religious practices and acts of speech by means of which a religious community is made possible. Our first concern, then, is with the possibility of a religious community. The existence and the continuance of such a community is the most worthy object of our religious contemplation. For in its continuing lies the possibility of the continuation and development of the religious life of its members. And although I contemplate my own life as bounded both in its origins and in its ending, I contemplate my community as having an origin, to be sure, but as without end. Although I perish, universal features about me survive with the survival of the community.

I say that a proper object of religious contemplation is the origin of a community—not that of the world or of the universe. My remark leads on to making good the warning against mislocation. For we are misguided by religious writers when we are subjected to a story about the creation or the origin of the universe—misguided in two particulars. First, an inquiry into the origin of everything introduces skeptical questions more appropriate to philosophy than to sacred literature. Second, one thing makes a beginning relative to other things. For example, the mark for beginning a race is set down relative to other things which do not form a part of the racing course.

You will say that you see nothing unique in the value which I place upon the existence and the continuation of a community. You will say as much for a secular community—say for a state, a university or even for a hunting lodge. I grant that we must look further to see wherein a religious community connists: We must consider its acts and emotional life.

By "its acts" I understand "communal acts and acts of communication or of speech." Let us think in particular of ceremonial acts; for their performance goes deep into the purification and maintenance of community.

The principal kind of ceremonial act relevant to our inquiry is that of reenactment: Through our participation in a ceremonial reenactment we recover for ourselves the original paradigms, standards and ideals of the community. Renewed contact with them may have one of two objectives: the possibility of binding the community together by reenactment of its institution and the possibility of effecting its proper emotional life. The benefit of the first is solidarity and continuity without change and that of the second is to complete the experience of the religious life.

I shall bring my letter to a close by taking up the two possibilities very briefly. A ceremony of reenactment has two parts: the performance of certain communal acts and the performance of certain acts of speech. There must therefore be both ceremony and language. We have no religion in a solitary thinker sunken in private meditation. The original act now reenacted must be of life size: Its heroes and people of perfection can be better than we are but not incomparably better. For we must, by means of our ceremony, be able to recapture it in all of its essential detail. The original hero, therefore, cannot be what some refer to as a god, a demon, a witch, a ghost, or an angel. All such talk that overwhelms and diminishes us without limit should be cast away as superstitious—talk which is alien to true religion. I hope that you will agree with me when I eventually unfold to you my Principle of Perfection.

The original story in which our hero forms our community can be a story with either one of two plot-lines: The first is that our hero brought into existence our community without dividing another; the second is that he struggled from within an existing community in order to found ours. For example, Jesus and Muhammad are represented as struggling against a given community in order to lay the foundations for another. There are other stories in which someone goes to a foreign place and there begins a community without struggle against other people. Their struggle may therefore be against nature.

To conclude my remarks let us suppose that there is an original hero who brings the community into existence against the efforts of his detractors and enemies. We who succeed him join him in a ceremony in which the original struggle and victory are reenacted. We thereby commit ourselves to a renewed attempt at sustaining the community against its enemies. The ceremonial drama has three major parts: the beginning, in which our own beginning can be celebrated; the middle, in which the struggle is acted out; and the end, in which the victory and the salvation are effected. The emotional life of the participants is a cycle of three responses: a reaction of hope and fear in the midst of the struggle; the experience of victory in the form of joy and exaltation, and finally gratitude to be in the community of such-and-such an origin.

I hope my letter finds you well. A sudden scholarly complication requires me to spend the next fortnight in Cairo. Write me there, if you wish, at the Nasser-Sadat Institute.

Your cousin and fellow pilgrim,

Ricardo

Majorca
April 25, 2076

My Dear Ricardo,

It was just as well your visit had to be delayed! Your spiritual odyssey has taken you *so far* from the position you held when last we were together! I fear we now seem to be almost as unprofitably divided from each other about religion as we always were in fact from pulpit-whackers like Phewlesse. But, if I say that we *seem* to be divided beyond hope of fruitful discussion, I do so only in the hope of reintroducing yet another sly distinction between Seeming and Reality.

76

Let me try to restate certain claims that you oppose. *First*, you oppose the idea that a worthwhile form of religion is going to take the attention of each solitary pilgrim away from his religious community to form a primary concern about the whole physical universe, about its design and origin. *Second*, you oppose the claim that when our solitary pilgrim is suitably racked by questions about the cosmos, he should next focus on the concept of a Transcendent Creator, of something which causes and designs and maintains the cosmos in being.

I can at least partly agree with you. You speak of "*mislocating our religious tasks*" and of "*rationalizing*" in the ancient Greek manner. Believers in Judaism, Christianity, and Islam do not purport to say very much as religious men about physics and biochemistry, let alone about the totality of suns, planets, stars, etc., conceived as a single system under the laws of thermodynamics. Of course, God is revered as the *Creator* of every other person and of everything else. But He is primarily revered as a moving force that is intimately experienced by one's particular community. He is experienced very often by people come together on certain ceremonial occasions. His power is also felt by many groups (as groups) in times of famine, good harvests, war, rejoicing, childbirth, death with burial, and so on. Such a God is believed to be at some times pleased with a society, at other times highly displeased with its "backsliding"—when God may be experienced by the devout as a force that punishes the society.

Yes, when various Jews, Christians, and Muslims became interested in Plato and Aristotle during the Middle Ages, there was an unfortunate turning away by some religious intellectuals from the model of the small group pervaded in obedience, affection, and ceremonies with God's presence. The new paradigm gradually came to be that of the isolated, scientific protocapitalist: He seeks to think of himself as a solitary competitive organism within the immense world of astronomy, an organism which can prove to itself that some timeless, unchanging Prime Mover makes the world tick. Prayer becomes less a social rite, and more a means of somehow inducing a God who does not change to take more interest in the individual supplicant's powers of competition. Where the Scriptures of Moses, Jesus, and Muhammad generally present God as unchanging or immutable with respect to His *personal perfections*—His steadfastness in Justice, Wisdom, Healing Power—the Hellenized religions' metaphysicians came to present God as a timeless abstraction like a square root or logarithm!—all this in spite of double-talk about His being a person whose wrath could soon be altered by our prayers.

The quest for a First Mover and a Final Cause of the universe led religious philosophers to further feats of mislocation and rationalizing—to borrow your words. Plato's and Aristotle's arguments, as Kant

77

finally pointed out after centuries of confusion, do not yield a Judaeo-Christian *Creator*. They can only offer at best a sort of coeternal engineer who keeps winding up, or magnetizing into intelligible action, our eternal machine of a physical universe. Such *mislocation* is all the worse if the winding up is said to be timeless! But the rationalizing sometimes becomes even more misguided if it is the God of the Testaments, the Torah, or the Koran whose existence needs to be proved.

Consider these pairs of questions and answers: "Why does the world *exist at all*?" "Because God is the world's Efficient Cause, as a sculptor is of a statue." "Why is the world *like this* and not totally different?" "Because God's plan in His mind results in this cosmic design." As you say, Ricardo, such questions would make better *hors d'oeuvres* for a banquet of skeptical philosophy than for a supper of meditation on Sacred Scriptures. For the skeptic merely replies to these cases of "Because"-answers: "But why does God exist at all?" "But why does God's plan go this way rather than that much more comfortable way for all concerned?"

Course after course of futility can now be sumptuously served. What the Judaeo-Christian religions usually offer as relevant "Because"-answers are replies that the members of a particular human community will accept as *justifying reasons* which *makes sense* of their existing here and now. I killed your bull because he was goring your wife. I hurt your child badly because it was the only way to get all the snake's poison out of his foot. I spent my last penny of the month on wine because I wanted everyone to have a good time. What of a society which preferred bulls to wives? Or one where snake poisoning is considered a sure way to Paradise? Or one given to frowning on wine and happy celebrations? In such a society, these "Because"-replies could not be used as reasons. In healthy religious groups, a certain constellation of codes, stories and messages, often deeply metaphorical, provide a sense of purpose and point to culturally-linked human families in living together. The Christian-turned-Greek-metaphysician *mislocated the kind of God that is relevant to his tradition or his community's needs*. I do not agree with you that everything worth calling a *rationalization* is alien to all religious people's social existence. For a crucial function of the group's ceremonies, with their interwoven codes, stories, and messages, is simply to give the participants a heightened sense of point and good reason for things being the way they are. Yes, in such ceremonies an increased feeling that all is well justified can be attained so that each is at home with his neighbours and environment.

Finally, let me praise your insistence that ceremonial, religious *acts* and verbal and non-verbal *doings* are very like a conceptually necessary condition for belonging to a community of religious believers. Most Western religious leaders, as opposed to most monarchs of speculative metaphysics, have required that the individual participate ritually with others in a shared language and form of life. That was wise from a logical point of view. For usually we can only speak of solitary researchers or mystics on the periphery of a Western religion if there is a firm and well-extended central space where many perform these verbal and non-verbal acts of worship together.

No doubt there's much that we should still disagree about together in private. But unless I have, as I fear, been very obtuse and totally misread you, we do hold a few good tenets in common.

Last night I saw this inscription on the wall of a hotel where everyone speaks English: "Come soon or I shall die of boredom. Lightning hit my library last night. Every book was burned to a crisp except Rawls' *A Theory of Justice.*"

Your eager host,

Jonah

May 10

Dear Jonah,

Many thanks for your spirited letter. It is kind of you to show so much interest in the critical notions of mislocation and rationalization. You go far in making out precisely how the notions apply to our own Western traditions. You do strike a note of discord, however, when you write, "I do not agree with you that everything worth calling a rationalization is alien to all religious people's social existence. For a crucial function of the group's ceremonies, with their interwoven codes, stories, and messages, is simply to give the participants a heightened sense of point and good reason for things 'being the way they are.'" I protest, my friend! Only under some circumstances should we be led to think or believe that things are right as they are, namely, when they are right! We must allow our religious community an epistemological platform capable of coming by and sustaining the insight that there are horrible things which can never be put right. (I will defend this possibility when I return to my exposition.) Further, when you write, "Yes, in such ceremonies an increased feeling that all is well-justified can be attained so that each is at home with his neighbours and environment," you express an optimisim to which I cannot in general subscribe. The sentiment reminds me too vividly

79

of the hollow—indeed, the shallow—optimism of Ralph Waldo Emerson.

In my last letter to you I allowed for laying foundations for a religious community and for continuing and sustaining it. I further allowed that in contemplating its continuance we contemplate our own lives as beginning, continuing, but also as ending. So within a dominating line of continuance we see a personal cycle of finitude: a cycle with a beginning, a middle, and an end. How, then, does the community accommodate the natural fact of finitude within the framework of its own life which continues without limit?

In my first letter I promised to expose my Principle of Perfection. Despite the complexity of its statement I will try to state it as briefly as I can. I lay it down as a principle of perfection that there must be a bringing to completion of dominant acts, actions, and activities of a given institution. I further make a demand upon such an institution: There must be resources adequate for making evident what it is to bring a dominant task to completion, and so when it is that a moment of perfection has come. I will extend the principle to those reared, educated, or trained within the institution: It should be possible for some of those nurtured and brought to maturity within the institution to recognize a moment of completion and to be honored for reaching it; it should further be possible to have emotions appropriate to one's knowledge or belief: satisfaction and peace, for example.

You will now see what I take to be a principal religious task: to reveal to its members what a rounded life is and what the marks are by means of which we can recognize a moment of perfection.

This much I can write now: Such a recognition can come only in the middle of one's life. To be quite specific, let me construct an ideal case. I will speak of Joseph, 85 years old. How long he lives is, of course, a matter of nature—but a matter within some control of his community. All communities and institutions accommodate them-selves to nature, whether in belief and statement they concede and agree that they do or not. All men are mortal, whether or not they accept my guidance in saying so. A proper community makes it possible to lead a rounded and completed life by living 85 years. The number of years may be divided according to my principle of asking for a beginning, a middle and an end. Let us mark the beginning as running from birth to 35, the middle from 35 to 65, and the end from 65 to death. Within the middle period, it must be possible both to reach a certain completion and perfection and also to achieve knowledge and insight that one has done so. It must also be possible both to fail to bring anything significant to completion and also to achieve knowledge and insight that one has failed. Of course, to say that one has failed to meet a certain ideal is to leave open the possibility that there are many degrees of falling short of the ideal. It is therefore equally important to know how far short of perfection one has fallen.

I call an unresolved life a life in which one has not come by knowledge or insight as to how close one has come to bringing one's principal tasks to completion. It is part of a religious and philosophical endeavor to come by such knowledge and in good time.

When it is achieved, appropriate emotions range from joy and peace to disgust and dismay. In the latter case it may be that there is no redemption possible. We must accept the possibility, my friend: There may not be, in the nature of the case, any way whatsoever of putting things right. Knowledge of the wrong remains a permanent possibility of disgust, sorrow and anger.

I know very well that the Christian tradition of people like Phewlesse works against my claim: There is a reckoning beyond that of our communities; there is still time for putting all things right!

They say so because they combine what knows no combination: complete knowledge, complete power, and a perfect will. What a monstrous conception to dislodge healthy and sound principles! If only you could bring Phewlesse away from such a position! In his case there is still time for reckoning. He must come to see the applicability of the Principle of Perfection: If a life cannot be fully resolved until one sees a supernatural god or a subnatural hell, we have not sufficient knowledge and means whereby to bring this life to completion; we cannot then lead a rounded life. He must see that resolution comes, let us say, by 60.

Before I sign my letter and post it to you, I would like to contrast and compare some of what I have been saying with some things which John Donne writes in a sermon preached at St. Paul's on Easter Day, 1628. The text is: "For now we see through a glass darkly, but then face to face; now I know in part, but then I shall know even as also I am known." Donne writes as follows:

> "These two terms in our text, *nunc* and *tunc*, now and then, now in a glass, then face to face, now in part, then in perfection, these two secular terms, of which one designs the whole age of this world from the creation to the dissolution thereof, for all that is comprehended in this word *now*, and the other designs the everlastingness of the next world, for that incomprehensibleness is comprehended in the other word *then*—these two words that design two such ages are now met in one day, in this day in which we celebrate all resurrections in the root in the resurrection of our Lord and Savior Christ Jesus blest for ever."

The knowledge and the clarity of mind which Donne allows can be secured in the "next world," I say must be secured in this world and in good time—secured in this world or the words "face to face/then in perfection" are vain symbols, groundless and misleading. Further, it is not for Donne to explain what can be meant when he writes that two such ages are now met in one day, in this day, in which we celebrate. Timelessness and time do not meet. We have in Donne brilliant metaphor, metaphor which challenges us not to meet and accept paradox but to dissolve it.

How then, you will ask, are we to solve the apparent paradox? Let us first replace the notion of resurrection by that of renewal. When we reenact a ceremony of renewal, we can perform the same ceremony performed for thousands of years. For a ceremony is a universal, and therefore not a particular which takes place at only one time and place. What the original hero did can be done again, even though the entire historical event is unique and past. But by following him and proceeding according to conventions essential to our community, we can now perform a ceremony and so celebrate the action originally performed. We therefore do not join two kinds of time, as it were: We fill up our own with an activity which moves us to peace and reflection upon the past; there is a harmony of mind, soul and public activity which moves us to emotions appropriate to a belief in permanence and security.

Your contemplative cousin
and ceremonial brother,

Ricardo

May 20th

Dear Ricardo,

What a splendid force your last letter has proven, compelling me to unravel and distinguish what must be kept apart. It was as if the soul of Ivan Karamazov had been wedded to a far more piercing intellect— far more than any that Dostoyevsky could devise in his novels for his partly psychoanalytic, partly philosophical dialogues on faith and reason!

I turn first to your most bitter paragraphs. There you touch rather scathingly on cosmic optimism. You sound as vexed as I am by any unwillingness to see how profoundly believers in the God of the Bible or the Koran are challenged by all the evil and suffering in this world of an allegedly perfect Creator. (Doubtless you'd prefer to say "made ludicrous" rather than "challenged.") But I know what the worst dogmatist would reply, for what that's worth. He would say that *most sorts* of believers in the God of Abraham and Joseph should feel challenged, but not his own sort.

"For," he would add, "I am a Voluntarist, not an Intellectualist. The debased majority of believers are Intellectualists. So they say: If God, being perfect, wills one thing rather than another to happen, this must be because God looks and sees that the former happens *to be good* and the latter happens *to be evil (or at least to be worse)*. But I, being a true man of Faith, am a clear-spoken *Voluntarist*, not a fork-tongued Intellectualist. I say that whatever God *wills* to make happen or *wills* to let happen is good because, and only because, almighty God wills this. Being almighty, He alone can make anything good or better by virtue of His omnipotent will. In the case of *infinite* might, might does make right. And, since everything that happens is caused or allowed to happen by God's so willing, Ricardo is absurd to complain of irremediable evil in the world."

Like you, Ricardo, I am "Intellectualist" enough to consider what is evil to be wrong, however mighty and dyspeptic the ogre who calls it wrong. But I remain a cosmic optimist.

For your part, you speak of the Judaeo-Christian tradition as combining what "knows no combination: complete knowledge, complete power, and a perfect will." You call this a "monstrous conception," though you don't say whether it's monstrous *just* to combine belief in these three, or monstrous to combine belief in these three with recognition of all the real evil in the world—or both. (Is Mary Baker Eddy just as monstrous in her Christian Science that asserts "the awful unreality of Evil"?) Your specifying which of these combinations you mean to despise might spare you many a theologian's spasms of indignation. And your consenting to separate your attack on Intellectualists from your protests against Voluntarists might enlighten all who would eventually be concerned—if I follow the drift of what you've written. Perhaps *you* could draw some new distinctions of your own?

As you do, I prefer a dogmatist like Phewlesse to come by some insight rather than a mere thrashing. Do I think this possible? Of course, but I do not expect a glimpse of wisdom in debate to alter such a dogmatist during one long afternoon of dialogue. Healers must let their medicine spread slowly through the great systems of his clogged veins before all those boils and carbuncles of inflamed self-importance can be finally purged away. (Phewlesses are among almost everyone's neighbours, it often seems.)

Now for your beginning remarks. Here I do, as I began this letter by granting, seem to be forced by you to draw some distinctions. Let me say of certain religious forms of life that they are purported to offer the *justification* of all that has been happening to a person and his community. Let me say by contrast of certain other groups' less central, more "philosophical" kinds of religion that they are only to be construed as offering *inspiration* and *consolation* to those who are truly faithful. The polytheist religion of societies described by Homer might be looked at in such a way: Life for all true servants of Zeus and the lesser gods is essentially tragic. Homer's Achilles tells us he would rather return to the earth as a serf worked to the bone by harsh farmers than remain in the underworld of Hades even as king of the dead. Men are born to flourish briefly in their flesh, only to depart to a sad, insubstantial form of "eternal life" as smokelike shadows below. Yet a person in middle age, as you prescribe, can find consolation within his or her own social view in having *excelled* at fighting, or bearing princely sons, or building ships, or weaving tapestries, or taming horses, or remaining loyal in temptation. The consolation is that one has indeed excelled without provoking gods or man by such primary sins as unbridled *pride* (*hubris*), *incest*, or *taking blood impurely*. Temporary excellence has been transformed into the eternal excellence or virtue of being a *wise* contributor to the group and its gods' demands. The achievements and wisdom offer inspiration to all one's family and peers, and even to one's (later) lonely ghost. Not so different, if I grasp some early Old Testament writers properly, is the consolation once found in certain Middle Eastern forms of *henotheism*, of communal faith in a community's one god who protects it against all other gods and nations. The followers of the tribal deity may be bound for extinction or at best a sad form of continued existence in some Semitic Hades called Sheol or whatever. Yet they can excel in specific tribal ways, not very different from the ways of Homer's most "heroic" men and women. They, too, can eschew blasphemous pride and the like, so as to reach wisdom with its consolations in middle age. They, too, can be an inspiration to their neighbours and descendants. Perhaps some of the more naturalistic religions of the Far East are not so different.

Again, to give your suggestions full credit, consider the life of an "inferior" like a slave or a concubine in such societies. The institutions make clear that, in doing certain tasks well and in avoiding other paths, such an "inferior" member can excel as a good slave or concubine, (to complement the excelling of the best aristocrats). They too, in a more limited way, but perhaps more easily, can reach the consolation of wisdom, can inspire others to excel in the nation's varied modes of virtue. Thus, for quite a spectrum of social agents, these more philosophical religions of consolation provide criteria of excellence, of due humility, of recognizable virtue and wisdom. Usually the training and attitudinal formation of children in the group will make the types of criterial realisation and accompanying emotional satisfaction that you speak of readily attained. And, as you also

84

suggest, Ricardo, the variety both of social criteria and of human responses will ensure, for as long as the society lasts, a dividing of the consoled from the self-frustrated.

"Why then are we at odds at all?" you may slyly ask. Because you are essentially a naturalist philosopher, while I am a philosopher who follows a religion committed to a Transcendent Creator and personal immortality. Because I must sadly shake my head at such restricted forms of religion which offer only consolation and inspiration, rather than provide each person with a justifying explanation. But what I take to be central forms of religion must seem to you to offer an absurdity— proclaiming justification (in the context of eternity) for all evil and suffering here and now. To me your favoured forms of religion seem nobly but unduly incomplete. The crucial function of a religion, as I paradigmatically use the term, is rejected in favour of what is largely or wholly a naturalist philosophy. What I call *central* or *paradigmatic* forms of religious life are those I consider to offer the best kinds of options.

But against a Phewlesse in some of his dogmatic trumpetings, I must still back you with regard to a crucial part of this matter of incompleteness. A serene Jesuit once told me of a colleague who kept outwardly cheerful, yet remained inwardly depressed from adolescence through old age. The serene Jesuit took the other for a saintly man. All saints of a human religion could hardly be like that! If all saintly men of my religious persuasion led gloomy lives devoid of joy and content- ment, but for grey moments of bloodless satisfaction in doing their duty, I would not think it odd for you to ridicule me. As you would probably add, a sane religion for men cannot put off happiness in recognition of achievements until death brings some Beatific Vision. I agree that there must be a *Comforter* of some sort or other. There must be some force whose ministrations mesh with most believers' socially guided reflexions on their inward and outward achievements, on their progress in wisdom and the like, long before senility offers them the joys of increasing anesthesia.

Where you and I seem to disagree most clearly is where the Alyosha and the Ivan of Dostoyevsky's *Brothers Karamazov* some- times most clearly disagree. (Tolstoy seems to love and respect both characters equally.) For Ivan the torture and murder of an innocent child must remain beyond all possibility of atonement. Ivan rails against the view that such a black little piece of reality can ever be redeemed by slipping any huge white piece into a vast spread of cosmic harmony. You write: "We must allow our religious community an epistemological platform capable of coming by and sustaining the insight that there are horrible things which can never be put right." I say that a good God must allow an honest man in a world like ours the epistemic chance of honestly, *virtuously* concluding that, because such horrors exist, no good God can exist. This I take to be something like Alyosha's own view in his soundest and most sympathetic moments of reflexion on Ivan's arguments for "giving God back His ticket." And I take this to be a question for disagreement between equally intelligent and honourable philosophers: Can all the terrible evils we encounter in this world ever be made up for in this world, or in a Heaven, or in a series of reincarnations? The person who replies yes has a chance of becoming a paradigmatically religious saint. The person who replies no has a chance of becoming a paradigmatically noble naturalist.

Yours ever,

Jonah

June 1st

Dear Jonah,

Many thanks for your lovely letter. I have felt somewhat ill the last week; your letter I found cheering, despite deepening disagreement between us. We have both insisted clearly that friends can disagree over profound things and maintain not only their mutual affection but also their mutual respect. You will not think me disrespectful if I touch upon a difference between us which perhaps goes to the heart of our disagreement.

You write of a proclaimed justification for all evil and suffering here and now. You continue, "To me your favoured forms of religion seem nobly but unduly incomplete. The crucial function of a religion ... is rejected in favour of what is largely or wholly a naturalist philosophy." You would further see religion providing each person with a justifying explanation.

My dear Jonah, I would not frustrate you for all the world in your desire for an explanation! In my last letter, I meant to plead for the possibility of an epistemological platform capable of coming by and sustaining the insight that horrible things can and do happen. If I can give you further satisfaction about my position, I will add this: We can bring our framework to bear in giving an explanation both as to why and as to how such things do happen. But as for *justifying them*! That we may not be able to do. I would complain further: You are unwilling to allow the possibility that the limits of explanation and of intelligibility are much wider than those of justification and exoneration. What would you exonerate and justify when awful and unfortunate things

86

happen? I urge you to reconsider your position in light of another glance at mine: We live in three worlds, one built upon and having the support of another. In the world of nature we can breathe, walk, and use our limbs; in the social world we lay down the forms of society and follow them; and in the world of communication we speak, write, and draw. The possibility of continuing and completing acts of the social world depends upon that of continuing and completing acts of the natural world. Without a natural world our social world would vanish; without a social world our world of communication would smack of insanity. Now let me return to the issue which divides us: When something goes wrong in a social or communicative act because of some abnormality in the natural world, we are not provided either justification or solace from nature. We are rather called upon to *adjust* and to *accommodate* ourselves. You, and others who speak of a transcendent creator, allow the notions of salvation and a justifying explanation to usurp a place reserved in truth for the notions of adjustment and accommodation. We deceive ourselves, my friend, taking up any other notions as serious instruments for understanding our place in the world of nature.

In my last letter to you I considered the relation between a personal cycle of finitude and the continuing life of our community. It is important for us to understand how, in our communal and communicative accommodation to the things and events of nature, we bring an enduring framework to bear on the finitude of a person's life. In my earlier letter I considered such a relation in light of our principle that we lead our religious lives subordinate to continuing that of the community. It is also in light of that principle that we inquire how an individual life can be brought to perfection while continuing an infinite life.

I hoped to continue that inquiry by speaking of the beginning, the middle and the end of a person's life. I ventured to set down a number of years in order to provide some guidance. I then suggested that at the close of one's middle period those acts, actions, and activities should reach the completion with which one had identified one's life; insight into that completion is necessary to perfect one's life.

I also spoke of a cycle of emotions which one has in response to one's participation in the community. I would now say that we will not have finished our consideration of the religious life until we consider the emotions of reverence, security, fear, and humiliation. You remember that I argued that there are emotions appropriate to the recognition that one has completed the middle of one's life—to a recognition of a successful turning, peace and satisfaction; to knowledge of an unsuccessful turning, sorrow and dissatisfaction. I did not then consider emotions renewed throughout the middle period of the religious life. I take that consideration up now.

I divide my inquiry with reference to a division between a mature person secure in his work and a young person in training. In the latter case we allow that urging and discipline may reach limits in threats and punishments. The emotion appropriate to a threat is fear, to being punished, humiliation. but just as threats and punishments are inferior functions of the community, so the emotions of fear and humiliation are inferior emotions in the life of the soul. Above intimidation and subjection, therefore, stands a display of the power of the community; since emotions appropriate to its recognition are reverence and security, the emotions of reverence and security are in general superior to those of fear and humiliation. That religion is therefore inferior in which the supreme exhibition of power and control is meant to move us to terror and trembling rather than to awe and reverence.

To maintain the life of our community, it may well be necessary to threaten and to punish. In sinning against the community one opens oneself up to threat, chastisement, and punishment. I say that such action is appropriate to the knowledge of sin. For just as it is appropriate to meet error and mistakes first by accusation and then by putting the person who errs in the right, so is it appropriate to meet sin by accusation and punishment and finally by correction. In the extreme case, there is accusation and punishment without correction. When it is held that someone no longer deserves to share communal life, he is either exiled or executed. So is our community purged and preserved.

Our best hopes, of course, are extended for the knowledge and recognition which lead to reverence and security. There may be such knowledge on those occasions when the religious community is focused in ceremony and shown in its fullness. At such a time we recover its institution and recognize the maintenance and the security both of it and of ourselves. Our recognition is then perfect when supported by the emotion of reverence. Thus sustained and renewed, we return to our ordinary life.

I do hope that you are well. I will close by relating a dream which I had last night. I suspect it was inspired by my considering yesterday how to answer your last letter.

When I first began to set down my thoughts in my journal (thoughts which I have now revealed to you), the reaction which I had to them in my dreams was profound and moving: A group of us were making a long voyage through mountainous terrain. We came upon a small chapel. I looked first inside and then outside, noticing that the statuary of Christ had been moved from the inside to the outside. As if with renewed appeal the inside became inviting and wholesome, offering a place for a new unity of our group. We eventually walked on and came upon a large assembly of people. We joined the assembly and humbled ourselves in an appropriate way, participating with others whose bodies were given over to a strange and satisfying ceremony.

Wait!! There is a final issue which it is necessary to take up, namely what the relation is between a religious community and the state. Should a state tolerate different religious communities? I shall try to answer the questions in a satisfactory manner by proceeding from the following premise: There are religious communities of the sort described in our letters which deserve the protection of a state. When some of the highest forms of the state are identical with those of the religious community, the state should not also be under obligation to support conflicting religious communities. Further, for the sake of the peace and the uniformity of the religious practices of the state, I argue that there should be only one religious community built up with the support of a given state.

We see again in our time, my good cousin, the folly of harboring two souls in the same breast. One is necessary, to be sure, but also enough. Let us suppose, then, that we have a state and a religious community in a secluded valley somewhere in the Rockies. So you pretend to be the Minister of State and let me be the High Priest. To our walls there comes a zealous missionary carrying the Bible and the message of some Christian sect that would spread itself about the world without state support or the support of a broadly-based community upon the wings of personal conviction and the dictates of a whispering conscience. He has come to convert our people. I reply, "My good man, to come to convert is to presume to change our religious community; to change our religious community is to change forms of the state. You are in no position to do that; you have no authority." I would then leave it to the Minister of State to return him to his path beyond our walls. We may quote to him from Donne's sermon, quoted in an earlier letter:

> If a wall stand single, not joined to any other wall, he that makes a door through the wall and passes through that door for all this is without still. One wall makes not a house; one opinion makes not catholic doctrine; one man makes not a church. Therefore, as we must be there, so there we must use the means, and the means in the church are the ordinances and institutions of the church.

Your everlasting friend and critic,

Ricardo

Ricardo, implacable Ricardo,

Your letter of June 1st brings us to several partings of our ways. It is as if two men had long thought they were brothers and then found they were orphans adopted from entirely different parents. Or better still: It is almost as if two old friends had come by some strange test to discover that they were beings of two quite distinct species. They remain friends. They can clasp hands warmly, but across a gulf of surds. Of course, as you say, there are many varieties of explanation and intelligibility beside the kinds supplied by a justifying, all-consoling answer. I hold that the religions and ideologies which offer such an answer correspond to what reflection, as well as basic human intuitions and feelings, reveals as a human need. I mean a need which may and should be fulfilled. What you hold is that sober reflection, armed with an understanding of man's trustworthy intuitions and satisfiable yearnings, reveals that the desire to justify human history in terms of a Supreme Good (a Muslim's Heaven, a Buddhist's Nirvana, a Marxist's millennium) is a useless passion. And, of course, you could be right!

But even if you are right, or if I am right, but not both of us, that disjunction is relatively *boring*. What is so striking here is that something which appears to each of us as sure as anything can be sure, which usually seems most ludicrous to question or debate, is not the same. *The opposition is perfect.* We share so many linguistic, cultural and moral intuitions, you and I, Ricardo. Otherwise we could not really be *talking* to each other, as you say, from points on a common social platform. Our earnest and teasing syllables would all be mere *flatus vocis*, which is unlikely. And yet *here* our linguistic, cultural and moral intuitions stand utterly apart. To repeat an analogy from an earlier letter: Dostoyevsky's Ivan Karamazov finds it intuitively plain that no amount of future good could redeem a child's suffering and—to use your word—*exonerate* a Supreme Being that let the child be hurt. His brother and dearest friend, Alyosha, finds no such certainty. You find it intuitively plain that there is no rational response for the sufferer and those who learn of the evil but to adjust and accommodate themselves to Nature as she is—presumably while struggling in family courts, medical laboratories, peace conferences, and the like to reduce the amount of future suffering by natural methods. And such a set of responses as those you recommend will surely be more reasonable than that morbid Ivan's obsession with evil.

Suppose it is asked: *Which of our views is more in keeping with Reason than the other?* This way of requesting a judgment upon us from some philosophical Solomon is typical of human tendencies, but quite misleading. As we were taught at school, it was only four hundred years ago that John Locke cautioned those who argued about Free Will and whether the Will could be free. Locke cautioned them about the tricks of language. He suggested that they lay aside such an abstract word as "Will" with a capital "W." He urged them to ask instead whether a concrete individual like a man, a person, is free and in what sense or senses is he "free."

In so many cases a belief is *reasonable* not because of its content or even its truth or falsity. We say that belief is reasonable in so many cases because the believer holds it in what is a reasonable *manner* for him to hold it. Now I say that *your* belief about religion is reasonable, though it startles me that your belief looks so absurdly different from mine. For I know that you have lived the kind of life in which your fundamentally Naturalist belief is embedded. You, Ricardo, have long been intimately exposed to people who believe in a traditional sort of God, but a great deal of experience and reflexion has led you to be a Naturalist. You are still willing to *discuss* the subject and to *clarify* your *reasons* for being a Naturalist. You recognize that you are *fallible* like any other philosopher. You completely reject the strategy of trying to *force* your Naturalism on those who disagree. You tolerate the tolerant, though you make no bones about your belief that even tolerant believers have made an unfortunate error. In a crucial sense of "reasonable," there are Naturalists and believers who are reasonable, while there are those like Phewlesse who would be unreasonable whether they stood on your side or on mine. So despite the very awkward gulf between them, some Naturalists and some who worship a transcendent God can still remain on philosophical speaking terms, embarrassed as they often are by their own supporters.

Yet suppose that we have a mutual friend whom we each admire as a reasonable, mature, widely experienced seeker of wisdom. He tells us that experience and reflexion leave him torn between your view and mine, though he has studied the many arguments for each over many years. He comments that he encounters what you have stressed: the human need to feel both reverence and security. (I couldn't agree more that our hunger to feel these arises from one of our primary human needs.) "But in which direction," he asks, "should I turn to satisfy these needs?" I suspect you are going to tell him that it's not just a question of whether belief in a transcendent God is plausible. You mean to tell him that the belief that God made the world makes no sense to anyone outside some Biblical circle; that it can't be understood by someone without a share already in a religious form of life. Ricardo, I can *hear* you shouting: "I believe it will be rainy tomorrow. I believe that I'll catch a cold. But I don't *believe* or *disbelieve* that the sun will rise tomorrow, or that my body will be made of flesh like everyone else's

91

tomorrow! The whole idea that one can stand outside any definite culture and choose between believing and not believing in a transcendent God is madness! We do not believe or doubt or argue about what underlies all our other beliefs! We can't be said to play chess on behalf of the rules or in opposition to them!"

But if someone asks me how he can decide between your Naturalism and my Faith, I say "*Gamble!*" I say, "Weigh all your experiences and reflexions and intuitions. Weigh them just as Ricardo did, slowly, almost involuntarily. For once Ricardo moved away from the supernatural beliefs of his community. He moved to sharing joyfully in their social rites, in their ceremonial aura of reverence and security, without any longer sharing their inward faith in the supernatural trappings."

Perhaps our mutual friend refuses to *gamble* on the direction to which his intuitions, experiences and reflexions begin to point. Of course, if they have not begun to point anywhere, the gamble could become a crime against all honesty. But if all these begin to point with persistence, although they offer no mechanical proof, let him realize that *this* kind of gambling is only a good variety of sound practical inference. Perhaps he is something of a pedant, an intellectual pederast with an insatiable appetite for juvenile figures on the blackboard. Well, let us set aside the chicken scratches of mathematical logicians. Just chalk up these two crude paths of reasoning on the board.

Argument A

Premise 1 My experience and that of many I admire suggest to my head and heart that trust in a transcendent God or in any Justifying Explanation of human history is silly and confused.

Premise 2 It will hurt me at first to live without trust in such traditions, but it is ultimately more rewarding to respect oneself as honest.

Premise 3 Some of those I admire have quite different intuitions and will be hurt by my new turning, but if they are honest people they would ultimately prefer me to be honest.

Argument B

Premise 1 My experiences and those of many people I admire suggest to both my head and heart that there must be a Justifying Explanation of human history and of all the universe.

Premise 2 The existence of a perfect, person-like Creator seems to me (after much puzzled reflection on experience and intuition) to be a good Justifying Explanation.

Premise 3 Belief in such a Creator seems, after my hearing many views, far more plausible to me by now than does any other religious or philosophical view purported to offer a Justifying Explanation.

Premise 4 The need for feeling security and reverence that such godly folk experience is a real need, but one satisfiable by a Naturalism that teaches love of community and culture and the ritual customs of generations.

Premise 4 I may, of course, be wrong, but in making such a commitment I seem to have the best chance of living in harmony with what William James called "the ultimate things" in speaking for the reasonableness of *some* people's making this commit-ment.

Premise 5 My living as a toler-ant believer threatens the free-dom of no one else.

Conclusion I am justified in "gambling," in committing my-self to a Naturalist's view of the world—and in explaining it to others who will listen *freely* and *gladly* to me.

Conclusion: I am justified in "gambling," in committing my-self to a Biblical view of the world and in explaining it to others who will listen *freely* and *gladly* to me.

When such chains of reasoning are scribbled down by and for those who have never tasted deep peace and puzzlement, or deep anguish and awe, they are just that, *scribblings*. Such scribblings have no intelligible place to rest or move about in any thought of any profit. But just let a person live and grow through the gathering cluster of clues and wounds that are expressed, if only quite grossly, by the scribbling of either chain! When it comes to these matters in the premises that divide us, Ricardo, and when it comes to the *manner* of slowly drawing one of the opposed conclusions that reunites us as reasonable beings, we each have reasoned our way through to feeling security and reverence as adults. We are each growing mature by middle age.

Thank God, you are not *absurd* like those humanizers of old creeds who deny all possibility of our comprehending arguments between those in different, exclusive "sacred circles" of belief. You do not try and so we can remain friends—to make those who disagree about religion believe that barriers of total unintelligibility separate them forever. How reminiscent such humanizing is (in a Paul Tillich or a D.Z. Phillips) of the religious fanatic's "Believe first, I insist—then you'll understand!" Human forms of Life are not like windowless Monads. Each human being's mind is strangely like most foreigner's minds five thousand year's ago.

Enough of this! Do send me one last letter to make clear what must stay unsettled between us. Then we can at least fashion a few bits and pieces together for a common shield: The wind and spittle of the doctrinaire world, that great belcher of dogmas, will soon be flying at our skins. Strangely enough, I can now look forward to this bombardment of bullying ideological burps—at least if you face it with me.

Your devoted friend,

Jonah

June 24th

Dear Jonah,

Tomorrow I join a caravan crossing the Sahara; we must therefore bring our series of letters to a conclusion. I have now reread our letters, casting a final glance over issues which we have discussed. Despite our disagreement I have observed great respect for reasonable differences of positions. I have tried to account for a framework in terms of which we can understand a broad genus of religious community—a genus containing many species. My account avoids the narrowness of some contemporary discussions which would cut off religious language and experience from scientific or philosophical language and experience. At the highest and most important level of religion and science I believe I can give the same account of the religious and the scientific community, emphasizing in both cases a triad of concepts, namely creation, obedience and recovery of a position adequate to that of those who did the creating and who do the training of those who would follow.

I must have confided in you that when I first went to college, I observed to a friend—doubtless somewhat pretentiously, but basically sincerely—that it was my task to reconcile religion and science. I would not now say that I have done any such thing; I have given an account of religious acts and achievements and an account of scientific acts and achievements which share the same basic concepts.

You will say that although the genus of which I spoke is broad enough to give the atheistic scientist and the naturalistic philosopher some comfort, it is too narrow for you and the views which you have stated in your letters. Let me review our disagreement.

I argued that a worthy object of our religious contemplation is its continuation without end. Even so we must work for its survival; its survival cannot be guaranteed. You, however, hold that each person survives—simply because of the nature of things.

In accounting for the forms of a community, I drew attention to

94

those ceremonies in which struggles of a hero are reenacted. I argued that certain ceremonial feats be of a size and a magnitude appropriate to us. For in such things we take heart and persevere in maintaining and developing our community. You, I suspect, hold to the possibility of miracles and allow us a response of being overawed. I would have us admire and show respect and reverence; you would have us worship, as if to worship a giant who, out of whim, may overwhelm and destroy us. Is this disagreement reasonable? Again, I say it is. For I understand the elevation of our deepest fears (as well as our deepest aspirations) to a status of supreme principle.

Although I can make peace with the idea that your views are reasonable, I cannot still a certain amount of sorrow—sorrow in response to the belief that by holding such beliefs you allow yourself to be misguided. I nevertheless allow that even by my canons you may more nearly bring your life to perfection and completion than I. For you have found your religious community; I am set upon a long journey still in pursuit of mine.

Yours,

Ricardo

Religious Experience and Aesthetic Experience

F.E. SPARSHOTT

Despite aesthetes on the one hand and iconoclasts on the other, art and religion persist in coming together in many ways; and analogous topics in aesthetics and the philosophy of religion often illuminate each other. This paper exploits that mutual illumination. It has to do neither with art and religion nor with beauty and God, but with what happens to the concept of experience when experience is qualified as aesthetic or religious, and how the things that happen are like and unlike each other.

The paper is in three parts. The first mentions some things ordinary people and philosophers mean by "experience" and asks what would happen if the phrases "aesthetic experience" and "religious experience" were used in these senses. The second part considers some of the things those phrases actually are used to mean, and asks whether the phenomena they pick out afford analogues for each other. The third part considers some of the general implications of the use of these phrases and ends with some brief remarks on what religious and aesthetic experience, in a suitably broad and vague sense of those expressions, have in common and what separates them. The first part of the paper thus demonstrates the impropriety of the last, and the last shows up the futility of the first. But wisdom is justified of all her children.

I

We habitually contrast the songs, or voice, of experience with the songs or voice of innocence. The experience thus opposed to innocence is worldly knowledge: Specifically, it is knowing how far things as they are fall short of things as they might be. To speak thus is to assume that the young expect the best until they get the worst, experience teaching that promises are seldom keepable and ideals seldom realizable, and that those which could be kept and realized seldom are. The contrast seems one-sided: Expectations of the worse are falsified as often as hopes for the best; threats prove empty as often as promises. But on reflection it makes sense. A planner must plan the best whether he expects it or not. What experience contributes is the knowledge of how little of one's plans one can expect to accomplish.

Do we habitually contrast religious experience and aesthetic experience with corresponding states of innocence? We do not. The loss is ours. The concepts are applicable. Young music critics often write in a state one would like to call aesthetic innocence, unaware of how little can be expected from performers and audiences; young artists and their friends as often take the manifesto for the deed. What they lack is experience, presumably aesthetic experience.

So too with innocence and experience in religious matters, as in Richard Garnett's story "The Dumb Oracle": The religious innocent expects each member of the communion of saints to be a saint; experience teaches us (as C.S. Lewis used to emphasize) that our unsatisfactory fellow-worshippers are as good as we are entitled to expect. Similarly, the innocent in the grip of the sense of sin will proclaim that he is the chief of sinners. Experience would have taught him that the competition is stiffer than that. But now we feel uneasy: Surely religious innocence is to be treasured. Has not truth been ordained out of the mouths of babes? Unworldliness has its place in religious life, and to renounce the world is surely to reject experience.

Not only in the context of religion, but in every context, the values assigned to innocence and experience are ambiguous from the start. We would not wish to recover the lost innocence we pine for: It was precious, but to prolong it risks preciosity. Experience, on the other hand, travelling the lugubrious road from the pleasure principle to the reality principle, may be blinded by excess of enlightenment: It is absurd to wish to be deceived, since things are what they are and their consequences will be what they will be, but there is something pathetic about a man who is never taken in even by himself. Innocence and experience alike are distressing unless tempered by each other. Nor is there any exact judicious blending that would avoid all offence, for no one can contemplate a perfectly wise man without sometimes wishing that he would drink hemlock. This is the unsuspected paradox of the Delphic inscription: "Know thyself" meant "Know that thou art mortal, and no god"; but perhaps only a god could really know that.

We have dwelt too long on this theme. In these terms there is no such thing as a distinctively religious or aesthetic experience, but only experience in general as manifested in a specific domain. We must pass on to a different use of the term.

A person is said to have experience if he is not a novice but has done something relevant before. Someone with managerial experience has done some managing; someone with secretarial experience has done secretarial work. Analogously, a person with religious experience would be one who had done appropriate things, such as joining a religious order, and a person with aesthetic experience might have subscribed to a series of concerts or managed a festival of the arts. But of course the phrases "religious experience" and "aesthetic experience" are not used in that way either. Again, the loss may be ours. That one becomes a certain kind of person by performing the appropriate actions is evident in matters of technical competence and has long been believed in morals. Perhaps art and religion too are things one has to work at; but, if so, our ordinary use of the word "experience" in connection with them does not reflect the fact.

In another common set of phrases, "experience" is used to distinguish between first-hand and second-hand knowledge. One says that "in my experience" such and such is found to be the case, or, more generally, that "experience teaches" that it is so. What is implied is that theory, in the latter case, and common report, in the former case, create a certain presumption; but it is found, or one has found, that matters turn out different from what was presumed. As theory is opposed to practice, expectation is contrasted with experience. On this analogy, we might expect to find religious experience contrasted with theology and with priestly lore, and aesthetic experience contrasted with aesthetic doctrine and critical consensus, the implication being that here as elsewhere things seldom turn out as one had supposed. Experience is the touchstone. And indeed references to aesthetic and religious experience do carry such an implication, with the difference being that the experience is contrasted less often with a theoretical expectation it belies than with after-the-fact interpretation felt to falsify its import. However, in the common contexts, the main point of using the word "experience" is to point out the contrast with theory or expectation, whereas with the phrases "aesthetic experience" and "religious experience" the contrast usually remains implicit. It would sound odd to say that aesthetic theory suggests that "one should tire of Mozart more quickly than of Richard Strauss, but aesthetic experience showed that the reverse was true"; the meaning would be plain, but the use of words would be strange.

The purport of our talk about experience, as we have seen, is that it can be contrasted in various ways. That is not true of the way we talk about experiences. If I say of something that happened to me that "It was quite an experience," I mean that it impressed me deeply. If I qualify and say "It was a horrible experience," I am saying *how* it impressed me. Moreover, a horrible experience is a characteristic sort of *event*. If I say I had a horrible experience this morning, it is natural for you to ask me what happened and for me to respond by describing an incident in such a way that you could tell what was horrible about it. If you could not tell, your question "What's horrible about that?" would amount to a protest against my calling it horrible. In general, what someone calls an "experience" of his is some incident he was involved in but did not precipitate, or at least the affective character of which was not due to his agency; and the adjectives that characterize experiences do so by saying how they affected the person whose experiences they are. As experience, then, is defined by overt incidents; it is called a certain person's experience in virtue of his passivity in relation to it; and it is called a certain kind of experience in virtue of the quality of that passivity. It is not simply an event, but an event as lived through by someone, as an episode in a person's inner life.

What, then, of religious and aesthetic experiences? Their cases differ in a way that proves interesting. Although theorists speak of aesthetic experiences and their characteristics, I have never actually heard anyone say "I had an aesthetic experience this morning." If someone did say it, it would sound odd, and the conversation could hardly proceed as it did with the horrible experience. If you asked him "What happened?" what could he say? Perhaps something like "I was walking through the art gallery when all of a sudden there was this great floppy hamburger. . . ." But would you expect to be able to tell from his detailing of incidents what was aesthetic about his experience, as you would expect to know from his description of a horrible experience what was horrible about it? Only, I think, on one of two conditions. He might tell you that the hamburger was a work of art, and you might agree that encounters with works of art are aesthetic by definition; but then "aesthetic" would not characterize the affect as "horrible" did, but merely classify it. Alternatively, he might qualify his experience with some epithet specifying the nature or degree of the aesthetic effect itself, such as "striking" or "lovely"; but then the specification of what it was he saw will have been neither necessary nor sufficient to warrant his claim to have had an aesthetic experience. "I had a horrible experience" means much the same as "Something horrible happened to me," but "I had an aesthetic experience" could not be paraphrased by "Something aesthetic happened to me." The one incident constitutes the experience in a way the other does not.

No one would really say "I had an aesthetic experience this morning." But someone might well say "I had a religious experience this morning," and you could suitably ask him what happened. However, the acceptable reply to this question would not be to specify an incident, such as assisting at mass or being stuck in a traffic jam behind a carload of nuns. Such a description would at most provide the setting for the experience itself, which would be an incident not in principle observable by others. A voice that says "Saul, why persecutest thou me?" is unlikely to be heard by Saul's companions, and it is certainly not necessary that it should be. Such incidents which took place overtly would be what Saul did—fell down, fainted, or whatever; and their significance in the description of the religious experience would be evidence that something was going on in Saul, which is quite different from the significance of the overt incidents in the horrible experience. In the aesthetic experience there is no necessary relation between stimulus and effect, so that a description of it has to specify the effect as well as (or instead of) describing the stimulus. But in the religious experience, as with the horrible experience, the stimulus is so described that its affecting nature is plain, although with the essential difference that in the religious experience stimulus and effect are inseparable if not identical, a single inherently affecting episode in one's inner life. It is because this connection is so firm that it makes more sense to speak of a religious experience than of an aesthetic experience—although religious experiences are seldom called that by those who have them, because the phrase smacks of a detached and clinical attitude that one would not bring to bear on anything of deep personal significance.

Like horrible experiences, religious and aesthetic experiences are not willed in their affective aspects. It is in one's power to fast or pray, to attend a concert or stare at a sunset, but not to command a beatific vision or a sense of visual delight. Because the connection between stimulus situation and aesthetic response, between worldly circumstances and revelatory stimulus/response, is not only thus unwilled but largely unpredictable, religious and aesthetic experiences are often thought of as quite gratuitous and fortuitous episodes in one's inner life, without any basis in one's mundane career. This goes too far, since there are notoriously and obviously things one can do to put onself in the way of having a religious or an aesthetic experience, just as one can put oneself in the way of having a horrible or delightful experience, without being able to guarantee the outcome. In a sense, though, the enumeration of things in common and different between these sorts of experience and others is beside the point: The difference is of a more radical sort than we have suggested. To call an experience horrible is to characterize it: I can describe what happened and say "It was horrible." But I cannot describe what took place in a religious or aesthetic experience and say "It was religious" or "It was aesthetic." These adjectives do not so much characterize as classify. A religious experience is not something that happened that had a religious character, but a special sort of happening. If I emphasize the "horrible" in "It was a *horrible* experience," I do so to stress how horrible it was; a comparable emphasis in "It was a *religious* experience" would not stress how religious it was, but would point out the contrast with aesthetic or some other sort of experience.

We may sum up this discussion of experiences by noting that the phrases we have glanced at suggest that experiences differ from events

100

in that they are viewed as episodes in someone's inner life, and that the cases we are interested in differ from others in that the episodes constituting them are treated not as happenings with affects but as affects loosely linked to happenings, or as inward episodes related to public happenings merely as events to their occasions.

This inwardness of "experiences" was not shared by the everyday uses of "experience" we started with. But it is a notable feature of "experience" as it is used in philosophical contexts, where the word leads a life markedly independent of everyday usage. Philosophers tend to use the word "experience" solipsistically, transposing events into terms of people's awareness of them. An English-speaking philosopher who talks about "experience" is almost certain to be an empiricist, one who dissolves the world into our knowledge of the world, volatilizing things and persons alike into impressions and ideas. This is even true, perhaps outstandingly true, of those apparently earthy persons who equate experience with sense-experience; for, after seeming to solidify thoughts into psychosomatic transactions, they then rarefy those transactions into their inward aspects and end up with a world of sense-data no less sublimated than that of the less thoroughgoing empiricists who preceded them. But in any case this philosophical use of the terminology of experience sheds no light on anything anyone wants to mean by "aesthetic experience" and "religious experience."

Things would be different if we used the vocabulary of the German *Lebensphilosophie*, which distinguishes *Erfahrung*, experience conceived as transactions of consciousness with the world, from *Erlebnis*, experience conceived as an episode in the inner history of consciousness itself. Things would be different, but perhaps not better; for then we should have to decide whether a religious experience involved a real object before we knew what to call it. So after all we had better confine our attention to the splendours and miseries of the English-speaking world. One can speak only one language at a time, and sometimes that is too much.

II

From a review of the concepts of experience and experiences in general as they relate to religious and aesthetic experience, let us now turn to some of the things people have in fact wanted to talk about when they spoke of religious and aesthetic experiences, and see what mutual light is shed.

Thanks to William James, "religious experience" primarily suggests to many of us the range of phenomena associated (chiefly in some forms of Protestant Christianity) with the concept of conversion: an emotional crisis involving conviction of sin and initiating a holy life. Such a crisis may be induced by a solitary discipline of prayer and fasting, or by the social excitement of a revivalist meeting. All three aspects mentioned seem necessary: Without a sense of unworthiness, and an emotional crisis, and at least a brief period of what the convert takes or means to be reform, we might hesitate to dub the experience "religious." But part of what makes an experience religious is its context, the way it is induced and understood: Few people attend Dr. Billy Graham's meetings without some idea of what conviction of sin is, and if they are ignorant there are plenty of people to tell them. Our feelings are our own, but it is from society that we learn how to name them, describe them, and interpret them, how important we should think them and what to expect as their outcome. A religious experience is differentiated from the aesthetic by its setting and by social definition.

Setting aside the social dimension just mentioned, what analogues can we find in aesthetic experience for the sort of religious experience we are considering? In the aesthetic domain as in the religious one, two routes are open: Aesthetic experience may be a solitary or a crowd phenomenon. It is one thing to listen to one's phonograph, and quite another to be in an audience. As for the three notes specified above as necessary to characterize such experiences as religious: Emotional crisis is certainly and notoriously possible, though hardly necessary, in aesthetic experience (though more in the case of music and the performing arts than with the plastic arts; for we should expect powerful emotional effects to be associated with processes extended and structured in time). Sin, on the other hand, when strictly construed as a sense of unworthiness before God, is inescapably religious. If we omit mention of God and speak only of a sense of unworthiness before something with which one is confronted, however, it also seems essential to at least some aesthetic experiences. But it is not what makes them aesthetic. On the contrary, it sets them apart from the common run of such experiences; whereas some would argue that no experience of any kind in which there was no sense of unworthiness could be deemed religious. The third note, amendment of life, involves the will, and since we expect no such consequences to stem from any experience we assign to the aesthetic domain, we do not try to bring them about.

In Plato's imagined republic things might be different: Who knows what reinforcement morality might derive from art if we thought it could and should? As things are, many people assert that art is uplifting or otherwise morally improving, apparently supposing that such benefits would flow from mere exposure to artifacts of the right sort. But we may doubt whether they are sincere, for they make no practical proposals in line with their pronouncements. Yet the emphasis on will may mislead us here: The religious convert may feel liberated and able to reform, whether he wills and whether he perseveres or not, and one simply does not know whether a similar sense of power might or might not be socially induced in connection with experiences socially defined as aesthetic.

Although we might concede that certain powerfully moving experiences of aesthetic confrontation have much in common with experiences of conversion, two differences will remain. First, in an aesthetic experience we shall construe whatever confronts "the experiment" as a series of sounds or a collection of sights, as such; in a religious experience, we shall assume that what confronts him is an object of worship, as such. Second, a religious experience as such is a turning point in one's life, but an aesthetic experience is over when it is over; in so far as it is more than merely an episode, we shall say that it is more than an aesthetic experience. The difference appears from the way we prepare for such experiences in their solitary modes: Prayer and fasting are training not for an experience but for a changed attitude to life and way of living, but aesthetic education is a sharpening of perception and widening of comprehension whose proper outcome is to make one more receptive in perceptual occasions.

Other modes of religious experience must be disposed of more briefly. There is a kind of religious experience that we may call the experience of the *transcendent*: We are made aware of the contrast between our finitude and imperfection in all its familiarity and an infinite, unknowable perfection—the negative projection, as it were, of all our limitations. And this experience, too, has its aesthetic analogue. Art is finite and definite, but at its best affords an awareness of possible perfection that in its own way imposes a contrast with the unsatisfactoriness of our everyday affairs. But the analogy is incomplete. Because the intimated perfection of art is only possible, not realised or realisable, it is in its fashion a transcendent perfection: We are aware of the unattainability of the perfection it exemplifies. But because it is indeed an exemplification of what must, therefore, be possible, its transcendence is qualified. To borrow the language of Karl Jaspers, religious experience of this sort would be an awareness of the transcending of our *Existenz* (that is, of that in us which lies behind all actual and possible experiences) by that to which we must be open. It is an experience of dependence and consequent finitude, of a contingency in ourselves and all that depends on us which, though doubtless total, is experienced as a contingency *in certain respects*. So, too, our openness to what transcends us in an openness *in a certain direction.* This directedness in the experience is what makes us relate it to religion rather than to metaphysics: The transcendent God of the philosophers, by contrast, is apprehended as an Absolute in relation to which our contingency is theoretically recognized and defined, but not lived, and our openness to it would be a general openmindedness, not in any way directed.

This language will be objected to by some and found nonsensical by others; but in any case it is language one could not well use of any aesthetic experience. One would not classify as "aesthetic" any experience in which dependence and contingency were either theoretically or existentially implied, even though it were to imitate one's finitude and imperfection and hence the possibility of an infinite and perfect being. And I would suppose that in any experience called aesthetic what was transcended would not be one's *Existenz*, but rather the structures of oneself as an experient.

The language of transcendence is not one that everyone wishes to speak. Closer to comprehension and the common tongue is the concept of the Holy—that which in its perfection demands our silence, contrasting not with our imperfection and finitude but with our sordidness and muddle.'One cannot experience the transcendent as such, but one can experience the Holy. Indeed, the Holy might be thought of as a mode of experience rather than as an object; and then the aspects of art that yield inklings of transcendence may be those that make it actually holy. One could say, however, on *a priori* grounds, that since the concept of art is that of a human productivity no work of art could be fittingly found holy. Therefore, the domain of the Holy in aesthetic experience could at most be that of natural beauty. But such a-priorities can be easily reversed: One can argue, for instance, that the experience of the Holy in art shows that the artist is merely the locus where the truth of being is revealed, or, on the other hand, that the aesthetic experience of the Holy is of a beauty not contained in but intimated by natural configurations and works of art alike. Things sufficiently like these have in fact been said, by Heidegger and Plotinus respectively.

The sacred is akin to the Holy, but does not connote infinity or perfection; if it demands silence, the silence need not be abashed. The sacred is contradistinguished from the profane: It is that which is separated from the everyday, to be handled or approached only at peril and in special circumstances, if at all. The gods are holy, their property is sacred. It is often felt, and sometimes argued, that the proper domain of the arts is the sacred, the mission of art being not to prettify or rectify the mundane but to set up or acknowledge the existing presence of a *hortus conclusus* or an *arcanum*, a special enclave in the world. If that is indeed true, then the arts have gone astray; but it is not news to be told that the arts have gone astray.

Akin to the transcendent, and associated with the sacred and the Holy, is the concept of the Wholly Other—that which reverses not only our limitations but everything familiar and is, therefore, an object of awe and dread. Of this there can be no experience—there can only be experiences that demand that the possibility of difference be recognized. But such experiences there seem to be. And contemporary art in its restlessness is full of intimations of difference: Our aesthetic experience is bound up with an art that insists on difference. But the intimated difference is a difference in detail, or in order, and instead of awe or dread evokes at most disorientation.

Thus far we have pursued a sort of *via negativa*, with the object of religious experience marked only by otherness, separateness, difference, or unknowability, not by any marks appropriate to a personal or providential deity. But the experiences that evoke the response "My Lord and my God" must be of another order, at the very least involving a power "not ourselves making for righteousness." But when we turn from experiences intimating a metaphysical or theological deity to those intimating a personal God, analogues in the aesthetic domain fail us. Were an experience classified as aesthetic to yield any such content, we would probably say that the aesthetic experience had afforded occasion for a religious experience. People who want to make a religion of art generally want to remain atheists. And we are even less likely to find plausible analogues of those more exalted experiences that prefigure the Beatific Vision, or of the more characteristic features of such experiences as are denoted by phrases like "being washed in the blood of the Lamb," or "accepting Christ Jesus as your personal saviour"; for the former is very specifically an experience whose object, in some sense, is the supreme being of the experient's cosmology, and the latter are explicitly tied to what is specific in a particular cult. Yet even in this area one might invoke a sort of negative analogy. Just as people who have religious experiences and talk about them as such may be contrasted with those who worship the God of Abraham, of Isaac, and of Jacob, so those people who have aesthetic experiences and talk about them as such may be contrasted with those who perform, compose and listen to string quartets, or with those who paint and look at pictures.

Finally, some might want to say that religious experience at least involves such inner peace or harmony as meditation might bring, although such inner peace would not in itself be called "religious" unless it were supposed either to be a gift of grace or a consequence of

105

specifically religious exercises. And here there seems to be an analogue, for many have urged that a form of inner harmony or repose is characteristic of aesthetic experience. John Dewey's *Art as Experience* even defines the aesthetic moment in experience as the moment of such repose. The analogy extends to the objections, which in both cases urge that what is thus singled out is but one aspect of one mode of religious or aesthetic experience. There is also a divine unrest and an agony of abasement, and an aesthetic excitement and involvement. In the religious case, however, it is supposed that any disturbance is ideally prelude to an ultimate peace; but in the aesthetic case such a peace would only be that of catharsis, release and exhaustion.

I have supposed throughout this discussion that those aspects and modes of religious experience that we describe or explain in psychological or metaphysical terms have recognizable affiliates in aesthetic experience, and those which we describe in a social context or refer to a personal deity have none. The former lack of connection is to be expected, but what of the latter? Is not a public related to the artist from whom its blessings flow as worshippers are to their god? Not really. The artist may be thought of as providence of the alternative world, the heterocosm, he creates, but his public are not in that world. And if the muses inspire him, they speak to him rather than through him. Or, if we were to follow Plato's *Crito* in supposing that the muses do speak through artist to public, we would have to admit that they are highly specialized deities. Besides, they have no worshippers nowadays, for it is only in etymology that a museum is their temple. Yet there is here a topic for elaboration: There is indeed an analogy between the problem of how a worshipper relates to the god revealed and concealed by the world, and that of how a public relates to the artist or other intelligence that activates or animates the work to which that public responds.

From the piecemeal comparisons we have been deploying we may now turn to some more general considerations. In principle, there are three ways of distinguishing religious experiences from others: by the felt quality of the experiences themselves, by the type of entity supposed to be experienced or to occasion the experience, and by the context in which the person who has the experience places it in relation to the whole order of his concerns. Similarly, by "aesthetic experience" one might mean experience having a certain felt quality, or experience of an object of a certain sort, or experience associated with a certain set of social practices and attitudes. But this triplicity could be reduced to unity again if one were to say that experience of the felt quality in question was aroused only by objects (works of art and things of beauty) apt to arouse it, and that the social attitudes and practices are wholly explicable by this coincidence of a kind of object with a type of experience. Thus too, and perhaps with more confidence, one might say that religious practices and institutions spring up around a Being whose nature is irresistibly intimated in experiences having a certain character: It is, for instance, because the experience of the Holy is the experience of an encounter that worship and sacrifice are performed.

Are these reductions of triplicity to unity descriptive or normative? If they are not normative, are they empirical or analytic? Is a beautiful object, for instance, one to which aesthetic experience is *appropriate*, or is it simply defined as whatever is experienced in a certain way? Is a religious experience one in which something is experienced *as* worshipful, one in which something is experienced which a church defines as "worshipful," or one in which something is experienced which in fact merits worship? If we define a god, as Ninian Smart has done, as "a proper object of worship, as such," it remains unclear whether we mean an object such that worship is indeed suited to it, a being judged by its worshippers worthy of worship, or a being which when experienced always or usually does evoke worship.

What is the evidential value of such experiences as we are considering? Even in the realm of art, people sometimes take their reactions to approved objects as evidence that they are doing something right: Either they have found something that was there waiting to be found, or they have learned a fashion of seeing or hearing that aligns them with a favoured social group. But the religious case is more serious, for some religious experiences are taken as evidence of a right relationship to God, and it is more important to be rightly related to God than to a painting. Moreover, while the painting itself is there for all to see, although its beauty may not be, God is not to be apprehended at all by those who lack this special experience that testifies to the rectitude of the relationship.

Generally speaking, one takes experience to be evidential when it is referred to some proposition that can be otherwise corroborated, whether by further experiences of one's own, by similar experiences of others suitably correlated, or by other forms of evidence. Evidence that is challenged can be checked against this other material. We speak of evidence only where such challenges and checks are possible. But religious experience is different, for how can there be such checks? Religious experiences are private to one person in their contexts. How then can one say that any such experience has evidential value? Or, if any experiences do, how can one say which they are and what they are evidence of? It is a perennially vexing question.

It would seem that the evidential value of religious experiences, if any, must be derived somehow from the character of the experiences

107

themselves. Presumably the experience must manifest a force or a perfection greater than the experient could evolve from his own resources operating upon previous experiences. But although the experient might well find himself compelled to believe that this was so, one hardly sees how he could be said to have sufficient grounds for believing it, for it is unclear what the criteria of sufficiency could be. *A fortiori*, neither his conviction nor its subjective grounds could serve as an argument to convince others.

One avoids that conclusion by saying that there may be marks by which veridical or authentic experiences can be identified. The objection that in the nature of the case one could not learn from others what those marks were is readily overcome, for here, as in other matters involving the subjective quality of experience, there might well be metaphorical ways of describing various types or grades of experience by whose legitimacy the initiate could tell how far along he had come on the road to Nirvana, Zion, or wherever. More telling, and perhaps insuperable, is the objection that the use of such marks and metaphors rests on the initial acceptance of some experience as evidential because authentic. Given this initial standard sample, one could certainly go by context (such as suitable preparation) and by the nature of the experience itself (the metaphors it evokes must be of the right sort). But the appropriate context, and the acceptable limits of description, can only be derived from the institutions and theology of a religion already taken as established and a set of experiences accepted by that religion as authenticated. And it is precisely the warranty for the authentication that is in question.

There is a further problem in this area, which we can only touch on. Mystical experiences given religious interpretations occur in the context of the institutions of different religions. If they have any evidential value, can it support anything in the different theologies of those religions? If so, do the experiences themselves vary in such a way that only adherents of the true faith have experiences of the right sort? Or do the adepts of all religions but one misinterpret their visions? Or do the expectations of the mystic, derived from his cult, induce variations in the visions themselves, so that to accept certain marks and metaphors as indicative of authenticity is automatically to endorse the claims of the relevant cult? Whatever may be the right thing to say in this area, it is hard to see how one could justify attributing a genuine evidential value to some experiences believed by the experient to be authentic and denying it to others.

Every experience is an experience *of* something in the sense that it has a determinate content and an intentional or internal object, but it need not be an experience of anything in the sense that its occurrence

108

involves an interaction of the experient with something other than himself. That an experience is indeed of something other than the experient can surely only be established through the accessibility of the object to multiple tests by any suitably placed and equipped observer. To the extent that that is true, it is hard to find good grounds for saying that the mystic vision is a vision of something other than the visionary. Any properties of the vision, however compelling, would be not merely inadequate but irrelevant. One could only say that the vision was occasioned by whatever could occasion such an experience in an appropriate experient. If dogmatic considerations are set aside, I think that no more is, in fact, usually claimed. But this may turn out to be a great deal.

Because the question of evidence applies, we have seen, asymmetrically to aesthetic and religious experience, it has sidetracked my discussion. Having seen the analogues aesthetic experience affords to standard accounts of this or that form of religious experience, let us now resume the main theme of our discourse and see whether standard accounts of aesthetic experience have analogues on the religious side.

Some say that "aesthetic experience" means nothing more specific than simply "contemplating works of art, or beautiful objects." They say it is just a myth that the variety of such experiences have any common characteristics. To apply the phrase to specific experiences with definite characteristics is to imply, tendentiously and arbitrarily, that such experiences have a special status i.e., are the only proper way to respond, or are the hallmark of the true art lover, or something of the kind. A parallel argument could be constructed for religious experience. That phrase, it might be said, can mean no more than all that part of life that involves religious behaviour, cult and objects, or that relates to God and his church and to the creation *qua* created. Attempts to specify the character of religious experience and experiences are almost certain to be intellectual weapons in interdenominational wars and are, in any case, discriminatory rather than discriminating. A narrow definition of religious experience excludes from the elect all to whom it does not apply. A Toronto theologian once said, "There are two ways of making a man a Christian: By conversion, and by definition"; but that is to define a Christian as a Christian by conversion, and "conversion" as usually understood seems to be a crisis in the emotions combined with effrontery in interpretation.

Various kinds of experience are singled out as "aesthetic." One kind is a certain rapture or ecstasy in the contemplation of beauty. Here the analogy with religious experience is obvious. An altogether different account is given by John Dewey who picks out a class of occurrences that shares some but not all of its members with those just

109

mentioned. Aesthetic experience, he says, is consummatory experience, a moment of rest between gratification and renewal of appetite, a psychosomatic equilibrium. Here the analogy with religious experience fails, for such an account of religious experience would be avowedly reductive. One can say of mystical experience that it involves at least a retreat or withdrawal from the world, and a devout secularist might classify religious and aesthetic experiences as coordinate species of such withdrawals or rests, or he might even make the religious a species of the aesthetic. In this regard Schopenhauer, for whom the experience of withdrawal is what constitutes the aesthetic, stands between Dewey and Plotinus, for whom even the aesthetic withdrawal represents the moment of Retreat to the intelligible Fatherland; for Dewey, rest is not withdrawal and has no necessary correlate. To Schopenhauer, rest is withdrawal and the experience has as correlate the platonic idea, but the experience remains, as it is for Dewey and as it is not for Plotinus, ineluctably aesthetic.

The term "aesthetic" is historically and etymologically associated with perception rather than participation, so that even those who recognize that experiences associated with works of art may be exciting, agitating, and transactional do not use "aesthetic experience" for such disturbances. Yet we may remind ourselves that Apollo and Dionysus are often named in this connection, Apollo as patron of calm and cruel arts and Dionysus as the alternate phase of abandonment and intoxication. Dionysus, Apollo, and the Muses are practically the only figures from the classical pantheon that still hold a place in our speech: They articulate our thought about the arts. Can it be that aesthetic experience is so inescapably religious that pagan deities must be conscripted to do the work that Jehovah declines?

Be that as it may, the phrase "aesthetic experience" is sometimes reserved for a peculiar sort of contemplation: an attitude of attached detachment, or tranquillized emotion, or psychical distance, in which our passions are partly cancelled out by and partly form the object of our contemplation. Without committing ourselves to the propriety of this usage or the significance or even the occurrence and identifiability of such states, we may say that an experience so described would differ fundamentally from any experience likely to be called religious. Serenity would be a self-centered abstraction if it were achieved not by turning from the world to something higher or by seeing the world in the light of something higher, but by making the world the plaything of one's subjectivity. One could take this to be a religious experience only by deifying one's subjectivity, distancing one's emotions by merging oneself with the world-soul or whatever. Something of this sort could be a religious exercise, though I am not aware that the

110

possibility is anywhere realized. And there is a related view of aesthetic experience which does seem to be allowed religious import. On this view, aesthetic experience is a contemplation of the appearances of things and the natures of kinds of things, abstracting from one's involvement with them as objects of use and hence abstracting from one's own nature as an appetitive being with a continuing nexus of vital purposes. To think of how things seem *to me* is to emphasize my subjectivity, but to emphasize how they *seem* to me is to reduce myself to mere observational correlate of what I contemplate. In this way artistic training becomes an important spiritual discipline, as a means to breaking down the illusion of the ego.

Sometimes again "aesthetic experience" is reserved for the awareness of order, detection of pattern or design, with or without a conformable harmony or synaesthesia of the perceiving mind or personality. In an aesthetic thus based, harmony and rhythm are the key terms, as they are for Plato. And some would say that the detection of order and design in the world is not merely an argument for the existence of God but the heart of religious experience itself, inasmuch as what is perceived as orderly is perceived as ordered and hence as having been set in order. Thus Marcus Aurelius thought one had to choose between chaos and providence as the only possible world views.

III

The very notion of aesthetic experience, as we have remarked, has recently come under attack. But even if we allowed the expression some meaning and usefulness, we might think it unfit for the role it has often been assigned: serving as the key term around which to order our thoughts about art. To think thus about art, it is urged, is to deny the spectator any vital relationship with the artist. As merely the occasion for such experiences, the work of art is treated as an "aesthetic object," as though it were a natural phenomenon in which one happened to take pleasure. Thus the work is dehumanized and trivialized, something that could enter one's life only as a toy or an ornament. The word "experience" itself, it may be added, reinforces these suggestions, intimating that the encounter with art is a mere transitory effect. A work of art is rather to be received as something someone has done and made, a means whereby human contacts are achieved, the point of clearest contact with the living traditions of our culture or with the otherwise irrecoverable heritage of the past. It is through the art of our own day that we become aware of, and part of, our society's changing modes of being. Alternatively, one may simply say that in the arts something of importance is obviously happening, though just what is

111

unclear. Therefore, the obvious way to treat a work of art is as an artifact in which some power is captured and transmitted: The work of art is indeed a sacred object and must be treated as such, even if in a cool hour we assure ourselves that the power it localizes is only the numen of the folkways. It may be hard to articulate any fully intelligible and rationally defensible doctrine on such lines; but on the negative side there is much to be said for Tolstoy's view that to think of art in terms of the aesthetic experience is at best a sophisticated hedonism that degrades and impoverishes the practice of the arts. Similarly, it may be held that to build one's thinking about the arts on the concept of aesthetic experience is to overvalue the inner life at the expense of the objectivity of artistic practice, distracting attention from the powerful and flourishing social institutions that shape artistic production as we know it.

A similar attack could be launched on an analogous emphasis on religious experience. Whereas the tendencies of the words "aesthetic" and "experience" converge to invite a double charge of excess subjectivity, however, the tendencies of the words "religious" and "experience" rather diverge. The word "experience," as we saw, connotes passivity, but by "religion" one usually means a system of beliefs, attitudes, and related practices, none of which are passive. To believe is to be intellectually active; to engage in a practice is to be physically and mentally active, to adopt an attitude is to be psychically active in taking a stand and organizing one's responses. It might then be thought that to make religious experience primary in religion is to subvert and trivialize it, to segregate it from the serious concerns of life and thus to transform it into something that is not religious at all. Faith and works alike are undermined. In a sounder tradition, it might be urged, religious experiences would be valued only as testimony to a relationship between worshipper and worshipped that would be valued for itself and of which the more important manifestations would be in the field of conduct and belief. The opposite view has its advocates, however. Popular advocates of hallucinogenic drugs have thought of them as harbingers of a new religion, the religious significance lying solely in the quality of the experience afforded. Now, those who say that God is dead must equate religion with a set of rituals, an ethical quality of action, an attitude to life, a set of experiences, or some combination of these; but, of them all, experiences seem the least likely candidates, acceptable only to those who have despaired of the world as well as of God and who cannot even summon the nerve and energy to cultivate their gardens. And, just as the emphasis on aesthetic experience distracts attention from the real and indispensable institutions of art, so even within an orthodox framework an emphasis on religious experience may devalue the sustaining institutions of the church, the visible body without which the spirit is only a ghost.

If there is indeed a tension between the terms "religious" and "experience," however, our values must be reversible. If the experiential reduction impoverishes religion, the religious imputation may sully experience. It seems a pity if one cannot enjoy a vision without preaching a sermon about it, or if one cannot speak with tongues without some official interpreter assuring the multitudes that one was really saying that we should all brush our teeth after every meal. If a religion of experience is a religion for the effete, experience defined as religious is experience anesthetized.

It is stupid to decry common practice as willful folly. If the emphasis on experience in religion is widespread, it must serve some purpose; and this purpose is not hard to determine. It satisfies the quest for certainty when other satisfactions are denied it. When the inerrancy of scripture is exploded by criticism of sources and by historical and archaeological sophistication, and the authority of the historical church is rendered incredible by historical criticism, and reforming zeal is blunted by anthropological self-doubt, nothing is left to take hold of but the experience of the believer himself, who thus becomes not only his own priest but his own prophet as well. Timothy Leary and his followers were only being more logical than their Protestant forerunners if, instead of taking their experiences to be evidence in favour of a creed they could not entail, or manifestations of a state of grace for whose existence there was no evidence beyond the experience itself, they valued the quality of the experiences themselves and the effects they were observed to have.

The aestheticizing of the arts could be justified in the same sort of way, though of course neither the function nor the frustrated quest is the same. The crisis in the arts is not one of certainty but one of interpretation. Art traditions in our complex societies develop so rapidly and so locally, and their products are so widely diffused, that the ordinary spectator has no chance of relating a work to the tradition whence it springs. This double change has been accompanied by a widespread renunciation, and a yet more widespread depreciation, of homiletic and representational modes. Thus one is faced with the choice of either abandoning all attempts to make anything of most of the works that confront one, or treating them as simply the occasions of such experiences as they may give rise to. And, as in the religious case, it is doubtless more honest to admit that this is what one is doing than to interpret one's experiences in some arbitrary way in order to endow then with a significance they cannot be shown to deserve. We know that we have had a powerful experience, but that does not entitle

113

us to invent stories about a power we have experienced. We may regret that vision can no longer be tied into the fabric of a continuing culture, but what seems to some to be a contrast between the savage and the civilized will seem to others to be a contrast between the free and the tamed.

Throughout this paper, the word "experience" has been taken rather literally. In practice, people generally use such phrases as "aesthetic experience" and "religious experience" far more loosely, to allude to broad cultural areas without any very specific connotations or demarcations in mind. The phrase "religious experience" becomes little more than a pointer toward all the behavioural and social phenomena that pertain to gods and so forth, and "aesthetic experience" points just as vaguely toward whatever pertains to the arts. Such vaguely indicative phrases play an important part in our everyday talk, where massive orientations are often called for: The risk of error and folly is grave, but must be run, for we could not otherwise get our bearings at all. Can we say, then, on the basis of all that has gone before, what these two areas or directions have in common that has enabled us to find so many analogies and suggestive differences between them? It is at least clear that both are contrasted with the workaday, that both relate to what is enjoyed rather than utilized, what is "prized" rather than what is "priced." Both are sources of values that are contrasted with moral and economic values by their independence of the values of survival. And it is these familiar facts, which are surely fundamental to all our thinking about art and religion, that give rise to the temptation to reduce both alike to terms of "experience" in the narrower senses we have been exploring. But that very reduction seems to betray a despairing belief that beyond the workaday there is nothing but objectivity: Not only is God dead, but culture, society, and certainly civilization were never born. This despair is falsified every waking hour of every day, for we show ourselves inescapably creatures of society and culture in everything we do and say. But the despair is so much a part of the intellectual fashion of the times that even those of us who do not share it find ourselves avowing it continually—so strong is the social pressure to deny the social dimension.

114

Encounters and Metaphor

C.G. PRADO

The legacy of radical theology as popularized in the '50s and '60s is that for some religion has become an existential response to crisis and a way of coping with evil and death, instead of an acknowledgement and worship of a deity. It is, moreover, a response and a way in which "God" figures only as a complex, symbolic form. The new conception of religion or of being religious is characterized by two cardinal items: religious experience and the view that religious language is essentially metaphorical.

When being religious ceases to be a matter of accepting a creed, of believing certain propositions about a transcendent realm, it can only have its source in and be sustained by personal experience or "encounter." The crucial thing about the abandonment of belief-centered religiosity is that the religious person must then find the roots of religiosity in himself, in his own life. It is also only within himself that the religious person can find the authority required for the commitment to the life dictated by the religious "vision" of the world. The religious experience is at once the "vision" and the authority for the implementation of that "vision." In rejecting revelation as a basis for faith, Sam Keen in *To a Dancing God* states that revelation

> *begs the question of authority and responsibility.* To the degree that I accept the principles of my faith from . . . external authority, I am living out another person's life.

At least as important as the foregoing is the new position that once being religious ceases to be a matter of holding certain propositions about a transcendent deity and realm to be true, religious language ceases to be importantly descriptive and assertive and becomes confessional and self-expressive. When God is no longer a being inhabiting a transcendent realm, and "God" becomes a symbol of the unconceptualizable, the main task of religious language is to define the subject of the religious "vision," "encounter," or insight. Thus, religious language becomes metaphorical and imagistic—at least in part because of the unwanted consequences that follow if it is allowed to be descriptive and referential.

Taken together, the reliance on religious experience as constituting religiosity and the recasting of religious language as metaphorical lead ultimately to what I would describe as an impossible religious solipsism, or an illusion of faith. What I want to do here is briefly sketch a view which I have developed more fully in my book, *An*

Illusion of Faith. I hold that religious experience will not bear the weight put on it by this conception of religion, once religious language ceases to be literal.

Religious Experience

In spite of what philosophers of religion tend to think, recourse to religious experience is rarely an evidential move. Religious experience is seldom thought of as a sudden *perception* of what was previously only *believed* to exist on faith. It is usually a somewhat dramatic confession of a certain perspective, a confession enhanced by reference to the usually profoundly moving mode of how that perspective was acquired. In this way recourse to religious experience can often be construed as a justificatory move, but it is not justification offered by the provision of evidence. This, however, requires qualification as to whether the experience recounted is *only* a complicated image or whether the account is offered as a description of an actual episode.

Now so long as religious language remains sufficiently literal, there seem to be at least five ways in which one might categorize a religious experience. I shall label them as follows: (1) vision-type experiences, (2) interpreting-type experiences, (3) numinous or feeling-type experiences, (4) oceanic experiences, and (5) cases of possession.

The importance of the distinctions is that the popular notion of religious experience is hopelessly vague. We must be clear therefore, about the implications which each sort of experience has with respect to its objects and to the claims each may support. It is also important to be clear about how the distinctions in question are blurred or denied when all or almost all religious language ceases to be literal.

(1) Vision-type experiences are special with respect to their objects, but not to the mode of apprehension. Classically, an entity seems to be seen and heard by the subject. It is crucial that the experience involve a recognitional aspect and can occur only against the background of a fairly complex belief-structure—even if the beliefs in question are not consciously held. In vision-type experiences the subject encounters *an angel*, or even the angel *Gabriel*, or the subject perceives some complex symbol (a cosmic serpent, a tongue of fire) which refers to a particular deity. The circumstances of the vision may be quite mundane, except for the apparition, or quite exotic: Compare Bernadette encountering the Virgin to St. John seeing a cosmic serpent. But in either case the experience is religious because it is perception *of the religious.* Philosophers are correct when they argue that there is nothing about the apparition that *requires* interpretation

116

in religious terms, but it is significant that as far as the subject is concerned there is no need to infer that the apparition is, for example, an angel. What makes the vision a vision is that what is encountered is *generically identified as* an angel, etc. There are cases—St. Augustine meeting a little boy on the beach or the disciples on the road to Emmaus meeting a traveler, for example—where it is only on reflection that the apparition is recognized as such. These, however, are borderline cases falling between the vision-type and the interpreting-type of experience.

(2) The interpreting-type experience is characterized by the absence of extramundane objects. While all five types of experience have an interpreting aspect, that in question is wholly interpretive in that it is not an experience or apprehension of something extraordinary. It is rather a realization that the mundane has a certain special, perhaps transcendent, significance. The interpreting-type of experience is based on perspective or attitude and is usually described in terms of a sudden realization, such as of the greatness of God or of the meaning of true humanity. The special character of the experience lies not in its objects but in the magnitude of significance attributed to the objects of ordinary awareness. The absence of special objects, then, raises the question: Why is an insight or realization of the type in question deemed a *religious* experience? The answer seems to be that it is religious only because it is deemed monumentally important. The insight may, of course, be more familiarly religious if there is also the claim that the significance perceived is attributed to a deity or something transcendent.

(3) The numinous experience, or feeling-type experience, is characterized by being a special *mode* of awareness, rather than by having extramundane objects or being a special (alleged) realization. This third type is perhaps best described by Rudolf Otto in his book *The Idea of the Holy*—though it is there mistakenly presented as the whole of religious experience. Essentially the experience or "encounter" involves being overwhelmed by awe and a sense of one's own finitude and contingency. Supposedly, the character or nature of the experience carries with it a concomitant object. The experience necessitates that its object be an object of awe, something on which we are totally dependent for our very existence. The experience is said to have "reference to an object." We are told that "the numinous is felt as objective and outside the self." (R. Otto, *The Idea of the Holy*, Oxford, 1958.) The object is not inferred, in spite of not being given in the experience: Rather "the feeling of a numinous object objectively given must be posited as a primary immediate datum of consciousness." Otto quite deliberately maintains a nice ambiguity between the numinous as

117

a feeling-element and as the object of the numinous experience or "creature-feeling."

What is important here for our purposes is that the third sort of experience is putatively a special mode of awareness. As such it is properly described as a *religious experience*, rather than an experience *of* the religious, in the sense of being an apprehension of religious entities or symbols. Here again, as in the case of the second sort, the question arises: Why should the experience be deemed religious? The putative object could be an indifferent universe. Or the experience could be deemed a profound metaphysical one. The experience can, of course, be attributed to a deity. But what seems crucial is that the awe and dependence experienced are themselves conceptualized in terms of awe and dependence in relation to something which, though unconceptualizable and described by Otto only as "the Wholly Other," is basically cast as a transcendent *agent*. The experienced dependence is conceptualized as a dependence on a creator, albeit possibly one whose personhood or nature is incomprehensible.

(4) The fourth, or oceanic experience, is the familiar, allegedly ineffable, mystical experience characterized by an alleged transcendence of the subject/object distinction. The experience is of unity, of a unity that transcends the thereby illusory diversity of the mundane. Freud used the term "oceanic" to describe an experience consisting of a momentary regression to the undifferentiated sentiency of earliest infancy. Allegedly there is an intense and somehow selfless and objectless awareness of the unity of reality. We do not have here a special mode of awareness nor awareness of special objects, but rather such a *level* of awareness that it is not to be differentiated from what would otherwise be its object.

(5) The fifth sort of experience is one about which I have some reservations as to whether it is a distinct type: *possession*. The experience of possession is not special in virtue of objects. Nor is it special because it is a special mode or level of awareness. What makes the experience special is that the subject experiences being displaced within his own body. "Speaking in tongues" is a classic instance wherein the subject utters words which he himself need not understand and has the no doubt terrifying, but possibly joyous, experience of being spoken *through*. What is crucial here is that, as in the case of the vision-type, there is a complex belief-structure in the wings.

Both the vision and possession cases are linked with the concept of an *alien will*. Being visited and being possessed are events which would occur as consequences of acts on the part of a being other than the subject of the experience. In this way, there is no special problem about how these are religious experiences, for both entail entities which are religious, at least in the minimal sense of being transcendent entities.

118

It is important to note that the interpreting, numinous, and oceanic experiences are essentially achievements of a sort and do not entail the existence of an alien will, as do the vision-type and possession-type experiences. Each of the former three types could simply involve an awareness of something gained independently of whatever the experience mediates.

The traditional orthodox Christian view of religious experience was that while such experience may enhance and perhaps even confirm religious faith, it could not be constitutive of religious faith. For one thing, the experience would at least be initially suspect: possibly a temptation of the sin of presumption. For another, as noted above, there is the crucial role played by background belief. When Saul/Paul was knocked from his mount and blinded by a great light his question was, "Who are you, Lord?" (*Acts*, 1:19). A genuinely nonreligious man would be perplexed by a visitation or by being possessed and would set about determining the cause of his experience. It would only be as a last resort, just prior to seriously questioning his sanity, that he would construe the experience as an act of God. It is clear that in cases of visions or visitations and of possession the conceptualization of something as a religious experience is an articulation or embellishment of previously held religious beliefs—even of previously unacknowledged religious beliefs.

In the case of the interpreting, numinous, and oceanic experiences, though possibly less so in the case of the numinous, what we have are experiences which can be constitutive and originative of religiosity at least in the sense that the experience can be the initial acquisition of a certain perspective or "vision." The experience will also be constitutive since by recurring it will sustain the perspective or "vision" in question. If the experience does not recur, the subject would eventually be in the same position as someone who accepts a creed on the basis of external authority. He would be like a man who has lost his sight and only remembers how things look; he would no longer have immediate grounds for faith.

The most important implication of the foregoing distinctions is that the vision- and possession-types require an alien will. Visions are revelations, either of entities or beings to be known through symbols, and as such they entail agency and hence will. If they were revelations which occurred without an alien intention that they occur, they would not be visions of the sort in question at all. Rather they, the visions, would have to be construed as the subject's own projections or characterizations of qualitatively different events. The only alternative is that an apparition, such as that of an angel or of a cosmic serpent, is in fact a *perception*, albeit a very rare and very special one. There would be obviously unwelcome religious consequences to

119

such an alternative. Possession, of course, entails will in an evident way.

The above distinctions also bring out certain implications about possible error. It is relevant to argue against appeals to vision-type and possession-type experiences that the religious awareness or perception is as vulnerable to illusion and hallucination as is ordinary perception; that so long as there are no public objects available to settle the issue, the religious person's claims cannot be taken as in any way conclusive. That argument is not applicable to the interpreting, numinous, and oceanic experiences, however, it is not even very clear how the interpreting-type can go wrong. At most it might be argued that a certain attribution of significance is exaggerated or inappropriate. But when we argue thus, we seem really to be questioning the credentials of the person doing the attributing, as opposed to the validity of the attribution itself. This is because we can readily imagine cases wherein the attribution would be rendered quite fitting by some consideration not immediately evident. While there seems to be no sensory content in the numinous and oceanic experiences (unlike the vision and possession experiences which can be deemed hallucinatory), the experience itself may be 'deemed *pathological* in some not-very-clear "psychological" sense.

If one takes religious experience claims seriously, one concedes that four of the five cases in question need explanation. Only in the interpreting-type experience does there seem to be nothing in need of special explanation. Although, in a sense, the experience itself should be explained because the subject does allegedly attain a momentous insight. But there is nothing distinct from the insight, such as an apparition. There is nothing which might initially puzzle the subject himself prior to his own conceptualization of what he might be undergoing *as* a religious experience. The significance of this point will become clear when we consider the consequences of construing religious language as metaphorical.

Further, the vision- and possession-types of experience are separated from the interpreting, numinous, and oceanic by the authority that each has. The authority of the first two is a function of the ultimate authority of the deity revealed in them. The mere occurrence of a vision or possession is insufficient—the credentials of the apparition or possessor must be established as acceptable. They may in fact never be questioned, but there is the possibility that the vision or possession is demonically inspired, for instance. On the other hand, the mere occurrence of a numinous or oceanic experience suffices with respect to the matter of authority, for these are essentially awareness *achievements*. The interpreting experience is also an achievement, but the authority here is not a function of the experience as such or of what is revealed therein. Final authority is here vested *in the subject*. The experience may in fact be little more than an acknowledgement or recognition of that fact.

Now what we have is roughly this: Of the five types of religious experience, four seem clearly to be special experiences or episodes in the sense that there is some content *of* experience which is extramundane. In two cases, that content is of a sensory sort and can be abstracted from the experience itself; in two cases it is identical with the experience. In the former two, the content may be deemed illusory or hallucinatory in a fairly familiar and reasonably straightforward way: That is analogous to other sorts of illusions and hallucinations. In the second two cases, the experiences may be deemed pathological as opposed to illusory or hallucinatory. The two types of experience which can be deemed hallucinatory, the vision- and possession-types, are such that—if they are genuine or veridical—they entail the existence of an alien will. The two types which may be deemed pathological, the numinous and oceanic, are—again, if they are veridical—achievements of a special nature and entail only what we might minimally describe as an extramundane realm. In the cases of vision and possession experiences, their specialness is a function of the specialness of their objects, and each is a *religious* experience in that it is an experience *of* the religious. The point here is that a complex belief-structure is presupposed and somehow operant. In the case of the numinous and oceanic experience, the mode or the level of awareness is special, and these are religious experiences in the full adjectival sense: It is the depth and nature of the experience which is described as religious. The first two cases imply the existence of religious *entities*; second two, as just noted, imply a level of existence or a realm accessible only in a special way.

What is crucial in the foregoing is that paradigmatically the vision, possession, numinous, and oceanic experiences are recounted or described in literal language. In spite of the claim that the experiences are in some cases ineffable, what is said about their occurrence is meant literally. The alternative is that what is said by the subject of experience in describing his or her experience is non-literal, so that the description or account of the experience is construed as a complex image or metaphor. What that account is then deemed to be an account *of* is simply an *interpreting* experience. In other words, it may be contended that accounts of numinous or vision-type experiences are no more than rather dramatic imagistic accounts of the interpreting-type experience: An experience where the actual and only content of the experience is the alleged insight gained. Accounts of religious

121

experience would, on this view, be taken as lacking descriptive content and as being imagistic in a way which primarily serves to define and articulate the insight gained for the subject himself. The variations, say between the vision- and oceanic-types, would be explained as a function of the subject's own limitations.

Once religious language is construed as essentially metaphorical, vision-type and possession-type experiences collapse into the interpreting-type because reference to religious entities becomes impossible. All that can be talked about is *symbols*. The Tillichean reason for prohibiting literal reference to the transcendent is the fear of idolatry: the construction, through literal predications, of a deity which, in being the subject of these predications, is precluded from having that degree of ultimacy which must belong to what "God" symbolizes.

The numinous and oceanic experiences collapse into the interpreting-type for slightly different reasons. The realms or levels of existence necessitated by the sorts of awareness in question must also be protected from the demeaning influence of comprehensibility. The moment that something becomes an object of awareness it is revealed as not sufficiently ultimate to be the transcendent; hence, again, what is experienced in the numinous and oceanic types must be symbolic of something further.

Aside from the vision- and possession-type experiences presupposing a set of operant beliefs, even if one could initially acquire faith and religiosity by encountering God, that possibility is precluded by the impossibility of encountering *God*. The consequence is that the vision- and possession-type experiences cannot be constitutive of religiosity. As for the numinous and oceanic types, we saw how they are reduced to the interpreting-type; and hence, if constitutive of religiosity, they will be so only *as* interpreting experiences. The interpreting experience lends itself well to constituting religiosity because it is the acquisition of a certain perspective and, therefore, constitutes taking up a specific view of the world or conceptual scheme—one in which there is room for "the sacred," however construed. Moreover, the interpreting experience is the right *kind* of experience, for it comes from within: It is how the subject comes to see the world; it is not something imposed on the subject. As such it is precisely the right sort of occasion for faith in that it is "existential." The authority of the interpreting experience need not be taken on faith: It is internal.

Most of what has been noted above is a direct consequence of the construal of religious language as essentially metaphorical for fear that literal religious language is only an invitation to idolatry. But religious language is not so construed only because of worries about idolatry, but also in part because of a desire to make it self-expressive and the need to accommodate the diversity resulting from the relocation of the source of religiosity in the individual's existential situation.

Metaphorical Language

It is a common view that there are certain universals of human experience which can be articulated or communicated only in complex ways—in a lengthy novel, in a moving play. Similarly, there are things we can say to one another only by bending language. In his *Models and Metaphors* Max Black correctly pointed out that there are some enlightening metaphors which cannot be replaced by or reduced to a literal statement, regardless of how long and complex or how carefully articulated. This is mainly because some metaphors bring together otherwise unrelated—or even incompatible—concepts in special ways. Religious language has always been held to be ultimately inadequate in the sense that it is merely analogical when it is about the transcendent. As noted earlier, however, some contemporaries now contend that religious language is *wholly* imagistic, "symbolic," or "metaphorical" in the sense that, like Black's irreducible metaphors, the *entire* idiom is uniquely nonliteral. Hence, unlike Black's metaphors, religious language is not parasistic on literal idiom. It is parasistic on the historical, conventional meanings of the various terms which provide the opportunity for using religious language to deal with religious awareness.

The claim in question is that there *cannot* be literal religious expressions and that all talk about the transcendent, or Tillich's "ground of being" (apparently the sole semi-literal expression tolerated), must be carried on in terms that are merely heuristic devices which serve to provide a kind of "picture," but have no descriptive or cognitive force. The "picture" is never a portrait; it is like an abstract painting in which others may see reflected their own religious awareness.

Religious language is "metaphorical" in more than just the sense that it imagistically captures something otherwise clearly present to the mind. The whole point is that the religious, as an object of awareness, cannot be comprehended as a "this" or as a "such-and-such." Imagistic or "symbolic" religious language is not as it is because it is inadequate with respect to its object but because it precisely reflects the symbolic and imagistic nature of religious awareness. Ramsey's "cosmic disclosures" are not tidy insights which because of their magnitude cannot be articulated; the whole point is that the "disclosure" is *itself* a complex image or symbol. Hence, the believer is committed to an endless modelling exercise because it is only through models and images that

123

he assimilates what has presented itself. The religious as apprehended is always seen through a dark glass, a glass which is partially composed of imagistic religious language.

It should be evident that we have been using "metaphorical" in a special sense—meaning a "palette of paints" rather than a part of language.

This is not the place to recapitulate the effects of certain doctrinal developments—the influence of Wittgenstein, generally, and. Flew's falsifiability challenge in particular—on the conception of the nature and role of religious language. Suffice it to say that religious language is no longer thought to have descriptive or referential force. This conception of religious language is one which, if not a consequence of, at least accords well with a conception of religion which rejects what Tillich called "supernaturalism." When the person-God is repudiated, however, it becomes necessary to give a new account of that discourse which apparently had as its main concern describing and referring to that God. What is it, then, that the metaphors and symbols "point to"? Here there seems to be a good deal of confusion, for often it sounds as if there is at least "the ground of being" to be "discussed," but more often it seems that God-talk is to be reinterpreted as really being about man and his relations and concerns. To say that the world is God-created, for instance, becomes a matter of saying indirectly that the world contains everything necessary for personal fulfillment and happiness.

The question that arises is: If religious discourse is not about a transcendent deity and/or realm, what makes it *religious*? The basically Tillichean answer is that what is described as our "natural" language and categories somehow cannot do justice to a certain aspect or dimension of human life. John Robinson, author of the trend-setting *Honest To God*, tells us that

> there are depths of revelation, intimations of eternity, judgments of the holy and the sacred, awarenesses of the unconditional, the numinous and the ecstatic, which cannot be explained in purely naturalistic categories without being reduced to something else.

(Robinson, reprinted in Card and Ammerman, *Religious Commitment and Salvation*, Charles Merrill, 1974)

We do not need religious language to refer to certain special entities. In fact, to make God an entity would be to fall into idolatry. Religious language, the transcendent, is simply about, the "unconditioned," the object of "ultimate concern." Tillich himself assures us that there are certain "deep things for which religion stands" which have nothing to do with deities: "the feeling for the inexhaustible mystery of life, the grip of an ultimate meaning of existence, and the invincible power of an unconditioned devotion."

It is tempting to say that on the above view religious language is only honorifically religious, in the sense that it is about the very *important*. This seems not to constitute a worrying objection, however. There is clearly a disposition to construe the religious as differing greatly in degree, but as essentially continuous with the ethical, the aesthetic, etc. It emerges that we are being offered a sweeping reconception of the religious, not just of religious language; a reconception in which experience plays a crucial role.

Tillich, when he wrote *Systematic Theology* and several other of his works, was willing to use religious language to do theology of a sort. More recent writers, however, have a more extreme view of the nature of religious language. It is still "symbolic," but its significance seems to have changed. The scenario we are offered by, e.g., Donald Evans and Sam Keen, goes roughly as follows: Crisis or deep dissatisfaction of a profound sort provide the occasion for a certain response, a response of assurance in the face of possible meaninglessness and the recognition of one's own contingency. To see the world as rational and ordered, as having overriding meaning is the religious response, and once made, it dictates the religious way of life. Religious language *historically* served the purpose of referring to a putative transcendent deity and realm. It next came to serve as a "symbolic" language, apparently to some extent adequate for "discussion" of the ultimate and transcendent; but it now seems to have come to have a rather different use: capturing or dealing with the individual's putative religious awareness—however it may be construed. It may, of course, also serve a secondary end—endorsing religiosity to others. In either case, it seems the only applicable test is the *effectiveness* of the idiom.

What begins to worry one about the foregoing view is just what it is that religious language deals *with*. It seems we have no independent access to what it is about, since that is the religious individual's religious awareness, Tillich was often criticized for inconsistency because, having said all he did about religious language, he often pontificated on the nature of a "transcendent" which was very reminiscent of the "supernaturalistic" person-God he had eschewed. But a Keen or an Evans seems not to be tempted by the idea of even an unconceptualizable God. They certainly talk enough about "God," but in the last analysis, "God" seems to be an integrated universe or a self-acceptance objectified. Religious language, then, is not even a set of symbols for dealing wth the transcendent, but seems more like an idiom which, like that of psychoanalysis, is designed primarily for the categorization of experience rather than for even an only symbolic representation of some glimpsed reality.

It would seem, then, that religious language has as its main function something like model-construction. Ian Ramsey tells us that ". . . the believer is committed to an endless exploration of countless models" in order to grasp what "confronts him in any and every cosmic disclosure." (Ian Ramsey, *Words About God*, Harper Forum, 1971.) Religious language cannot be used to articulate doctrines, for doctrines are not "photographs of God,"—they are not true descriptions but only "rules for significant stuttering." (Ibid.)

Ramsey's "cosmic disclosures" are precisely what we have been calling interpreting-type experiences. But most important, they are all that can constitute the significance of religious expressions used by an individual. The significance of those expressions cannot be propositional content, e.g. communicated to the speaker, for there are no doctrines. A man might parrot the expressions in question, but unless he has himself had the requisite religious experience, and hence is using those expressions to come to terms with what he "encountered," the expressions will be without significance. They may have their conventional, historic meaning, but that will only be what makes just those expressions useful for dealing with the religious experience. That meaning can no longer be taken as their actual significance and force: This is to construe those expressions as being about a divine entity, etc. It is only in virtue of the individual's own experience that the expressions have significance—insofar as they are used to construct an image or model or complex metaphor which "gives" or captures the "vision" or insight, the content of the "cosmic diclosure." Stuart Brown, in his *Do Religious Claims Make Sense?* (SCM Press, 1969), defends just this view in arguing that "religious beliefs are unintelligible to the unbeliever by virtue of his being an unbeliever." Brown maintains that it is only through having a conceptual scheme-changing "insight" that a nonbeliever comes to understand a religious belief or claim or expression, for that matter.

Religious expressions are thus called meaningless, with reason, despite all conventional meanings, unless they are used by an articulate individual to come to terms with a religious "vision." In this way they might be described as having only what Austin called *perlocutionary* sense for the speaker; that is, they are used to *do* something. Their conventional—what Austin would call their *illocutionary*—sense is only important insofar as it renders them likely candidates for being used as the speaker uses them. Radical theologians had to claim that

126

God had died—an absurdity—in order to pry traditional, culture-determined conventional meanings from religious expressions, and so to render them capable of being used in the model-constructing way in question.

Now, I am not claiming that the religious contemporary has a naive theory in which the meanings of expressions are so many ideas in the mind. The point is more complex. It is not denied that religious expressions have intersubjective conventional meanings, but those meanings are "symbolic": We must not make the mistake of looking for the *referents* of religious expressions. So long as the expressions in question are used only in their conventional meanings, they are uninteresting. The expressions gain significance when, largely because of their conventional meanings, they are employed by a particular individual to come to terms with his or her religious "vision" or "encounter." The expressions are used to capture his religious "vision," and that is done by constructing one or more models. Thus this person may speak now of having "encountered" a loving father, now of having witnessed the unity of reality, now of having been overwhelmed by the majesty and awesomeness of God.

When religious expressions are used in this way, they, of course, retain their conventional meanings. But those meanings really become irrelevant, and the nonbeliever, attending only to them will, of course, understand nothing of what is being said by the religious man. The nonbeliever will take it that deities are being referred to or claims made about the existence of another world, etc.

The real significance of the expressions will be what the speaker "encountered," and the nonbeliever will have access to *that* only when he has himself had a similar "encounter" and has used religious expressions to capture it. He will then not so much understand the other's remarks as have come to learn to wield religious language as that other does. In that sense he will understand the other speaker.

How can we best understand what is "encountered"? Perhaps in terms of a Wittgensteinian "picture." The user of religious expressions acquires a certain picture, a certain perspective; he has a "vision." He may come to see the world in a special way, and himself in that world in a special way, a way that regulates his conduct: He now conceptualizes himself and his fellows as, say, worthy of love and respect. But it is crucial for our purposes that the "vision" is private to the subject. This is evident in that the search for religion is an introspective one, and the job of religious language is primarily capturing what one finds within oneself. Keen remarks:

> Is there anything in my experience which gives it unity, depth, density, dignity, meaning, and value—which makes graceful freedom possible? If

127

we can discover such a principle at the foundation of personal identity, we have every right to use the ancient language of the holy. . . .

The reason is that "any language is authentically theological which points to what is experienced as holy and sacred." (Ibid.) But to experience something as "holy and sacred" is not to experience something as pertaining to a deity; it is to experience something "unconditioned" and "ultimate." To encounter a person-God is, as noted, to "symbolize" to oneself the unconditioned and ultimate *as* a divine person.

The answer to how the religious experience constitutes the significance of religious expressions is that those expressions serve as elements in a "picture" of the religious "vision" or insight. The picture will be inadequate, of course, and many pictures or models will be used to attempt to capture the "vision." The conventional meanings of religious terms will be operant only as bases for analogies or metaphors. The speaker will employ those analogies and metaphors primarily to make concrete *for himself* the insight he has had and which by its very nature, magnitude, and scope begins to elude him from the moment of its occurrence.

The importance of religious language as a vehicle for doctrine and as a source of cognitive constructions emerges at just about zero. All religious language need do is afford the subject of religious experience a way of coping with his "vision." As for its intersubjective importance—it need only signal the occurrence of religious experience. Users of the idiom will understand its expressions as they use them to deal with their "visions," and hearers will either "understand" the idiom in the sense that they will know how to employ it in like manner, or they will understand only the expressions' conventional meanings. There will be no possibility of using religious language to formulate doctrine. For, first, there can be no doctrines about deities, and religious language allegedly cannot be referential or descriptive; and, second, the significance of religious expressions is private to each user of those expressions.

Conclusion

In the section on religious experience I pointed out the kinds of religious experiences and how the conception of religious language as metaphorical restricts religious experience to one type. In the section on religious language I explained what I understand to be the underlying structure of the view in question and to bring out the importance to that view of religious experience in that only such experience can constitute the "real" significance of religious expressions. In this section I want to suggest that, on reflection, it seems that the content of the religious experience may, in fact, be wholly irrelevant and that the "visions" or "cosmic disclosures" may at best serve only to authenticate a commitment to a certain way of life. It is in keeping with the root sense of "religion" that its focus be a way of life and not a deity, and to this extent the suggestion is not a radical one.

First note that the insistence on religious experience may amount to no more than a requirement that an individual take up a certain way of life for profoundly personal reasons, rather than on the strength of some authority, or because of "mere" intellectual commitment to the truth of certain propositions.

The importance of the religious way of life is evident in the thought of even a relatively conservative contemporary religious thinker such as John Hick. In answering a question about the difference religion or the religious "vision" makes, Hick remarked that

> to experience the world as having a certain character is . . . to be in a dispositional state to live in it in the manner which such a character . . . renders appropriate. And to experience it in a way derived from Christ's own experience is accordingly to tend to live in the kind of way that he taught and showed forth in his life.

Hick, "Religious Faith As
Experiencing-As"

If we factor in Donald Evans' notion of religiosity as a response of assurance to the confrontation of possible meaninglessness, we can get some idea of this "character" which Hick speaks of: The revelatory aspect of the religious experience can be thought of as an alleged insight into the (putative) integrated nature of the universe. The "vision" of an integrated universe produces an extraordinary object: the world as a whole of which one is an infinitesimal part. That "vision" will include the place of others like ourselves, and it may evoke a profound feeling for the necessity of community and mutual love. As an experience of restructuring of perceived reality, of reshaping of priorities, it will dictate conduct and only certain behaviour will now appear appropriate. But as noted earlier, the scope of the "vision" will require the use of religious language to "capture" it. Moreover, worship and ritual also will now have a new sense and role. Worship will no longer be homage paid a deity. It will be what John MacMurray somewhere called "a celebration of community," a ritualized way of sharing the religious "vision," and perhaps of symbolically acting out its more important implications.

Now in the above scenario the role of religious experience seems to be fundamental: That which dictates the way of life. But consider:

129

No criteria exist by which to determine whether any two individuals have had *the same* "vision," other than how they live. Consider further that there can be no way to establish the veracity of an interpreting experience. All we have access to is how the subjects of such experiences live. For Keen, it is important that men live "gracefully"; for Evans, that they live in an assured manner—that they not despair in the face of death and possible meaninglessness; for Hick, that men live in accordance with the "character" they discern the world to have. But what dictates those ways of life, if it is argued that the various descriptions come to the same thing? There can be no appeal to an idea that each subject of religious experience discerns the will of an independent agent, God. Nor will it do for each subject to discern the pattern of an objective reality—even one that somehow includes or incorporates value; for the whole thrust of contemporary religious thought is that religiosity must be *existential*. The apparent fundamentality of the religious experience, then, seems to require a wholly subjectivist interpretation. What really counts is that an "authenticating" experience take place—but there can be no way to specify the nature or character of such experiences. At best, they may be taken to be necessitated by how a man comes to live, in effect postulated as explaining why that man lives as he does.

If religious language is nonliteral there can be no descriptive, cognitive content in accounts of religious experience. Nor can a religious experience be conceptualized, in the last analysis, as other than an interpreting experience, one requiring no special objects. Moreover, the subject of an interpreting experience will not be able to articulate what he allegedly learns: The experience cannot yield doctrine. Yet the religious experience is, nonetheless, somehow supposed to dictate a way of life. What emerges is that while we can form some idea of how a religious "vision" might restructure a man's priorities and shift his perspective on the world, we have no idea how the religious "vision" gives rise to *particular* ways of life, much less how apparently diverse "visions" seem to give rise to very much the *same* way of life—the desired *Christian* way of life.

It seems that the contemporary religious thinker faces a dilemma: Either he makes religious experience the *sine qua non* of religiosity and adopts a wholly subjectivist position with respect to the nature and content of religious experience and to how it defines religiosity. Or he renders religious experience unimportant by conceiving of religiosity in terms of a certain way of life, thereby relegating religious experience to a kind of authenticating or legitimizing role. The trouble with the first horn of the dilemma is that it renders the notion of religiosity vacuous since nothing can be excluded. Being religious will be whatever it *seems* to a man it is to be religious. There can be no intersubjective *or* subjective criteria for determining the correctness of the judgment in question.

The first horn has in fact been embraced by some contemporaries. Frederick Streng, C.L. Lloyd, and J.T. Allen, in their *Ways of Being Religious* (Prentice Hall, 1973), warn against parochial conceptions of religion and offer eight ways of being religious, which range from encounters with a person-God, through mysticism, to "achieving an integrated self through interaction," to "creating the full life through sensuous experience." They define religion in terms of "ultimate transformation." An individual, prompted by a felt-need or profound dissatisfaction objectifies a goal or god and then strives to attain what he comes to conceive of as the ultimate state. His striving is his religion, and in spite of lip service paid to not making the conception of religion too permissive, it is clear that nothing can be excluded without circular appeal to some set of cultural or religious values which would allow us to distinguish between the important and the trivial.

Aside from rendering the notion of religiosity vacuous, the first horn is also dangerous since while most characterizations of ways of being religious are ethical, some may not be. There is a sanguine expectation that all will be ethical, and a readiness to reject as not "truly" religious those which are not; but these attitudes are indefensible so long as there are no standards which allow religious "visions" and ways of life to be evaluated other than in prudential terms.

The second horn of the dilemma—defining or conceiving of religiosity in terms of a way of life and having religious experience play only an authenticating role—is also unacceptable. If the religious way of life is defined in terms of its ethical and social aspects, and ritual is construed as nonessential, then we cannot differentiate the religious way of life from a moral, just, virtuous, but *non*-religious way of life. On the other hand, if ritual and the use of religious language are taken as essential, there will be behavioural criteria which will be logically adequate for the ascription of religious experience.

The latter alternative may seem to some to be perfectly acceptable. It will seem that no further criteria can satisfactorily be demanded in the case of religious experience than are satisfactorily demanded for ascribing pain to someone. There are, however, significant differences between the two cases. Perhaps most important is that the religious experience must play a legitimizing role with respect to behaviour. That is, assuming that religious experience is ascribed on the basis of logically adequate behavioural criteria, what are we to say about the claim that the subject is going to engage in certain ethically significant behaviour *because* of the religious "vision" so ascribed? The matter

131

here is not like explaining that someone is or will act in certain ways because of a debilitating pain; for while pain may *excuse*, it cannot *justify* conduct.

It is also noteworthy that in the case of pain we understand that, as a punishing sensation, pain can have certain behavioural consequences. Unless we want to say that all it *means* to say that someone is in pain is that he or she is behaving in a certain way, we must acknowledge that what we take the behavioural criteria to be adequate *for* is the presence of a punishing, distracting, or debilitating sensation. The character of the experience ascribed explains its function as something that causes, and excuses, unusual behaviour. Consider, though, the difficulty in trying to give a parallel characterization of the religious "vision." The trouble here is precisely with giving a characterization of the experience which is uniquely religious and is not reducible to an ethical or aesthetic characterization. This is exactly the question of the necessity of religious language.

What we want to conclude is that if the religious man is willing to allow that there are logically adequate behavioural criteria for the ascription of religious experience, then what I described as the authenticating role of religious experience becomes a fail-safe device. A man leading a way of life indicated by certain exemplary moral leaders and using religious language in certain ways will simply *have* had the religious experience and be authentically religious. That the life led cannot be distinguished from the moral life will seem irrelevant: It will be maintained that the religious is to be found not in the life itself *but in the nature of the commitment* to the moral life. The religious man will be one profoundly committed to the moral life, a life which, it is implied, is understood more fully by him than by one committed to it for, say, intellectual reasons.

We now have contention that the religious experience, like pain, is an inner process with outward criteria. As we cannot demand that pain be exhibited to legitimize pain-behaviour, we cannot demand that religious experience be exhibited to legitimize the use of religious language. Yet in both cases the behaviour is a consequence of the experience.

What the role of religious experience can be on the view in question, and whether on that view the notion of religious experience can have any content needs clarification here. As noted earlier, in the case of pain we understand the connection between the experience and the behaviour. And skeptical worries aside, human beings are sufficiently alike that little trouble arrives about the nature of the experience which is somehow responsible for pain-behaviour.

Religious experience, on the other hand, seems not to be characterizable, as pain can be characterized as a punishing or debilitating sensation. First, there is a question whether the religious "vision" is *uniquely* religious and not describable in terms of an ethical insight, etc. Second, there is a question whether the religious "vision" can be so characterized to relate it closely to one or another way of life. The main difficulty is that the "vision" cannot be characterized in terms of *doctrine*. That is, it cannot be characterized as the realization that such-and-such, since any "doctrine" will be only an image or metaphor.

Given the difficulty of characterization, a further question arises: How is the religious experience *recognized* as such? The answer will be that, as in the case of pain, we undergo certain training, based on the responses of others to our behaviour, and thereby come to associate certain concepts and expressions with what we experience. But again, we understand why the associative process works in the case of pain; we do not in the case of religious experience. It begins to look as if a religious experience is *whatever* the subject comes to associate with certain behaviour.

Many will feel that it is enough to characterize the religious experience or "vision" in terms of the pervasiveness and depth of outlook on moral matters or some such thing. What is wrong here is that while such a claim makes the religious-experience case more like the pain case, it does so at the cost of the alleged uniqueness of the religious: We are brought back precisely to the question of the alleged necessity of religious concepts and language to describe something like a moral insight or perspective.

There is clearly no conclusion to be drawn here except that, in the absence of religious *doctrine*, we have no reason to believe that religious language and concepts are necessary to deal with certain aspects of experience. All we have is the insistence that they are—an insistence based, allegedly, on some sort of first-hand experience of an aspect or dimension not adequately dealt with by our non-religious concepts and language. What is extremely difficult to understand is how the subject of such awareness *knows* religious concepts and language are necessary for dealing with the aspect or dimension of which he is supposedly uniquely aware. The religious man owes us an account of how he comes to understand the applicability of and necessity for an idiom—an idiom which, being essentially imagistic or metaphorical, is incapable of describing that to which it is somehow applicable prior to the initial experience of whatever it applies to. How, moreover, can he ever know he has got it *right*?

It seems that the only possible answer will be an essentially behavioural one: It will turn out to be a matter of living a certain life and using a certain idiom. But if that is the case, the notion of religious experience is an empty one.

Background Texts

Text 1: Saint Thomas Aquinas on Proving the Existence of God:

The existence of God can be proved in five ways.

The FIRST and more manifest WAY is the argument from motion or change. It is certain and evident to our senses that in the world some things undergo change. Now whatever is undergoing change is being changed by something else; for whatever is being changed is in potentiality to that to which it is being changed, but something brings about change inasmuch as it is in act. For change is nothing but the reduction of something from potentiality to actuality. Now nothing can be reduced from potentiality to actuality except by some being that is in actuality. So something that is actually hot, as fire, makes wood which is potentially hot to be actually hot, thus moving and changing it. Now it is not possible that the same thing should be at once in actuality and potentiality in the same respect, but only in different respects. For what is actually hot cannot be at the same time potentially hot, but it is at the same time potentially cold. It is therefore impossible that in the same respect and in the same way something should be changer and changed, i.e., that it should change itself. Therefore whatever is changed must be changed by something else.

Then if that which changes it is itself undergoing movement or change, this too must be moved by something else and that by something else again. But this cannot go on to infinity, because there would be no first mover or changer, and consequently no other mover, because subsequent movers bring about change or movement only in so far as they are being moved by the first mover, as the staff moves only in so far as it is moved by a hand. Therefore it is necessary to come to a first source of movement or change, which is not changed by anything, and this everyone understands to be God.

The SECOND WAY is from the nature of the efficient cause. Among things perceptible by the senses we find that there is an order of efficient causes. There is no case known, nor is it possible, that something should be efficient cause of itself. Then it would be prior to itself, which is impossible. Now in efficient causes it is not possible to go on to infinity, because in all efficient causes following in order the first is cause of the intermediate cause and the intermediate is cause of the last cause, whether the intermediate cause be several or only one. Now if the cause is eliminated, the effect is eliminated. Therefore if there is no first cause among efficient causes, there will be no last cause nor any intermediate ones. But if efficient causes went on to infinity, there would be no first efficient cause, then there would be no last efficient cause, nor any intermediate ones. This is plainly false. Therefore it is necessary to admit a first efficient cause, which everyone calls God (Thomas Aquinas *Summa of Theology* 1.2.3).

Then Aquinas proceeds to outline the OTHER THREE WAYS, from necessity and contingency, from degrees of perfection and from tendencies to goals in the universe.

Text 2: Plotinus Concerning the First Cause of All That Is:

Since the nature of the One is generative of everything, it is nothing of what things are. It is neither something, nor of such quality, nor so large, nor mind, nor soul, neither in motion nor at rest, neither in place nor in time, but unique in form or rather formless, being prior to every form, prior to movement and to rest; for these are attributes of being which render it multiple. . . . To call it "the Cause" is not to affirm any accident of it, but of us, since we receive something from it, while it remains in itself. To speak accurately we must call it neither this nor that, but try to express our own notions, hovering about it, so to speak, sometimes close, sometimes falling back baffled by the enigmas involved (Plotinus *Enneads* 6.9.3).

Text 3: "Dionysius the Areopagite" on the Unity of God:

[The Cause of everything is] one because it is all things in unity according to the eminence of its unique oneness. For none of the things that are lacks a share of unity, but just as every number shares in unity (for we say "one pair," "one decade," "one half," "one third," "one tenth"), so everything and every part shares in unity, and by being one each thing is a being. The one Cause of everything is not one of the many, but is prior to all unity and plurality and determines all unity and plurality ("Dionysius" *Divine Names* 13.2).

Text 4: Saint Thomas Aquinas Regarding the Meaning of Predicates such as "Good," "Wise," "Just," etc. When Attributed to God:

In accord with the opinion of "Dionysius" (see *Divine Names* 13; a small portion is quoted above in Text 3) it must be said that predicates of this kind signify the substance [or essence] of God, although in a deficient and imperfect way. This is shown as follows:

Every agent acts insofar as it actually is, and consequently produces what is in some way like itself; hence the form of what is produced must be in the agent. This is so in different ways:

(a) When the effect equals the power of the agent, that form must be in the producer and in the produced in the same way; then the maker and the product belong in the same species. This is so in all univocal causes: A human being generates a human being, and fire generates fire.

(b) But when the effect does not equal the power of the agent, the form is not in the agent and in the product in the same way; it is in the agent in a more noble way. According as it is in the agent, the agent has the power to produce the effect. Hence if the whole power of the agent is not expressed in the effect, then the form is in the agent in a more excellent manner than it is in the effect. And this we see in all equivocal agents, as when the sun generates fire.

Now it is certain that no effect equates the power of the First Agent, namely God; otherwise only one effect would be produced by his power. But since we find many effects of different kinds produced by his one power, we can see that any one of them falls short of the power of the Agent. Therefore no form of any effect of God is in God in the same way in which it is in the effect. Nevertheless it must be in him in some superior way. Hence all forms which in diverse effects are distinct and separated are united in God as in one common Source [literally power]. Just so, all the forms produced in this lower world by the power of the sun are united in the unique power of the sun. All things generated through the action of the sun are made like to this one power. Likewise the perfections of created things are made like the unique, simple essence of God.

Now the human intellect, since it receives its knowledge from created things, is informed by the likenesses of perfections found in creatures, such as wisdom, power, goodness, etc. Hence, just as created things by their perfections are like God in some way, but deficiently, our minds are informed in a similar manner by the species [likenesses, concepts] of these perfections. . . . Hence, when an intellect informed by these species predicates these perfections of God, it is true that they exist in God; he corresponds to each one of these predicated notions inasmuch as they are all like him.

. . . But the species we are talking about is not a complete likeness of God's essence, as has been said. And so, although predicates of this kind which the intellect on the basis of such conceptions attributes to

God signify what the substance of God is, they do not signify it completely as it is, but as it is understood by us.

So then it must be said that any one of these predicates indicates the substance of God, not as comprehending it, but imperfectly. For this reason the name *He who is* is most fitting for God because it does not signify a definite form, but *being* in an indeterminate way (Thomas Aquinas *On the Power of God* 7.5 from the body of the article).

God, the Null Set, and Divine Simplicity

C.B. MARTIN

There is an argument that should have been put forward by St. Thomas but wasn't. It is implicit in much of what he wrote and ranges over explanations of what happens in the world of higher and higher degrees of generality. I shall express this argument informally:

1. If an explanation does not preclude the possibility of what it explains being explained by a still more general explanation, then it is rational to suppose that there is such a more general explanation.
2. Explanations of higher degrees of generality are not endless.
3. Conclusion: It is rational to suppose that there is an explanation (or set of explanations) that preclude the possibility of what is explained being explained in a still more general explanation.

It is hard to see how a scientific explanation or set of scientific explanations would preclude this possibility of there being a still more general explanation.

If we call an explanation that would preclude such a possibility a basic explanation, then I think we must conclude that a scientific form of explanations will not be basic.

If we call items figuring in an explanation "explaining items" and items figuring in a basic explanation "basic items," then we should be able to see what features a basic item must have or lack in order not to allow of explanation. Here, St. Thomas is of great help. We might ask for an explanation of why something has changed or has not changed. In order to keep this from being askable, St. Thomas suggests that the basic item must be logically incapable of alteration because it is pure act having no potency or tendency for change.

We might ask for an explanation of why something is the way it is rather than some other way. In order to keep this from being askable, St. Thomas says that the basic item must lack a complex nature, must lack composition. Thus, all its apparently distinct properties must ultimately be identical with one another.

We might ask for an explanation of why something exists at all. In order to keep this from being askable, St. Thomas says that the basic item must have the necessity of its existence in itself. This it does, not only by having its properties identical with one another, but also having them identical with its very existence. Its essence and existence are identical and inseparable. With the basic item the *kind* of being and

138

the *fact* of being are one and the same. Understanding that, one sees how the question "Why does the kind of being exist?" is inadvisable —there isn't anything to *happen*. Here we have the simplicity of God attributed to the basic item. If the basic item is to be logically inexplicable, then there must be *ways* of making unaskable the questions that make explicability thinkable. How then can the basic item fall short of having the Thomistic simplicity?

St. Thomas' doctrine of the Divine Simplicity shows *how* the stopping place in explanation must be *logically* inadmissable of further explanation. Thus, St. Thomas is not touched by the thrust of Hume's argument in *A Dialogue Concerning Natural Religion*. Hume's *Dialogue* is a sophisticated, witty, and profound development of the child's question "Who made God?" Hume asks the challenging question, "How is God a more final stopping place in explanation than is the world itself?" St. Thomas answers in terms of the Divine Simplicity. And here an answer is given as to *how* the basic item in the stopping place of explanation rules out of court all questions concerning its explanation.

With the massive grasp of genius, St. Thomas saw where he must go, and go he went. Is there another alternative? Almost twenty years ago, I suggested one that was later taken up by some writers. It is worth raising again in this context.

Let the basic item be a factually necessary being, which is defined as a being that is causally necessary and sufficient for everything else and nothing else is causally necessary or sufficient for it. On this account the most plausible candidate for a basic item would seem to be the world's stock of energy. If we believe the law of the conservation of energy, it does not come to be or pass away. And it does the work of any change that occurs. But then, of course, it is *just* a fact and an unexplained fact that the basic item is basic. And this is so whether the basic item is divine or worldly.

There is another very different alternative. A basic item might be defined as one whose existence is logically necessary and whose possession of its basic properties is logically necessary. Thirty or forty years ago, a sophisticated arch of the eyebrows would have been quite enough to devastate such a suggestion. Now, despite the efforts of Quine and others, intelligent.men and women have made the indecent categories of modal logic at least respectable.

There are able philosophers who get paid well, who believe in the existence of sets, and in particular the null set, and who also employ the modal notions. I think it is clear that at least for these people, the null set should be a logically necessary being. The null set is that set having no members. The non-existence of something determines the null set. A contradiction designates what does not exist in all possible

139

worlds. What does not exist in all possible worlds determines the null set for all possible worlds. As to logically necessary properties, for all possible worlds the null set has the property of lacking numbers.

It might also be said that in every possible world something does not exist. For any possible world if A is standing at a particular time, then A not standing at that time does not exist. So for any possible world something will not exist and so determine the null set.

Further to logically necessary properties, if we allow occupancy of space-time (something which sets, for example, lack) to be a property of something, I cannot help but think it is a logically necessary property of that something under any possibly true description and under any possible change. If it can change, for example, into the number two or the null set, then of course I am wrong.

However, God's properties of goodness, wisdom and power do not *seem* to be the sort that could be logically necessary. They seem to be just the sorts of properties that something *could* cease to have. When it is argued that it is different when they are applied to God and in ways we cannot understand, it is fair to reply that it is no longer clear that those properties that we have some understanding of are still *being* applied at all.

It would not seem to be entirely philosophically outlandish for someone to explain the basic item's defiance of explanation in terms of its logically necessary existence and its logically necessary possession of its properties. So far there has been no mention of the Thomistic simplicity. I do not think, however, that this can be avoided.

The assertion of logical necessity is not sufficient. There is also the need to make it to some degree apparent. It is hardly a category for casual attribution. We could see *how* the null class might be thought to be a necessary being. Now we have to be brought to see *how* the basic item, let us call it God, might be thought to be a necessary being. There is an obvious reply, namely in terms of the Thomistic simplicity of God. And I am not sure that there is any other reply whatsoever to such a reasonable request.

If God's properties are all one with one another and one with his very existence, then there is no division between what he is and that he is. If that is so, the question how does such a kind of being come to be, is critically malformed. A *way* to be cannot come into or pass out of existence. Indeed, if it is said to be at all, it *must* be. So, if the existence of something is identical with its way of being, then it *must* exist.

The trouble, however, with the idea that the basic item's properties are one with one another and one with its very existence, namely that God's goodness, power, and intelligence are one with one another and his existence, is just that it is hogwash. I mean there is no deep or

140

profound difficulty needing to be researched by experts. It is simply that three obviously distinct properties are said in a particular instance of their application to be one and indeed one with the existence of the object to which they are applied. And I am not gentled into acquiescent non-comprehension by being told that these simplicities are not to be made coherent to the finite mind. I am reminded of how F.R. Tennant, that unusually intelligent and crusty theologian, began a book review with the sentence, "Let us call nonsense by its name."

But the real point is that it took the genius of St. Thomas to see that one has to go to the absurd lengths of the simplicity doctrine to show *how* the basic items' nature rules out and disallows all question concerning its explanation. It is ironical that establishing the consistent demand for a basic entity that disallows all such question only leads to absurdity. It is worth learning that the stopping place of explanation, wherever it may be, *must* fall short of such a basic entity. One of the main drives of cosmological forms of argument is therefore lost. The moral is that any explaining item must be at least logically, if not actually, capable of being itself explained.

For those who *insist* on raising the issue of the ontological argument whenever and however the logically necessary existence of God is discussed, the following comments may help: The ontological argument for the existence of God takes many forms. It has sometimes been put in such a way that the very concept of God involves the idea of God's existence as a logically necessary being. That is, from the concept of God as the most perfect possible being, it can be seen that a being whose non-existence was logically possible is less perfect than a being whose existence was logically necessary. The concept of God as the most perfect possible being is consistent with the attribution of logically necessary existence to such a being. It is further argued that, unless one can show that such a concept is somehow incoherent or that the existence of such a most perfect being (incorporating logically necessary existence) is logically impossible, one cannot stop short of attributing logically necessary existence to it.

There have been many attempted refutations of this rough form of the ontological argument. The most frequent is that the idea of a logically necessary being is incoherent, that it is logically impossible that any such being could exist. This attempted refutation is weakened by my earlier argument that the null set could be plausibly, even if wrongly, thought of as a logically necessary being.

It is important, however, to remember the obligation to give some coherent account of *how* to conceive the logically necessary existence of the null set which cannot simply be asserted. In the case of God, I tried to argue that the only way of conceiving the *how* of God's

141

logically necessary existence seemed to be in terms of the Thomistic doctrine of Divine Simplicity which, at least, appears to be incoherent. So, the argument that there is incoherency in the concept of God as the most perfect being (whose perfection includes logically necessary existence) is on a different footing and is stronger than ever.

To return to our original argument: I have tried to show that it is a *reductio ad absurdum*. The conclusion has absurd and incoherent implications. Which, then, of the two premises is false? The second premise is that explanations of higher degrees of generality are not endless. I don't really know how to argue for either the truth or falsity of this premise, and I can't remember anything particularly profitable having been said by anyone else. I find myself inclined, however, to believe that it is true and to like the idea of its being true. (I can see that if space-time is infinite and if there are an infinite number of *kinds* of elementary particles, then the second premise would be false. But I still know of no argument that would show this is the case.) So I shall turn to the first premise:

> If an explanation does not preclude the possibility of what it explains being explained by a still more general explanation, then it is rational to suppose that there is such a more general explanation.

This premise, as well as the second, has been assented to by a number of philosophers of my acquaintance who flinched from the conclusion and its implications. The oddity is that it has the form of going from "possible that" to "rational to suppose that." Only one colleague noted this, and even he thought this obvious howler of inference might still hold in the special case of explanation. It clearly is geared to hold in certain modal contexts ranging at least over numbers. When pressed no one could say why it should hold with explanation. Why then should the premise have seemed so plausible?

I think the answer may lie in the sociology and history of human explanation-giving and explanation-seeking. By and large we have not lived with problem-free explanations of great generality. For any particular explanation there have been problems that needed a still further explanation for resolution. Though it seemed for a while as if we almost achieved it with Newton, we have not lived with a problem-free physics. We may lack the intelligence to develop the unity of science with an over-arching, problem-free physics. Let us suppose, what many consider supposable, that two hundred years from now such a unification of science is achieved and is problem-free. For three hundred years the most brilliant minds attempt to find a problem and fail. If after that time we actually were in, or even if we were only to think we were in, such a problem-free theoretical state, then I believe we would not find the first premise of our argument intuitively plausible. That is, we would rest content with the "stopping-place" explanatory items and their known and understandable properties, though granting still that their further explanation was not in unthinkable logical absurdity, but just a needless logical fantasy.

My theme has been that the only way I can see of making apparent how the nature of the basic item or set of items of explanation *necessarily* excludes the thinkability of explanation is *via* something in the form of St. Thomas's Simplicity of God—and this seems contradictory and incoherent. One can of course apply necessities where they are not apparent, but that would seem *ad hoc*.

Clear and Distinct Explanations of God

FRANCIS FIRTH, C.S.B.

Professor C.B. Martin expresses considerable admiration for Saint Thomas Aquinas' "massive grasp of genius" and makes generous efforts to be fair to his demonstrations. But in spite of this distinguished scholar's good intentions, I would call into question his success at being really fair to the philosophy of St. Thomas.

I. An "Obvious Howler"?

Martin begins by formulating an argument which, he claims, is implicit in much of Aquinas' writings. The initial premise is as follows:

> If an explanation does not preclude the possibility of what it explains being explained by a still more general explanation, then it is rational to suppose that there is such a more general explanation.

Near the end of his paper he points to an "obvious howler of inference" in this premise: from "possible that" to "rational to suppose that." It seems to me this howler is to be attributed to Martin, not to Aquinas. St. Thomas—whether he is right or wrong is not now in question—insists that in the experienced universe there are many things which necessarily require a more basic source, a source of movement, or of causality, or whatever. Then he reasons that this source in its turn must require a still more basic source, and so forth. He does not leap from the possibility of a source to its actual existence. Rather he proceeds from the necessity of presupposing a cause of observed phenonena to the actual existence of that cause.

II. Is Divine Simplicity Really "Hogwash"?

Professor Martin's principal claim in his article has to do with Aquinas' insistence on Divine simplicity—that such attributes as God's goodness, power, and intelligence are in reality absolutely one with one another and with his existence. Martin first shows the importance of this contention; then he rejects it as absolutely impossible:

> It is simply that three obviously distinct properties are said in a particular instance of their application to be one, and indeed one with the existence of the object to which they are applied. And I am not gentled into acquiescent non-comprehension by being told that these simplicities are not to be made coherent to the finite mind.

I maintain that here he has misconstrued Aquinas' position. He understands Saint Thomas to say that properties which are obviously distinct are in fact identical in God, but that our limited human intelligence cannot understand how they can be identical.

This is not Aquinas' position. True, he insists that in God *his* power, and *his* wisdom, and *his* goodness are identical. But these are not properties, either one or many; in fact, they are not what we understand by power, and wisdom, and goodness. We know them only as they are found in creatures. As such, they are properties and are obviously distinct; they could not be identical. In God as conceived by Aquinas, there are no properties in the strict sense of the word. A property is an actuality modifying some reality, which must have the capacity to be so modified. In God there is nothing to be actualized; he is pure actuality itself. This actuality includes in itself all of the perfection or actuality that is found or could be found in anything else, but in a much better way: the way of the unique Self-existent.

Aquinas finds various parallels to this within this world of man and his affairs:

> Something like this can be found in the knowing and operative powers of man. For by its one power the intellect knows all that the sensitive part [of the soul] grasps through a diversity of powers—and much more besides. So too, the more perfect an intellect is, the better it can know by one [likeness] what a lesser intellect gets to know only through many [likenesses]. So too, a king's power extends to many things over which diverse authorities under him have control. In this way, then, through his one simple *being* God possesses every kind of perfection that other things come to possess, but [they] a much diminished [perfection] through diverse [principles]. (*On the Truth of the Catholic Faith* 1.31.281)

St. Thomas explains his meaning at greater length in one of his public disputations. The reader is directed to Background Text 4, offered before Professor Martin's paper. In this text the example of the sun and its relations to other things is typical of many uses which Aquinas makes of the physics of his day. We in the twentieth century are quite aware of the great differences between the physical speculations of his time and our modern physics, which is based on far more carefully controlled experiments. Nevertheless his use of this example can enlighten us concerning his meaning. Aquinas does not understand that the physical characteristics of animals or plants (other than warmth) are found in the sun. Rather he sees in the sun a superior nature, source not only of the warmth, but also of the generative activity of plants and animals on earth, and hence of the nature of each animal and plant so generated. These latter natures, he understands, must in some way be found in the sun to the extent that its superior nature is able to produce them. Analogously he sees in creatures many perfections derived from the unique, absolute perfection of God. These characteristics of creatures must be in some way like their Source. Thus, he reasons, the source can be said to contain all their perfections in the unity of its one essence.

So Aquinas does not claim that obviously distinct properties are identical in God, but rather that his absolute unity in its simple perfection is the Source containing all that is positive or of value in all properties with none of their deficiencies. This position cannot be rejected out of hand as "nonsense."

III. Is God Really Wise and Powerful and Good?

However there is another objection which might be directed against this position, even perhaps by sincere Christians. This is expressed by Cleanthes in the *Dialogue* of David Hume mentioned by Professor Martin:

> A mind whose acts and sentiments and ideas are not distinct and successive, one that is wholly simple and totally immutable, is a mind that has no thought, no reason, no will, no sentiment, no love, no hatred, or in a word no mind at all. (Part 4)

This sort of objection might be phrased as follows: If Aquinas claims that God has no properties, that he is not wise or powerful or good as we understand these terms, then what right has he to say that God is wise or powerful or good in any real sense?

To help in unravelling this dilemma, a dilemma of which St. Thomas was acutely conscious, it would be well for us to recall that Aquinas did not invent the notion of Divine simplicity. Long before, it had been used and taught by Saint Augustine of Hippo and by many other Christian writers. When Aquinas began writing in the thirteenth century it had long been accepted as standard doctrine in the Christian schools. Augustine and other fathers of the Church had found its basis in the teachings of Plotinus and of other neo-Platonists; these in turn had developed their conception from the reasoning of Plato, who in turn had been influenced by Parmenides.

Plotinus wrestles with this problem and arrives at insights that are deep and penetrating. He argues that the First Source of everything must be absolutely simple; nothing can happen to it, for there is nothing to happen. It is not intelligent or active, for that would imply that it needed to be perfected by intelligence or activity. "As Plato rightly says, it is above intelligence" (Plotinus, *Enneads* 6.7.37). "Immune from intellection, the Good is purely what it is, not fettered

146

by the presence of understanding, which would annul its purity and unity" (*Enneads* 6.7.40). Rather than attribute intellectual activity to the First Principle of all, he speaks of "august repose." Yet immediately he sees difficulties with this word "repose"; inactivity can be like the passivity of something dead. In the end, he finds it "more august and venerable and truly venerable" to attribute repose rather than intellectual activity to what surpasses every process of reasoning (See *Enneads* 6.7.39). Thus Plotinus finds himself at a loss for words. He strenuously denies to the First Principle all duality or multiplicity, all definite, limited characteristics; then he has to keep explaining that he does not mean that the Good is in any way inferior; rather it is superior to the perfections found in the things caused by it.

Many Christian writers, as well as some non-Christian followers of Plotinus, have carried this reasoning a step further. If the absolute Unity is superior to all attributes, they argue, it can be said to include those attributes in a superior way. What is "above intelligence" is said to be *super*-intelligent; in this sense it can be called intelligent. It is truer and less misleading, they claim, to ascribe such characteristics to God than not to ascribe them. One is reminded here of the little girl mentioned by C.S. Lewis whose parents described God to her as "perfect substance," carefully avoiding any such "anthropomorphic" language as "knowing" or "loving." She got the general impression that God was like tapioca. And she did not like tapioca!

One who developed reasoning about God's attributes with considerable subtlety was an otherwise unknown Christian Platonist who wrote c. A.D. 500 under the name "Dionysios the Areopagite," as if he were the convert made by St. Paul about 450 years earlier (see *Acts of the Apostles* 17.34). He developed a theory about the way in which predicates can be affirmed and denied of God. In connection with the disputation quoted above in Text 4, Aquinas confronts himself with a Plotinian objection based on the works of this author: "No name which signifies the substance of anything can be truly denied of it. Now Dionysios says that concerning God negations are true, affirmations inappropriate" (Aquinas *On the Power of God* 7.5 obj. 2).

After expounding his own teaching, a good part of which has been quoted above in Text 4, St. Thomas replies to this objection as follows:

> Dionysios says that negations of these names are true of God, but not in the sense that affirmations are false or inappropriate. As regards the reality signified, they are truly attributed to God; for this reality is in him in some way as has been shown. But as regards the mode in which they signify, they can be denied God. For each of these names signifies some definite form, and thus they are not attributed to God, as has been said. And so, in the absolute sense they can be denied of God, because they do

not belong to him in the mode signified, i.e., the mode they have in our minds. They belong to God not in this mode but in a more sublime way. So affirmation of them is said to be inappropriate because it is not entirely fitting to ascribe them to God on account of a difference of mode.

So, according to the teaching of Dionysios [see his *Celestial Hierarchy* 2; *Mystical Theology* 3–5; *Divine Names* passim, esp. 1.5–8, 4.1–17, 5, 12] these properties are mentioned in relation to God in three ways. First affirmatively: We say "God is wise." We should say that about him because in him is a likeness of the wisdom which is caused by him. But because wisdom as we understand and name wisdom is not found in God, it can truly be denied. We can say "God is not wise." Again, because we do not deny wisdom of God because he falls short of wisdom, but because it is in him in a more eminent way than is predicated or understood, therefore we must say that God is superwise (Aquinas *On the Power of God* 7.5 answer to obj. 2).

St. Thomas thus distinguishes between the reality signified by such a name on the one hand, and on the other the manner in which the perfection in question exists in created material things which we know. In them there are many different properties. God's unique reality contains all that is positive and good in his manifold effects.

Many of the predicates which we apply to creatures, says Thomas, contain in their notion some deficiency or lack. Such are all that contain matter or necessarily belong to material things, for example "fire," "coloured," "angry," "rock." These can be truthfully predicated of God only in metaphor. In a literal sense they do not belong to him at all. Included here, too, are all those that imply change, such as "reasoning" or "improvement." The predicates which are the main subject of our discussion are those such as "wise," "powerful," and "good." The meaning of these terms, he says, is such as not to imply the existence of any imperfection. But as we understand the qualities expressed by these terms, and as these qualities are found in things of our acquaintance, they seem to involve imperfection, including the imperfection of diversity and difference. What is different from something else lacks something that the other has. But the essential meaning of each of these predicates, he maintains, does not involve such deficiencies; rather these defects belong to the mode of realization of these qualities in created things, and hence affect our human thinking about them.

Thus Aquinas maintains that in some real sense God should be called wise, and powerful, and good, even though in him there are no such properties; rather he is one perfect Reality superior to them all. But while this reality is absolutely one, creatures can be related to it in different ways, and the use of some relational predicates, such as "Creator" or "Ruler," to describe God appropriately must express such differences. For example, talk of God's power implies that various distinct things can be produced by him. These things are distinct from one another and from God; their dependence on him is very real. But the Source of them all and of this dependence is the unique reality of God himself.

This reality St. Thomas conceives to be identical with God's own existence—God is held to be pure actual existence, not limited by one or other manner of existing. His manner of existing is just simply *to be* without limit or qualification. But since we cannot conceive this clearly, we can reasonably ask, "Does such a being really exist?" Aquinas thus does admit a distinction between *saying* what God is and *saying* that he is. To God himself it is clear that these are identical, but not to us human beings in this life on earth.

IV. Analogies from the World of Science

In the world of our ordinary experience and in the history of scientific investigations, many instances could be pointed out in which one reality can be known, conceived, and spoken about in two or more different ways. Among primitive people it is not always realized that the magic power by which a physician cures people is the same as the knowledge and understanding which he has acquired by poring over books and experimenting in the laboratory. Not everyone realizes that the heat which feels warm to the touch, which expands and softens iron and makes it glow, is understood by the scientist as a swifter movement of molecules within the iron itself.

Because of the success of modern science at proving the identity of apparently distinct objects of human experience and providing explanations that fit many different observations, most people nowadays are ready to accept from scientists explanations that seem quite contrary to normal experience; they are anomalies, not flat contradictions. So it is with the conviction of Aquinas, along with many other Christian thinkers, about the absolute simplicity of God: It involves not logical contradiction, but anomaly. God's essence is not identified with many properties, but in its absolute unity surpasses, and so virtually includes, all that is positive and all that can truly be called "perfection" in the properties of other things. In this sense only can these properties be predicated of him.

V. God of Our Fathers?

This reasoning might satisfy the logician, but should a believing Christian, or for that matter a believing Jew or Moslem, accept such

149

conclusions? Can this be the God of Abraham, Isaac, and Jacob, who spoke through the prophets, who is believed to exercise providence over this world? Can this be the God to whom religious people of many faiths pray as to a personal Lord and Father? To ask this question is to show that one has forgotten what the scriptures of all these traditions have to say about the mysterious, hidden nature of God, who is not like popular images and conceptions. As St. Paul says, "The depths of God can be known only by the Spirit of God" (1 Cor 2.11). Aquinas by his reasoning does not eliminate this obscurity, but rather emphasizes it. He himself and many other devout believers have found nothing in such a theological conception incompatible with personal devotion to God, with a life devoted to prayer as well as to study and research.

VI. Clear and Distinct Ideas?

One event in the history of human thought that has made it more difficult for believer and unbeliever alike to accept St. Thomas' understanding of God is the resolution taken by René Descartes "to carefully avoid precipitation and prejudice in my judgments, and to accept in them nothing more than was presented to my mind so clearly and distinctly that I could have no occasion to doubt it" (*Discourse on Method*, Part 2). There is much to be admired in such a resolution; for one in Descartes' situation it is quite understandable. Yet this same resolution involves something rash: He who adheres to it without reservation accepts by implication that clarity is the first test of truth. This has had unfortunate results. It has led to the rejection, not only of metaphysics, but also of ethics, as meaningless; it has driven some into skepticism, others into solipsism; it has led to that kind of philosophy which rejects God's non-complexity as "hogwash."

The reasoning of Aquinas shows that any knowledge of the First Principle of all reality cannot be clear and distinct. To look for clear and distinct ideas about God is thus a hopeless task; this explains the difficulty which many find with "proofs" for his existence. But although such clarity and precision about him is beyond the human mind, we can still find in the universe genuine indications of God. Correct reasoning about this world does not "prove" his existence in the Cartesian sense, but it points to him. A discerning mind can come to realize the dependence of this universe on a First Principle and can find that it points, not clearly and distinctly, but truly and cogently, to something such as that personal God which Jews, Christians, and Moslems acknowledge and worship.

150

VII. Conclusion

Of course there is much more that might be discussed about St. Thomas' arguments concerning the existence and nature of God. I do not hold that, as he presents them, all of them are cogent. The first of the five ways, for example, is still too closely connected with Aristotle's physics, which does not allow for what we call "momentum." But I hope to have shown by now that some of Professor Martin's objections to Aquinas' reasoning are not convincing either. Aquinas does not reason from possibility to actual existence. He does not identify obviously distinct properties, but points to a source for all properties which is a Being of absolute unity. Although this Being is not understood by "clear and distinct ideas," but "in a glass darkly," neither is it completely beyond the reach of the human mind.

Can Faith Be a Christian Virtue?

WAYNE GRENNAN

Ever since St. Paul singled it out as a quality Christians must possess, faith has been considered a virtue by the Church (see I *Corinthians* 13:13). In this paper I shall argue that belief in the Christian God militates against seeing faith as a virtue deserving the place of importance given to it. This conclusion is the unexpected outcome of the way Roman Catholic and Protestant theologians talk of faith, when this is taken in conjunction with the claims these groups make about the nature of God.

My approach will be to examine the accounts of religious faith generally accepted by the Roman Catholic and Protestant traditions, rather than presenting some account of faith that I take to be true and judging Christian positions in terms of it. This would be an external approach in contrast to my internal one. I am concerned with what has been said about faith within Christianity, and this is best done by assuming with Christians that the Christian God exists. Consequently, I shall not consider at all the atheist's argument that religious faith cannot be a virtue because there is no object for such faith. This argument is sound if the Christian God does not exist, but it seems to me quite uninteresting because it tells us nothing about religious faith as a crucial religious concept.

Let us begin with the traditional Roman Catholic account of religious faith. A succinct version was provided by the First Vatican Council, and according to the *New Catholic Encyclopedia* (to be referred to as "*NCE*") this account represents "the most important and complete doctrinal statement on faith . . ." (*NCE*, vol. 5, p. 797).

According to Vatican I, faith is ". . . a supernatural virtue by which . . . we hold as true what God has revealed, not because we have perceived its intrinsic truth by our reason but because of the authority of God who can neither deceive nor be deceived . . . (*NCE* Vol. 5, p. 797). The article also supplies a definition for faith in general which ". . . is to be described as a firm persuasion whereby a person assents to truths that are not seen and cannot be proved but are taken on trust in the reliability of another" (*NCE*, Vol. 5, p. 798).

On this account faith is a propositional attitude reached in a special way. The person who has faith is firmly persuaded of the truth of some proposition or set of propositions. This attitude comes through trust in the reliability of a putative authority on the matter of what has been said.

As Roman Catholic writers describe it, faith can be contrasted with what we might call "unmediated belief," one arrived at through immediate acquaintance with the direct evidence for a proposition. I may come to believe, for instance, that water turns to ice when cooled to a certain degree by perceiving that certain things happen when water is cooled. This is an unmediated belief since I am not relying upon anyone else's testimony. On the other hand, if I were a native of some hot country, I might very well have arrived at the same belief by trusting someone I took to be in a position to know about such things.

These two sorts of belief are epistemologically connected, it seems. If I have mediated belief, it will be based upon my belief that some particular person is an authority on this sort of topic. If I am rational and prudent, I will form my judgment about the competence of the putative authority on the basis of direct evidence for such competence. Thus, to the extent that direct evidence for competence is favourable, this represents indirect evidence for the mediated belief.

The foregoing is something of a digression. The question to be answered is: "Is religious faith a virtue?" I should like to deal with it by first presenting the definition of a virtue generally accepted by Roman Catholic writers: "a habitual, well established, readiness or disposition of man's powers directing them to some specific goodness of act" (*NCE* Vol. 14, p. 704). Without serious distortion we can streamline the definition fairly satisfactorily by saying that a virtue is a habitual disposition to act in a certain meritorious way.

The first point worth making is that faith, as a propositional attitude, is not the sort of thing that can qualify as a habitual disposition. Therefore, it cannot be a virtue. This consideration seems to have been in the minds of the participants at the Council of Trent where, we are told, ". . . there was reluctance to employ the technical term 'habit' . . ." (T.C. O'Brien, *NCE* Vol. 14, p. 704). Although this reluctance amounts, nevertheless, to a reluctance to call faith, hope, and love, "virtues," the writer assures us "that these infused endowments are best described as true virtues is theologically certain" (*NCE* Vol. 14, p. 706).

It seems then, that faith, religious, or other, cannot be a virtue if we accept the Roman Catholic definition of "virtue." This is not to say that particular examples of faith cannot be praiseworthy. But because virtues are praiseworthy, it does not follow that every praiseworthy human attribute is a virtue.

At this juncture, two realistic alternatives are open to the Catholic theologian who accepts our conclusion: Either he can say that although religious faith as he defines it is not a virtue, it is nevertheless a meritorious condition to be in; or he can alter his definition of "faith" to fit the definition of "virtue" so that faith does qualify as a virtue. This amounts to adopting a Humpty Dumpty policy about word meaning: "Faith" means whatever one defines it to mean. To get away with this, one's subsequent use of the term must conform to that definition, however. Otherwise, one would be involved in an inconsistency.

Setting this consideration aside, what would the new definition of "faith" be? If a virtue is an habitual disposition to act in a certain meritorious way, then "faith" might be defined as "an habitual disposition to become firmly persuaded of the truth of a proposition on the basis of trust in the reliability of another."

Now is there anything essentially meritorious in the disposition to become firmly persuaded of the truth of a proposition on the basis of trust in the reliability of another? If there is not, then we again can say that faith (so defined) is not a virtue. And, in fact, it seems that the disposition described is neutral with respect to merit and, therefore, does not stand up as an adequate definition of a particular virtue. At first sight, it appears that it is laudable to become persuaded of the truth of a proposition to the degree to which one trusts its author. But this will only be true when one's trust in the author as an authority is based on good grounds. Trust is a very subjective attitude since it can be generated by all sorts of factors not relevant to establishing that a particular individual is a genuine authority.

Thus, the definition proposed does not exclude individuals who are gullible, and gullibility is no virtue. To exclude these cases, the definition must stipulate that the disposition is that of being persuaded in proportion to *well-placed* trust. Adjusting the definition this way makes it a description of a meritorious quality, but unfortunately the merit does not come from the right source. The quality described is actually one form of prudence, one of the recognized virtues. But if we discount any merit arising from prudence, the remainder (if there is any) seems to be due to trust. Some people will want to say that faith is trust, so that the definition is satisfactory after all. If Roman Catholic theologians take this line however, they will be abandoning rather than adjusting the Vatican I position. That position involves essential reference to propositional attitudes or dispositions to propositional attitudes.

Thinking of faith as a personal attitude—the Protestant view—is quite different. Here, the sponsors of the new definition might retreat a bit and argue that religious faith is a praiseworthy disposition to become firmly persuaded of the truth of propositions *God* asserts on the basis of trust in the reliability of God. In other words, it is laudable to be disposed to assent to whatever God says.

154

It is odd to talk in this way about propositions revealed by God. In everyday situations, we commonly try to identify the proposer and his qualifications when something is proposed for our assent. But what do we do when the proposer is identified by us (correctly or incorrectly) as God? In this case, because God is omniscient, omnipotent, incapable of deceit, there is no question of withholding assent. All reasonable persons will assent to what God declares. This is what prompts Hobbes to remark that "... not only Christians, but all manner of men do so believe in God, as to hold for truth all they hear him say, whether they understand it, or not; which is all the faith and trust can possibly be had in any person whatsoever . . ." (*Leviathan*, Part One, Chapter 7).

That the situation is an extraordinary one when God is presenting claims for our assent can be shown in another way. In ordinary cases, it is logically possible to doubt the truth of a claim in spite of the fact that we trust implicitly in the reliability of the proposer because even the most competent human authority can make a mistake. Perhaps the claim being made is contentious within the discipline and ultimately turns out to be false. Or perhaps the authority blunders in arriving at his findings. But if the authority is the Christian God, he obviously cannot propose anything false for our belief, so that doubt is logically precluded. It is logically precluded because to doubt the truth of God's claim is at the same time to doubt that it is God who has made the claim.

There is, then, nothing especially meritorious in a disposition to be persuaded of the truth of a claim on the basis of trust in the reliability of God. Furthermore, the merit associated with the disposition is the merit associated with a disposition to act rationally. The individual who believes that God asserts "P" must give his assent to it, since "God asserts 'P'" entails "P." His action is no more and no less praiseworthy than his assenting to the conclusion of any valid argument whose premises he accepts.

An important point here is that Roman Catholic theologians may be unable to accept faith as a disposition, since it seems that one can have a disposition to be firmly persuaded of the truth of God's claims without actually assenting to any Christian doctrine. This is possible because one can possess a disposition without ever having acted from it. Since all rational people have the disposition in question, the theologians will be forced to say that even those who have never heard of Christianity possess Christian faith—an implication so absurd that it seems to call for denying that faith is a disposition at all.

In light of these considerations, the other alternative seems more promising. The theologian can insist that faith, as a propositional attitude, is sometimes a meritorious condition to have. Obviously, he will have to admit that being firmly persuaded of the truth of a claim is not meritorious when one's trust in an authority is ill-founded. But he will want to say that being persuaded of the truth of propositions revealed by God is a meritorious condition.

Unfortunately, some of the same objections apply here that applied to viewing faith as a disposition. Just as, given the nature of God, a disposition to be persuaded to accept what he says is true is no specially meritorious quality, neither is actual assent specially laudable.

It can be pointed out that I am assuming that the merit in an action is proportional to the effort required. That is, there is less merit in assenting to what God says because God is infinitely more reliable than any human authority. It seems that these claims go against our actual practice of conferring praise on the basis of merit which is reflected in the definition of virtue as an habitual disposition: one that is exercised effortlessly. Consider, for example, two trapeze artists, both of whom sometimes perform the very difficult triple somersault. One, however, can do it whenever he pleases, but the other finds it more difficult, and sometimes fails in the attempt. Without doubt more praise is directed to the former than the latter, for whom it is more of an effort. Does this show I am wrong in thinking merit is proportional to effort? No, because there is a confusion here about the object bearing the merit. Praise can be given for particular actions, but it can also be given for being accomplished at that particular kind of action. In the example, the difference in merit arises because one performer is more accomplished than the other, and greater accomplishment is— other things being equal—the result of greater effort. So merit is proportional to effort after all.

But suppose that other things are not equal: Suppose that one performer has more natural ability than the other, but that they are equally proficient. In this situation, we are likely to accord more praise to the less gifted individual, and I suggest that this is because we know he has had to make a greater effort to achieve the same result. It is not, therefore, the effortlessness of an action that is the basis for praise, but rather, what that effortlessness represents—a high level of accomplishment. And since a high level of accomplishment is usually the result of considerable effort, this preserves my assumption that merit in a particular action is proportional to the effort expended and its consequent—that assenting to God's assertions is not specially meritorious.

Someone will no doubt object that some people do not become persuaded of the truth of what God has revealed. The Bible, which contains God's revelation, is not universally accepted by those who are exposed to it. Therefore, it will be said, some individuals do not have a disposition to be persuaded of the truth of what God reveals, and this shows that it must be logically possible to doubt God's word.

Without arguing about the origin of the Biblical revelations, I should like to point out that the above argument reflects confusion about the object of trust in religious faith. The existence of doubters and atheists has presented a problem for Catholic theologians ever since they began thinking of religious faith in the way they do. Why do some who have been exposed to the Christian message acquire faith, while others do not? The generally accepted answer is that in the former cases, God has intervened: By his grace the will of the individual is influenced in the right direction.

It seems to me that this answer creates new and unnecessary difficulties because the original problem is only an apparent one. For it demonstrates not the possibility of doubting God, but that most people's religious faith is based upon trust in witnesses for God, not trust in God himself. They doubt whether or not religious doctrines have been communicated by God which is not at all the same as doubting what we know God to have revealed. We might go on to say that the "problem of faith" for the would-be Christian is two-fold: (1) that the Christian God exists, and (2) that the Christian revelation does indeed come from God. The concept of God being what it is, to become persuaded of the truth of the latter is simultaneously to become persuaded of the truth of the revelation.

This completes my scrutiny of the Roman Catholic view of religious faith. Given the Catholic definition of "virtue" and the Christian concept of God, I have argued that (1) the definition of "faith" as a firm persuasion of the truth of propositions revealed by God disqualifies faith from being a virtue, since it is an attitude and not a disposition or habit; (2) even if the definition of "faith" was altered so that it becomes a disposition, faith would not be an especially meritorious virtue. It would, for example, be no more and no less meritorious than the disposition to assent to the claim that Socrates is mortal on the basis of accepting that all men are mortal and Socrates is a man. Finally, I noted that construing faith as a disposition has the implication that even rational individuals who have never heard of Christianity will have to be counted as having Christian faith.

The only reasonable alternative to seeing religious faith as a propositional attitude seems to be the one accepted by Protestant thinkers, i.e., that faith is an attitude toward a personal being. The Protestant account has, from the beginning of the movement, stressed the personal relationship with Christ and God rather than assent to a

157

set of propositions. As one writer puts it, "'faith' in classical Protestant (as in modern Biblical) theology means obedient trust or trustful obedience towards God as he is revealed in his Word" (P.S. Watson in A. Richardson (ed.), *A Dictionary of Christian Theology*). The writer goes on to elaborate what faith involves: ". . . such faith that we look to Him for all good and for help against all evil, and are ready to do or endeavour to do whatever he may command."

The use of the phrase "obedient trust or trustful obedience" reflects some uncertainty in the writer's mind about whether trust or obedience is the primary element in religious faith. This uncertainty is quite common among Protestant theologians. Some, Brunner for instance, see obedience as primary: "Faith is obedience, nothing else; literally nothing else at all." (*The Mediator*, O. Wyon, trans.) This view is extreme, but it is worthwhile to consider whether faith, as so conceived, can be a virtue. The question reduces to: Is obedience a virtue?

Obedience seems to be only conditionally a virtue. In a soldier under battle conditions, we think it is a virtue. In a newspaper publisher in his relations with government, it definitely is not. What about obedience to God? Well, if we conceive of the God-man relationship on the model of father-child, as most Christians do, we shall be forced to admit that obedience to God is a virtue. But we need not admit that faith in God is a virtue. It is simply false that faith is obedience. This can be argued fairly convincingly by means of an analogy drawn between religious faith and faith in human beings: "[Faith] is analogous to the confidence a man may have in another man. In so far as I have confidence, for example, in my doctor, I take him at his word when he assures me I am going to get well, and I take both his advice and his medicine even when they are unpalatable. My confidence in my doctor rests, of course, on what I know of him, whether from my own observation or the testimony of others" (P.S. Watson, op.cit.).

If "faith" is synonymous with "obedience," then obedience is both necessary and sufficient for faith. One might obey a doctor's instructions, however, because we are afraid to disobey even though we have grounds for doubting his medical competence. This shows that obedience is not sufficient for faith. Again, one might have confidence (trust) in him yet fail to obey from lack of interest in getting well; so obedience is not a necessary condition either. It seems that if faith is to be identified with either obedience or trust, the latter is the most logical choice. This choice is entirely in accord with the view of the first great Protestant: ". . . Luther's teaching on justification by faith alone stressed the voluntaristic side of faith. . . . The chief moment in it was trust (fiducia). . . ." (F.L. Cross, ed. *The Oxford Dictionary Of the Christian Church*, (2nd edition).

At this point, we might compare the Roman Catholic and Protestant accounts of religious faith. The latter takes faith to be an attitude toward a personal being—faith is trust in God. The former holds that faith is a propositional attitude, a firm persuasion of the truth of certain propositions. Recall, though, that this firm persuasion is based upon trust in the reliability of God. Recall, also, that I argued that this trust is not especially laudable since nothing can inspire trust more readily than God. The same argument holds for the Protestant account of faith as trust in God.

In applying the argument, we must first note that Protestant thinkers typically conceive of putting one's trust in God (coming to have faith in God) as something of a venture:

> Christian faith in God has its rooting in a venturesome moral attitude similar to that which is involved in every act of loyal devotion—a willingness to trust beyond the evidence.
>
> W.M. Horton
>
> *Theism and the Modern Mood.*

The reference to a venturesome moral attitude here suggests that there is an element of risk involved. W.M. Horton is assimilating religious faith to the secular faith of which faith in one's doctor is an example. In Protestant thinking, and in the thinking of many Catholics subsequent to Vatican II, religious faith is putting oneself in the hands of God. In taking a doctor's medical advice and consuming the medications he prescribes, one is putting oneself in his hands. Each case involves trust and an element of risk. After all, physicians have not been found infallible: The wrong medications might be prescribed. In one crucial respect, however, the two cases are different in the matter of the competence of the individual in whom faith is placed.

Physicians are fallible; so there is always risk involved in following their instructions. But God is thought of as omniscient, as incapable of deceit, and as loving his creatures. In following his instructions, it is not even logically possible to see risk involved, and so there can be no moral venturesomeness. The concept of God allows no possibility of God's instructions being wrong. Where someone does have misgivings about instructions that seem to come from God, we must conclude either that he doubts that the command really is from God, or that he doubts that God is as Christians describe him. These alternatives are quite different from doubting the Christian God's competence.

One might object that there have been many cases in which doing

God's will involved risk, and risk of which the would-be servant of God was well-aware. The argument given above would, it seems, imply that martyrdom in a Christian context is never praiseworthy.

It would be outrageous if I claimed that no Christian martyr was courageous. Very likely even the best of them had doubts that made them conscious of risk in what they were doing, and thereby worthy of the praise Christians bestow on them. But these doubts cannot be construed as doubt about the soundness of God's judgment or about whether he can and will keep his promises. They must, as noted above, be doubts about whether the commands really are from God or whether God really is as he is said to be.

If I am right, then, the common tendency of Protestant theologians to consider religious faith a highly praiseworthy state is based upon the wrong ground. The merit of faith is taken to reside in its venturesomeness but this can only be involved when doubt about the soundness of the instruction or command is possible. As we have seen, this sort of doubt cannot arise when religious faith is defined as trust in God as one who commands us. It is important to note, however, that the impossibility of doubting God's competence does not entail that we cannot have faith in him. It is tempting to see a parallel between the Wittgensteinian slogan "If you can't be wrong you can't be right," and the claim that if you can't doubt, you can't have faith. But there does not seem to me to be anything problematical about having faith in an individual who cannot betray that faith, even when the "cannot" is a logical one.

To summarize my treatment of the Protestant account of religious faith: I began by noting that Protestants take faith to be trust in God manifested by obedience to his wishes. Next it was pointed out that Protestants see faith as meritorious because it involves a venture, which prompted me to present an example of secular faith that they would accept as similar to the religious case. I then pointed out that these cases are crucially different because the individuals in whom faith is placed do not have the same status: There is room for risk when faith is placed in a fallible authority, so that acting on faith can require courage which is sufficient to make the action meritorious. But where the authority is infallible, there is no room for risk, and the attendant ground for merit is removed. The Protestant theologians, then, are mistaken in according merit to possession of faith in God, insofar as they take it to be a venture.

The somewhat bizarre-sounding conclusions of this paper are implied by the accounts of faith accepted by Christian theologians when these are taken in conjunction with the traditional account of the nature of God. That my conclusions seem bizarre suggests, to me

160

anyway, that there is something wrong in the way Christians think about faith. Alternatively, or in addition, there may be something wrong with the way they think about God. I have not, of course, provided any grounds in this paper for preferring the latter alternative.

Could Christian Faith Become a Vice?

CATHERINE DAFOE

Professor Grennan has argued that Christian Faith, as the supposed virtue of Faith is understood by many Catholics and Protestants, cannot be a virtue. His arguments seem sound enough when addressed to the Christian thinkers whom he has in mind. But it would be a pity to stop here. May it not sometimes be the case that Christian Faith is neither virtuous nor morally neutral? I ask the question with these points in mind: The branches of Christianity are typical forms of organized religion; such forms demand much obedience of the believer. This will be obedience either to a single leader like the Pope, or to a collective entity like a Council of Bishops or Elders, or to a more abstract source like an approved item of "Revelation"—such as some authorized interpretation of the Bible—or to the conventions of fellow laymen in the know, and so on. When the believer is a Christian who allows organized religion to become a convenient means of avoiding personal, moral decisions, it is almost necessarily true that Faith is *valueless* or worse.

In the tenets of an organized religion faith will often, it seems, present the individual with a moral dilemma in which his private, personal belief is contradicted by some tenet of the organization. The organization usually exhibits such a subtly dictatorial nature that each person becomes afraid of refusing to adhere to *all* of its tenets, however counterintuitive or unreasonable they may appear. The believer who tries to be faithful finds himself not only bound to let many moral decisions be taken from him, but also on occasion drawn by fear of taking a solitary stand into allowing his own conscience to be over-ruled. This double sacrifice of personal autonomy and responsibility is a likely source of moral decay.

A particularly striking example of dubious moral taste is furnished by certain sectarians who make themselves prominent from time to time in the news of the day by refusing to accept medical care which they or even their children obviously need. Consider the case of a mother whose baby cannot live without a blood transfusion. If her Faith is that of certain religionists, her fellow believers will urge her to "keep to the Good Word" and protect herself from "gross immorality and sacrilege." Suppose that she yields to them against her better judgment: She decides against her conscience to follow a plan which alleges to save her child's soul from "corruption." It may be that the baby dies soon afterwards, and she begins to wonder in her grief whether some outrageous wrong has not been done. She may even ask if she is not partly the wrongdoer since she overruled her own conscience to satisfy the faithful.

A somewhat similar case is that of a parent with more children than he can look after effectively. He becomes convinced as a matter of conscience that birth control is morally right or even, in cases like his own, obligatory. He now considers it wrong for a man to bring unwanted children into the world; he also considers it monstrous to destroy the viability of his marriage and family ties by denying sexual relations to his wife and himself. But after a time of being made to feel "out of step" with his group, he decides to let his personal convictions be overruled by decrees of celibate clergymen.

The mother in the previous example committed a double wrong by overruling her own conscience and allowing her child to die. In this case the parent is also doubly at fault: He ignores his own convictions to oblige his tribal peers and their witch doctors; he also brings unwanted children into the world despite his well-founded belief that this is cruel and inhuman.

Then there are all too many cases of faithful believers who hold, when their own Faith is threatened by other groups, that each person should be free to make his own decisions about moral and religious matters. And so these believers are often disturbed (at first) when *their* Church gains enough power to force its views on those who have different ideals. But if their Faith triumphs over such samples, a multiple injustice—not just a double wrong—is likely to result. The believers first sacrifice their inner consistency and integrity by denying that they should act tolerantly towards others as their own church had once said all men should act towards their neighbours. Then they compound this betrayal of another person's autonomy and right to do as he sees fit by endorsing their Church's further attempt to force the "non-believer" to do what they themselves (privately) believe is something doubly immoral for anyone to do: to violate his conscience and reject those who love and depend upon him. Thus a Catholic follower of Louis XIV might have made himself help and even praise his Church when it tried to force French Huguenots to "convert" to the "true Faith" and to betray recalcitrant members of their own families to those who would massacre them like cattle. Of course, the German Protestants who similarly betrayed their long respected Catholic neighbours in the Thirty Years War to some army of "holy avengers" compounded a similar set of crimes against their own and others' humanity. We should be sure to note that in these examples there is a progression from the simple failure to do what a person's conscience *demands*—this could be likened in part to a sin of omission—to doing what his conscience *forbids*, which is more comparable to a sin of commission.

It is certain that not all of the moral dilemmas presented by the conflict of one's conscience with religious tribal tenets are likely to generate as much evil as would arise from these last examples. Many compromises made in the name of Faith by believers are more subtle and seem to have less sinister implications.

There is the less dramatic case of some Mormons who privately believe that the black man is no different from any human in dignity, yet almost gladly accede to their church's refusal to let blacks become Elders. They may do this because it appears extremely convenient to let a conventional figure of authority dictate most of their moral decisions to them. Or they may be led more by a wish to avoid "rocking the boat" of organized complacency. In either case they violate their own consciences and integrity.

There have been too many communities who once harboured someone of alien beliefs; who were drawn to admire, then to love, and even to *imitate* such a person because he seemed to be wise and a true friend to all; who then suddenly turned against their neighbour to oblige their clergy; and who ended by denying themselves his wisdom, shunning him as an infidel "damned to eternal torment."

There have been sectarians who believed in education and a fuller life for their children. Some of these have denied their children any advanced education for a fuller life, lest the young be subverted by pride in the intellect, or lest adolescents learn of new religions and political options and so be enticed from the narrow conventions of unreflective orthodoxy. Such parents have not only denied each of their own children the birthright of a free human being (though they themselves often acknowledge, at convenient times, that moral growth comes from confronting rival options seriously), but they have also denied their own religious community the benefits of new knowledge, enhanced capacity of reason, and even the increased humility and wisdom which education helps to make possible.

In the last three paragraphs I have focussed on examples where the violation of a person's reason and conscience seems to be rather less destructive of others. But the question still arises: Can any such violation or compromise of the dictates of one's own conscience be anything but serious? Some of this quite deliberate appeasement of officers of organized religions are less clearly going to have grave *outwardly observable* consequences. Some such consequences would be hard for another person to detect in the appeaser, but they could be no less destructive of his conscience after the compromise. On the other hand, even if all the consequences are truly slight, the very *act* of compromise is enough to tarnish the ideal of Faith that is advocated by too many leaders of organized religion.

Professor Grennan points out, quite rightly, that "unmediated belief" in God is not possible. A characteristic of organized Christian religion is that the believer's Faith *is* mediated and that it is mediated thanks to his deliberations and decisions: A believer is not permitted to form his own beliefs about God on the basis of personal experiences which he trusts, nor on the basis of the experiences of others (not in ecclesiastical power) whom he strongly trusts.

Much of what we say we *know* about the world is "mediated" by the language, symbols, and concepts of a relatively secular society. In the same way what many claim to *know* about God or God's commands is "mediated" for them, as they choose to allow, by the language, symbols, and concepts of religious organizations. And organized religions capitalize on this human situation by censuring any attempt to query those forms of "mediation" that its officers endorse —they may well be *secular* forms dear to a Church, and not only religious forms, as Galileo came to realize at great cost when he denied that the universe turns round our Earth! Such religious leaders similarly censure most novel, unauthorized attempts to appropriate fresh modes of "mediation." Too often the individual is (willingly) induced by such pressures to accept without question a conceptual scheme that is saturated with his Church's values and attitudes as a "TOTAL PACKAGE."

It should be clear by now that the *Christian Faith* or *Faiths* of which Professor Grennan speaks cannot be identified with a purely personal belief in a Christian God. His references to typical theologians make clear that his subject is the type of Faith which is moulded and manipulated by an organization claiming a sacred mandate from God himself to communicate and interpret his words for men. Not every religious believer's Faith is of this kind, though Grennan usually seems oblivious of this, or simply not interested in it. There are some, like Immanuel Kant two hundred years ago, whose Faith is guided by *consulting* others, but afterwards only by personal reflection and heed to private conscience. For my purposes here, their Faith is not morally objectionable, though it should not be inferred that I would automatically praise it. I am tempted in sadder or more sceptical moments to speak of it as *morally neutral*. If, however, as in the case of conflict between one's conscience and some organization's doctrines, one bows to the authority of that sect, then, to the extent to which a compromise or violation of one's conscience is required, that "Faith" could be taken as a vice.

165

Paradox and Faith in Kierkegaard

ALASTAIR McKINNON

Though Kierkegaard made many important contributions to religious thought, I shall concentrate in this paper on only one, which, I confess, is problematic and, perhaps appropriately, paradoxical. Very briefly, I shall argue that, despite his apparently repeated insistence that Christianity involves belief in the paradox and the absurd, he has, perhaps in and through his use of these terms, pointed the way to a faith which is beyond paradox at least in most senses of this term. More specifically, I shall argue that, correctly interpreted, he sees the Incarnation as a "coherent" event from which the Christian can and should derive his conceptions of God and man, and that in this he represents a clear and important advance upon traditional or orthodox Christianity, or, as he *might* have preferred, a return to New Testament Christianity.

To avoid misunderstanding, I shall state my thesis on orthodoxy as clearly as possible. Quite simply, I hold that, at least since the time of Aquinas, Christian theology has in fact followed what I shall call the "way of paradox"—it has conceived faith as the capacity to believe what, in the rest of one's mind, one knows to be in some sense untrue. In the case of the Incarnation, it means professing belief in the reality of that event while simultaneously holding fast to conceptions of God and man in the light of which the Incarnation is and must have been impossible. Orthodoxy has traditionally avoided the use of the word "paradox," but there is, I think, no better way to describe its treatment both of the Incarnation and, though perhaps to a lesser extent, of some other central beliefs of Christianity.

Consider the following typical, if perhaps not historically important, example. In his book, *Christ, the Christian and the Church*, E.L. Mascall begins by saying in effect that, by the light of reason, he knows God to possess properties x, y, and z and, by the same light, that he knows man to possess properties -x, -y, and -z. He then suddenly remembers that he is a Christian and, as such, that he is bound to believe in the Incarnation. How, he asks, in consternation, is this possible? How could two natures which are totally unlike be united in one person? One can understand the seriousness of his problem from the nature of his answer: With God all things are possible. Not that he admits that the Incarnation was, strictly speaking, logically impossible—were that the case, even God's efforts would be of no avail. But it is a strange, improbable, perhaps inappropriate event, utterly at odds with human reason, and therefore possible only through a kind of special, divine intervention. But we need not trouble ourselves about the postulated divine mechanisms, for in the final analysis they are not what really matters. The crucial point is that Mascall imagines that we can simultaneously believe both in the Incarnation and in those other conceptions which render it unintelligible and, indeed, impossible.

There are two points to be noted in this connection. Mascall hopes to solve his problem by appealing to his belief that with God all things are possible. I have absolutely no difficulty with this belief, but it does not help him out of his difficulty: The problem concerns the union of two logically incompatible natures and, as he himself concedes, even God cannot do or be conceived as doing the logically impossible. In short his claim, though religiously unobjectionable, does not solve his problem.

The second point is more problematic but nevertheless interesting. In the course of his discussion, Mascall refers to the Cartesian problem of the alleged interaction of Body and Mind; indeed, I suspect that he thinks that the two cases are in some way comparable. Now Descartes appears to have thought that the question concerned the means by which Body and Mind might interact. In attempting to answer this question, he proposed the pineal gland and, beyond that, a supervenient divine intervention. But in fact, Descartes mistook the nature of his own problem. The question is not the mechanism or means by which Body and Mind interact, but rather how they could conceivably interact. Put another way, Descartes' is not a scientific but a conceptual question, answered not by proposing a scientific or pseudo-scientific answer (about possible means), but rather by revising one's conception of Body and Mind, so that the problem disappears. This follows the sound principle that, if interaction takes place, it must be possible and is therefore a fact to be taken account of in our conceptions. Put another way, if we build the admitted interaction into our conception, the problem does not and cannot arise. In fact, it is puzzling that Descartes should have got himself into this situation, and it is difficult to avoid the suspicion that the real explanation is that he was much closer to orthodox scholasticism than many are prepared to admit.

It is interesting to compare the treatment or, rather, the two different treatments of the Incarnation in the contemporary Protestant theologian Karl Barth. In his early work *The Epistle to the Romans*, Barth presents Christian belief—and, in particular, the Incarnation— as requiring the sacrifice of the intellect, the crucifixion of the understanding, and as being in itself paradoxical and absurd. I personally think there is no doubt that, his protests notwithstanding, Barth's terminology at least is derived from Kierkegaard or, more correctly, from the phantom Kierkegaard by whom he was perhaps unduly influenced. But whatever his real motives for refusing to acknowledge the influence of Kierkegaard, he was at least partly justified by his primary concern in this work: to make explicit and articulate the nature of Christian belief according to the orthodox account.

Barth's treatment of the Incarnation in his later works (for example, *The Knowledge of God and the Service of God*) is very different and, in my view at least, much more interesting. In these works he no longer proclaims the Incarnation as the paradox or the absurd, but instead as "the most natural of all natural events." The explanation of this dramatic change is simple but very important: By this time Barth has clearly rejected all so-called natural theology and has resolved to derive his conceptions of God and man from the event of the Incarnation. In fact, he argues that the *Christian* conception of God and man must be derived from this source and that the Incarnation is the primary datum for all Christian belief. Of course, Barth would not argue that he had wholly succeeded in articulating such conceptions, but it is absolutely clear that he understands that this is the task for theology and that it is idle to talk about believing in the Incarnation while at the same time holding conceptions which would make it impossible.

Barth attached great importance to this break and said that it was the line which future theology must follow, that in it he had gone beyond Kierkegaard. I accept the first claim but have grave reservations about the second. In fact, as I have argued elsewhere, it would be more correct to see Barth's movement as an escape from the phantom Kierkegaard to catch up with the real one. In any event, or so I shall argue, his last position is substantially that which Kierkegaard had reached almost a hundred years earlier. But this, of course, is something which has yet to be demonstrated.

It is perhaps worth noting that Barth is not the only modern theologian to have come to this position. For example, in his quite excellent book *God Was in Christ*, D.M. Baillie writes, "If the Incarnation has supremely revealed God, shown Him to us in a new and illuminating light, put a fresh meaning into the very word that is His name, *that* is the meaning that we must use in facing the problem of the Incarnation, because that is what God really is." Baillie does not here make the same claim for our understanding of man, but it is, I think, implied in his whole position.

In this brief historical introduction, I have described two very different accounts or treatments of the Incarnation. In what follows I shall attempt to show that both are present in different parts of

168

Kierkegaard's writings. As is so often the case, the question, therefore, is which of these represents the real Kierkegaard.

It should be frankly admitted at the outset that our interpretation of Kierkegaard is inherently implausible, certainly paradoxical, and perhaps even absurd. His writings frequently refer to the Incarnation as the Absolute Paradox, to Christian belief as involving the acceptance of the absurd, and to belief or faith as possible "by virtue of the absurd" and as requiring "the crucifixion of the understanding." Obviously, then, there is a certain plausibility to the traditional view that he is an irrationalist or, at best, a kind of fideist. But whether this is the whole or even a part of the real Kierkegaard is, of course, the question which has to be answered.

I pause at the outset to seek a simple understanding with the reader. What Kierkegaard has to say is perhaps ultimately very simple, but his works are extremely complex and difficult. For example, at one point the *Philosophical Fragments* asserts "Faith (Tro) is not an act of the will" and, a few pages later, that "belief (Tro) is not a form of knowledge, but a free act, an expression of the will." Such difficulties may be due to unresolved ambiguities in his thought or, as I think more likely, to his own perception that a totally consistent revolutionary thought would be simply unintelligible and that one must, therefore, continue to use the language one seeks to replace. In any event, I do not want to claim that Kierkegaard is always consistent or that my own understanding of him is adequate. And certainly I do not wish to suggest that I can adequately convey his thought in the space here at my disposal. I so, however, think that our question is an important one worthy of the serious interest of any intelligent person, and I hope that my account may at least provide a useful introduction to this important aspect of his thought.

I propose to devote much of the space at my disposal to those "pseudonymous" works which in fact contain virtually all of Kierkegaard's uses of the terms "absurd" and "paradox." First, however, I shall distinguish some of the main senses in which he uses the term "paradox" and, on this basis, comment briefly upon some of his related key conceptions. (By "pseudonymous," of course, I mean "published under a pseudonym.")

Kierkegaard's most distinctive and characteristic use of "paradox" can perhaps be best described as its existential sense because it stems entirely from the fact that the knower is, in Kierkegaard's language, "an existing individual." This is clear from the case of Socrates who, in Kierkegaard's view, provides the proper introduction to Christianity precisely because of his emphasis upon the knower as an existing being. It is this alone which explains why the truth is a paradox in this particular sense. As he writes in the *Postscript*, "Socratically the eternal essential truth is by no means in its own nature paradoxical, but only in its relation to an existing individual." Similarly, ". . . the fact that the truth becomes a paradox is rooted precisely in its having a relationship to an existing subject." Plainly, then, paradox in this sense results from the conjunction or juxtaposition of the realms of existence and truth in the life of an existing individual. The sense is fundamental to his thought, and all the others, I am inclined to believe, are in some way subordinate.

It is worth noting that, according to Kierkegaard, Christianity is paradoxical in precisely this sense, or more correctly, that it is more strictly so because it accentuates existence more strongly than the Socratic view. Unlike that view, it is also paradoxical in the various logical senses of that term. The fact of this connection is instructive: Reality and logic may be totally disparate, but the corresponding senses of "paradox" are nevertheless connected.

When we turn to the various logical senses of "paradox," the situation is somewhat more complicated. Here there are at least five distinct senses: the dialectical, the systematically incomprehensible, the *Self*-contradictory, the historically dependent, and the apparently contradictory.

The first, or dialectical sense, appears in the following *Journal* entry: "The paradox is really the *pathos* of intellectual life. . . . It is only the great thinker who is exposed to what I call paradoxes which are nothing else than grandiose thoughts in embryo." Though the closing words fail to do full justice to the complexity of Kierkegaard's conception, the sense intended is quite clear: A paradox is a thought containing a contradiction which can and should be untied, and it is precisely the business of great thinkers to untie them.

The second, or systematically incomprehensible sense, appears in another *Journal* entry which reads in part as follows:

> . . . the inexplicable, the paradox, is a category of its own . . . it is the duty of the human understanding to understand that there are things which it cannot understand, and what those things are. Human understanding has vulgarly occupied itself with nothing but understanding, but if it would only take the trouble to understand itself at the same time it would simply have to posit the paradox. . . .

Kierkegaard's point is, of course, one about the nature and operation of the human understanding as such. He is asserting that any coherent understanding rests and must rest upon something which cannot itself be expressed in terms of that understanding. He is claiming that any system of thought rests ultimately upon something which cannot be understood in terms of that system, upon something which is systematically incomprehensible. Anyone who doubts this point has only to reflect for a moment upon contemporary views about the place of primitive postulates in a deductive system.

The third, or *Self*-contradictory, sense is more closely associated with Christianity and particularly with Kierkegaard's assumption that there is an implacable opposition between its goals and those of natural man, especially when, as in the Hegelian philosophy, the latter are identified and bound up with human reason. Whether these goals are in any sense rational is really beside the point. For Kierkegaard Christianity is unalterably opposed to them and hence can only be experienced and accepted as paradoxical in the sense of *Self*-contradiction.

The historically dependent sense is closely linked with the preceding, but it is concerned more with the form than the content of Christianity. In particular, it is connected with Christianity as an historical religion, so that the believer must base his faith upon what is in some sense a merely historical fact. Kierkegaard has Hegel, particularly, in mind, but his point can perhaps be best understood with reference to Hume. Against Hegel's claim that the historical facts of Christianity are merely helpful illustrations of timeless and eternal truths, Kierkegaard insists that these facts are vital, since without them we are incapable of imagining or conceiving these truths. Like Hume he wants to point out that our beliefs are dependent upon the facts of experience, but with one very important difference: We may well be annoyed that our knowledge of the properties of bread is apparently derived from experience. Yet we are bound to be offended that even our salvation is similarly based on historical fact. This is *one* of the reasons why, particularly in the *Fragments*, paradox is so closely linked with offense: We are offended because Christianity proposes to base our salvation upon some merely historical fact.

The apparently contradictory sense is much more familiar, straightforward, and closer to common use. Apart from the existential sense, it is also the one which figures most largely in Kierkegaard's authorship. When he declares Christianity to be a paradox in this sense he is simply saying that it, or any other new view for that matter, *appears* and must appear to the would-be believer as a contradiction. His point, at least in this case, is simply that as a new view, it necessarily conflicts with the would-be believer's earlier conceptions, and that one can *become* a believer only by first accepting a claim which is, or at least appears to be, logically self-contradictory. Many of Kierkegaard's reiterations that Christianity must be accepted as a paradox are, I believe, to be understood at least partly in this way. I put the matter deliberately thus because, of course, many of his uses of this term actually involve more than one of the senses which I have identified.

It is perhaps worth noting that this use of "paradox" seems very close to Kierkegaard's concept of *the absurd*. That the Eternal has come into being in time, that God has existed in human form, that the Eternal is the historical—all these are described as both paradoxical and absurd. Further, Kierkegaard's presentation of the absurd suggests that it is somehow essentially self-contradictory. For example, in the *Postscript* he speaks of "the contradiction that something which can become historical only in direct opposition to all human reason, has become historical. . . . It is this contradiction which constitutes the absurd, and which can only be believed." This might prompt one to think that such claims are really unthinkable and genuinely self-contradictory, but that impression stems, I shall argue, from the very peculiar focus and concern of the authorship. Indeed, as I hope to show, Kierkegaard's position is that even those claims which appear to unbelief as absurd or contradictory are not essentially, permanently, and incorrigibly so. This is a view whose foundations have yet to be established.

I trust that the above distinctions will help the reader to pick his way through the difficult terrain which lies ahead. But it is clear that if we are to understand Kierkegaard at all, we must deal with him much more concretely and, particularly, that we must understand the strategy of what he called his "authorship." Very briefly, he saw his contemporaries as living in *aesthetic* categories and he sought in and through his writings to lead them from the *aesthetic*, through the *ethical*, to *Religiousness A*, and finally, as he describes it, to *Religiousness B*, or *Christianity*. The former is the essentially Socratic religiousness of immanence and has only human nature in general as its presupposition. Paradox, in the existential sense of the word, appears within this sphere, but apart from this one exception, like the absurd, it is associated with the transcendent and specifically with Christianity. This is the terrain in which it occurs, and the background against which it must be understood.

It should be noted that Kierkegaard connects the aesthetic mode of existence of his contemporaries with his belief that Hegel had transformed Christianity from an "existence-communication" into a speculative doctrine which asks only to be understood. Worse, he had made the understanding of Christianity a higher and more important thing than being a Christian. Kierkegaard judges this a confusion and says that if anyone thinks that this is so then "the existential security police had better be called in." In a very real sense, his pseudonymous authors are such a police force; their task is to remind the reader that he is an existing individual, and that Christianity, with its concepts of faith and the paradox, represents the greatest possible emphasis upon, or accentuation of, existence. It is, in fact, the one true affirmation of existence.

It is important to realize that Kierkegaard does not identify the absurd with absurdity or nonsense as such, for which, indeed, he has neither time nor patience. Like paradox, it is rather a concept or category. As he writes in the *Journals and Papers*, "The absurd is a category, the negative criterion, of the divine or of the relationship to the divine." In the pseudonymous authorship he attempts to delineate this category and to demonstrate its necessity. He knows that this will be extremely difficult because the modern mind in its superficiality no longer has any understanding of such things. But he thinks that perhaps it can be done. As he writes in the same entry, "The absurd is a category, and the most developed thought is required to define the Christian absurd accurately and with conceptual correctness."

We are perhaps now in a better position to appreciate Kierkegaard's peculiar sense of the word "belief" and thus to have some inkling of the nature of the revolution mentioned above. We ordinarily think of belief as more or less continuous with knowledge, and thus find no difficulty in saying, for example, "Yesterday I believed X, but now I know that X is true." Kierkegaard almost always uses this word in an entirely different sense. For him belief is a passion or resolution, a decision by which we move from fathomless uncertainty to absolute certainty. It is action as, for example, in the case of Abraham. It is what one does when one actually trusts in the forgiveness of sins, i.e., when one actually believes that his sins have been forgiven. This is why he later links belief with obedience, and why he has an almost pathological fear that belief might somehow be transformed into understanding, a fear which makes no sense if they are indeed part of a continuum but which is entirely justified if they are instead of entirely different orders. Of course, this also explains his repeated insistence that faith is a sphere of its own and that there is an absolute heterogeneity between it and reason. It is, of course, this belief or faith by which one apprehends the absurd or paradox.

With this as background, we are now ready to consider the individual works in which Kierkegaard uses the terms absurd and paradox all of which are, I remind the reader, published under one or another of his various pseudonyms. These works are, respectively: *Fear and Trembling* (1843), *Philosophical Fragments* (1844), *Concluding Unscientific Postscript* (1845), *Two Small Ethico-Religious Discourses* (1847), *The Sickness Unto Death* (1848), and *Training in Christianity* (1848). I begin with the first partly because it seems to

173

have been the chief source of the traditional, irrationalist interpretation of Kierkegaard, and mainly because, though it scarcely mentions Christianity, it introduces into the authorship most of the conceptions central to our present concern. Our aim, again, is to see what light, if any, its treatment of Faith, Paradox, and the Absurd sheds on Kierkegaard's own final position regarding the Incarnation.

Fear and Trembling is a beautiful and lyrical treatment of Abraham's response to God's command that he sacrifice Isaac. Johannes de Silentio, its pseudonymous author, shows how, believing and acting by virtue of the absurd, Abraham became the father of faith. Johannes stresses the fact that he cannot himself understand Abraham; he speaks repeatedly of the paradox of Abraham's life and says that it is so paradoxical that it cannot be thought of at all. But, significantly, he adds, "in a certain crazy sense I admire him more than all other men." In fact, it is plain that, like Kierkegaard, he regards Abraham as the right figure with which to confront an age which has forgotten the nature and meaning of faith and which even lacks the passion to observe the fundamental distinction upon which this concept rests—that between what is humanly possible and what is not.

Because he is presented as essentially unintelligible, Abraham is set in contrast to two figures which the reader can more readily comprehend. The knight of infinite resignation, similarly commanded, would also have sacrificed his son. Yet he would have done so as an act of resignation because he knows that, humanly speaking, it is impossible that he should both sacrifice Isaac and have him back again. Abraham, like the knight of faith, responds quite differently. He, too, knows what is possible—humanly speaking. But he goes where the knight of resignation will not go; he believes and acts by virtue of the absurd, in virtue of the fact that with God all things are possible. He is able to sacrifice Isaac because he believes that God will somehow give him back again. He is able to act because he believes what is impossible for the merely human understanding.

Both knights express passion in distinguishing between what is humanly possible and what is not. In one vital respect, however, they are very different. Though the knight of resignation surrenders everything that is dearest in his life, his is a purely human act of renunciation of which any human is capable and which, so far from being an act of faith, is rather only the last stage prior to faith. The knight of faith also performs this act of infinite resignation but, having thus understood himself, he goes on to believe by virtue of the absurd and thereby regains the whole of existence. His is that "paradoxical and humble courage" which "is required to grasp the whole of the temporal by virtue of the absurd, and this is the courage of faith."

Abraham is also contrasted with the tragic hero as instanced in Agamemnon, Jephtha, and Brutus. In appropriate circumstances this hero is also prepared to sacrifice his offspring and, like the knight of resignation, he remains fast within the context of human understanding. Indeed, he conceives his action as a higher form of the ethical and, therefore, has comforters and advisors with whom he can communicate. But Abraham's situation is totally different: He has broken with the ethical and has opted for a private relationship with God. He is, therefore, completely unintelligible to anyone and hence arises the dread, distress, and torment that are repeatedly associated with the paradox of his life.

This comparison of Abraham with the tragic hero is immediately preceded by the words, ". . . faith begins precisely there where thinking leaves off." Here we have a hint of the nature and complexity of faith. The last four words refer to human thinking as such and the quotation implies that faith comes after what is humanly conceivable. This is consistent with the preceding account and with Johannes' own words, "Anything beyond my mere eternal consciousness is paradoxical and requires faith." But "where thinking leaves off" also refers to action, and this appears to be an essential part of what Johannes has in mind. Thus, he says Abraham "acts by virtue of the absurd." He means that he was able to act by setting aside all merely human thought, by believing that with God all things are possible. And it is of course in this same act that he becomes the father of faith.

There is much else in this book deserving discussion, but the following is particularly relevant. Though Abraham and the knight of faith understand that, humanly speaking, all is lost, both proceed to act by virtue of the absurd; both step outside the world of the merely human understanding. But Johannes observes that there is no absurdity in this for the understanding which "continued to be in the right in affirming that in the world of the finite where it holds sway this was and remained an impossibility." Or, as he puts it a few lines earlier, "The absurd is not one of the factors which can be discriminated within the proper compass of the understanding. . . ." Plainly then, while the understanding has its rights, it has no valid objection if the individual chooses to act, in Johannes' characteristic phrase, "by virtue of the absurd."

Philosophical Fragments, the first work of the pseudonym Johannes Climacus, does not even mention Christianity until the second last page for purely tactical reasons. In fact, it is an indirect attack upon the Hegelian trivialization of Christianity and its concepts. Its underlying strategy is to show what Christianity must be like if it is to go beyond Socrates.

175

Socrates is presented as holding that the learner has the truth already within him, that knowledge can be only an occasion of recollection, and that in the final analysis the learner cannot owe the Teacher anything. Climacus seeks to show that if we are to go beyond this position we become involved in all the traditional Christian claims: that the Teacher must bring with him both the Truth and the condition by which the learner recognizes it as such; that the Teacher must be the God himself; that the learner must be responsible for his own error and hence in Sin; that there must be a Saviour and Redeemer, an Atonement and a Judge; that there must be Conversion, Repentance, and the New Birth; that the Teacher must come in the Fullness of Time which is the Moment; and that his coming as a Servant must be an expression of his Eternal Purpose. This established, Climacus then deals with the reader's supposed objection that this "thought project" is simply a poem, "a wretched piece of plagiarism," by pointing out that while man might have imagined himself as the equal of God, or God the equal of man, it could never have occurred to any man to imagine that God would make himself into the likeness of man precisely because of his need for him. In fact, he concludes, the poem is "not a poem at all, but the *Miracle*."

The next chapter argues that, unable to conceive absolute unlikeness, the Reason goes astray in its attempt to determine the Unknown or the God and ends by conceiving the unlike as the like. Since the God is absolutely unlike man, and since this is a self-contradiction for the Reason, such knowledge must come from the God. But even though it has been given this knowledge, the Reason cannot understand and possess it since it cannot understand what is absolutely unlike or different from itself. Here we seem to be confronted with a paradox which Reason cannot understand: that the God is absolutely unlike man; that his unlikeness is due to sin of which, however, man can become conscious only insofar as the God consents to become a Teacher. Thus our paradox has a double aspect or proclaims itself as the Absolute Paradox "negatively by revealing the absolute unlikeness of sin, positively by proposing to do away with the absolute unlikeness." The Reason sees this as threatening its downfall but, paradoxically, it is precisely this which the Reason, like the Paradox, desires. Indeed, like self-love and love, they are "at bottom linked in understanding; but this understanding is present only in the moment of passion."

This passion is subsequently identified as Faith or the happy coming together of the Paradox and the Reason in a mutual understanding of their unlikeness, this as against an encounter where such understanding is absent and which is called Offense. All Offense is

176

essentially a misunderstanding of the Moment, which is the Paradox in its most abbreviated form, which Paradox "unites the contradictories, and is the historical made eternal and the Eternal made historical." In fact, the Moment is the Paradox and the only proper and happy relation to both is Faith. But since "no knowledge can have for its object the absurdity that the Eternal is the historical," it follows that "Faith is not a form of knowledge." In fact, "the object of Faith is not the *teaching* but the *Teacher* . . . the Teacher who must be both God and Man." Such a Teacher is not immediately knowable but can be known only as he himself gives the condition. But this is an eternal condition and there is therefore no essential distinction between the immediate contemporary and the disciple at second hand. Put another way, belief is the real or true contemporaneity.

There is much else in this work which is interesting and important. There is one further point which is *vital* to our present discussion. Climacus claims that whereas the "what" of a happening—for example, that a star is there—can be known immediately, the fact that it happened can never be thus known. This "coming into existence" aspect of a happening is always uncertain, and belief with respect to it is essentially the negation of such uncertainty. Hence it is not a form of knowledge but an expression of will. Belief is a resolution which excludes its opposite passion, doubt, and yields a certainty beyond that of mere sensation and cognition. With respect to the *coming into existence* of the God, however, we must make a distinction. As an ordinary historical fact it is the subject of belief or Faith in the direct and ordinary sense whereas, as "a fact based upon a self-contradiction," it is the subject of Faith in the eminent sense. This distinction is taken up again in the *Postscript*.

Climacus' second book, the *Concluding Unscientific Postscript* is, as its subtitle indicates, a postscript to his earlier *Fragments*, despite its being approximately five-and-a-half times the length of his earlier work. But this is just one of its jokes. In fact, while the *Fragments* is severe and even algebraic in its argument, the *Postscript* is a gay romp through philosophy, a kind of fun book or, at least, a kind of philosopher's fun book. But we must leave that aspect for the reader and concentrate instead upon the points relevant to our own thesis.

Like its predecessor, indeed, like most of Kierkegaard's writings, the *Postscript* is concerned with what its author takes to be the real ills of his time. Climacus believes that his contemporaries, whether in thoughtlessness or in stupidity, have forgotten what it means to exist as human beings. The knowing subject has become a fantastic entity, and the truth has become a fantastic object for this fantastic entity. This he ascribes to Hegelianism, partly because of its direct influence upon the thought of the time, but most particularly, because Hegel had trivialized the concepts of Christianity and thereby transformed it from what Climacus calls an "existence-communication" into "a doctrine which asks only to be understood." The connection may seem strange, yet it is clear to Climacus, who holds that Christianity is the one great and sure guardian of existence and that reason, in its cunning, has marked it as such. To make the reader aware of the real situation, Climacus begins again with Socrates a champion of existence in his own way, whose "ignorance is an analogue to the category of the absurd," just as his "inwardness in existing is an analogue to faith." But for Socrates the truth becomes a paradox only in its relation to an existing individual. If existence is to be ultimately and finally affirmed, the truth must itself be the absurd or the paradox. Climacus is quite explicit about its nature: "What now is the absurd? The absurd is—that the eternal truth has come into being in time, that the God has come into being, has been born, has grown up, and so forth, precisely like any other individual human being, quite indistinguishable from other individuals." Again, he writes, "That God has existed in human form, has been born, grown up, and so forth, is surely the paradox *sensu strictissimo*, the absolute paradox." Such things cannot be assimilated by human thought which, as always, is rooted in immanence. They cannot be thought or understood but only *believed*. They put a halt to speculation and show unmistakably that the real task is not to understand Christianity but rather to become a Christian. It is this which Climacus has in mind when he insists that Christianity is an "existence-communication" and that it poses an "existential contradiction."

Climacus has some difficulty with his view that Christianity is not a doctrine but an existence-communication, and he is not helped by his creator's Danish having only one word (*Lære*) to express what we would call both teaching and doctrine. Indeed, he devotes a long footnote to this problem which, however, is too extensive to quote here. There are several briefer passages which are relevant. Criticizing the preaching of his day he writes: "Orthodox doctrine is expounded, and at the same time the teacher (the Christ) is decked out in pagan-aesthetic categories." Again, in a passage which is obviously relevant to our own problem, he speaks of his attempt to formulate the "existential contradiction posed by Christianity. . . . If I were to say that Christianity is a doctrine of the Incarnation, of the Atonement, and so forth, misunderstanding would at once be invited. Speculative philosophy would immediately pounce upon this doctrine. . . ." We can perhaps understand Climacus' fears about speculative philosophy, but I am not convinced that his distinction between doctrine and existence-communication is altogether happy or sound. Recall, for example, his insistence that in Christianity the truth must be paradoxical both in itself and in its relation to an existing individual. Consider also one of the most famous and frequently quoted passages from near the end of this work: "The thing of being a Christian is not determined by the *what* of Christianity but by the *how* of the Christian. This *how* can only correspond with one thing, the absolute paradox." Surely, if this *how* thus corresponds with the absolute paradox, there cannot be any final disjunction between Christianity as doctrine and as existence-communication. But this is a relatively minor objection and does not in any way invalidate his claim that Christianity has primarily to do with existence rather than with understanding or, as he might have said, that the task is to force individuals back into existence.

The *Postscript* is a long book and shows evidence of considerable internal development. Connected with this it also anticipates future themes and emphases. I briefly note the following: concern with the question of the relation or, more precisely, the kinship of the temporal and eternal; the emphasis upon God's coming into existence in time as *a particular man*; and the final description of the paradox as "that Christ came into the world *in order to suffer*."

Christianity is often regarded and dismissed as otherworldly, and Kierkegaard is generally held to err in this same direction. Before leaving the early pseudonyms, I must, therefore, comment upon what I can only describe as their aggressive worldliness. Abraham's act makes him unintelligible and so threatens human community. In fact it expresses the passion from which real community is to be established at another and deeper level. Climacus sometimes sounds like the champion of Christianity for its own sake. Yet even a superficial understanding of his work reveals that he also values it as the only sure guardian and ultimate guarantor of human existence. He knows that only its categories provide the framework for a truly human life. The aesthete in the first volume of *Either/Or* thinks he has the answers; Climacus knows that Christianity is the last and highest of the existence stages.

The *Postscript* was to have been Kierkegaard's last work; certainly with it he hoped to lay aside forever his pseudonymous pen. It represents the end of a development, the logical culmination of a particular line, the last work in a series meant to lead his reader into becoming a Christian. I shall, therefore, pause to consider briefly the possible bearing of these works upon Kierkegaard's treatment of the Incarnation. In this same connection I shall also note certain aspects of some other writings most of which are from the period after the *Postscript* and before the late pseudonymous works.

Though he is at pains to deny that Christianity is a doctrine,

179

Johannes Climacus is not entirely able to avoid treating it as one. Despite this, it should be noted at the outset that both he and Johannes de Silentio treat the objects of their concerns as existence-communications and that they understand and use the words *absurd* and *paradox* primarily in what we have called the existential sense. The contradiction with which they are primarily concerned is one which arises as the existing individual seeks to give expression to the truth in his own life. I do not claim that the precise meaning of this is perfectly clear, but I am convinced of its importance.

The next point is much simpler: As they are at pains to insist, neither of these pseudonyms are themselves believers. Though they can admire and applaud belief, they yet stand on the outside. They describe belief from the point of view of one who is not a believer. Hence, insofar as they describe belief as involving the acceptance of paradox, in some logical sense they may be understood as intending what we have earlier described as the apparently contradictory sense. They are reporting that it conflicts with their previous conceptions. Of course, I do not deny that they may have intended some other sense as well. But I think that we should not neglect the possible presence of this one.

The next point is very difficult and complex, but nevertheless unavoidable. It concerns the nature and status of the pseudonymous works and, perhaps more particularly, that of the early pseudonyms, some of which we have been discussing. Briefly, the matter is as follows: In the "Declaration" which he appended to the *Postscript*, Kierkegaard roundly and unequivocally declared that each of the pseudonyms was a distinct literary personality; that each had his own distinct point of view; that they contradicted one another; that anyone could make him look like a fool simply by quoting one pseudonymous work against another; that anyone who ever quoted from a pseudonym should kindly do him the favour of citing the name of the pseudonym in question, etc. Further, he declared that he was not responsible for one single word in the pseudonymous works, whereas he was, by contrast, responsible for every single word in his own acknowledged works. There is abundant evidence that this apparently remarkable declaration is quite serious and entirely justified. To choose a particularly appropriate example, the words *absurd* and *paradox* are, as our distribution table shows, confined almost entirely to his pseudonymous works. So, too, for that matter, is the word *stages* which provides the foundations or framework for the pseudonymous authorship. I am not prepared to take the extreme line that, since the former pair of words are thus virtually restricted to the pseudonymous works, we are therefore justified in pretending that Kierkegaard himself never used them. Yet that would, I suggest, be much more defensible than the traditional practice of ascribing them to Kierkegaard without qualification. I do, however, think that this is a quite remarkable and deliberate feature of the authorship, and I note that in his religious works he discusses Christianity at great length without even using these words. Why, we have to ask ourselves, do the pseudonymous works present Christianity as paradoxical while Kierkegaard himself does not?

It is generally agreed that, at the time of the writing of the *Postscript*, Kierkegaard was himself a Christian but that, wanting someone to chart the transition to belief, he assigned this work to Climacus. I think that there is much in this view and, as the reader will note, I have in some sense already accepted it. I would, however, suggest another quite compatible possibility: that, not psychologically identified with traditional orthodoxy, Kierkegaard needed someone to embody this position and chose Climacus to fill the role. This is suggested by a number of facts: Kierkegaard's own attitude towards orthodoxy was ambiguous; he seems to have been more concerned about other matters; all the uses of this word are confined to the pseudonyms (see the distribution table) and most are by Climacus. It helps to explain why Climacus uses *absurd* and *paradox* while Kierkegaard does not and gives added point to the latter's apparently outrageous claim that he was not responsible for a single word in the pseudonymous works. It may also help us to understand Kierkegaard's own need to "distance" himself from some of these works. But if there is anything in this suggestion, it would follow that Johannes Climacus should be seen as attempting to rehabilitate certain notions which he saw as central to orthodoxy and that Kierkegaard should be seen, in general at least, as accepting our account of orthodoxy as following the "way of paradox." More generally, it would follow that the pseudonyms' emphasis upon the absurd and paradox in Christianity should be seen more as an historical thesis about the nature of orthodoxy than as an account of Kierkegaard's understanding of the essential character of Christianity. Of course, there is much more to the matter but I suggest that this may be an important element.

In this connection it is worth recalling that the word "stages" is totally absent from Kierkegaard's freely acknowledged works. This is important because since the stages culminate in faith as belief in the absurd, they are often cited as evidence of what is generally regarded as Kierkegaard's irrationalism. In fact, the absence of this term from his own works must mean that this doctrine forms no part of his belief. It is rather, as I have suggested, simply the framework of the early pseudonymous authorship.

181

	Early Pseud- onymous Works	Late Pseud- onymous Works	Reli- gious Works	"Attack" Litera- ture
absurd (7) (122)	115	3	—	—
paradox* (16) (572)	501	63	—	1
Christianity (4) (2,447)	624	297	372	1056
orthodoxy (7) (52)	42	8	—	—
stages (4) (120)	108	1	—	—

NOTE: The first number in brackets following the word is the number of variants included, and the second the total number of occurrences. Discrepancies between individual and overall totals are accounted for by works not belonging to any of these four main subsets of the "authorship."
*Including three forms of, roughly, "the paradoxical religious."

Distribution of Selected Words in Kierkegaard's "Authorship"

Shortly after the appearance of the *Postscript*, Kierkegaard was attacked by the theologian Magnus Eiriksson writing under the pseudonym Theophilus Nicolaus. In his unpublished reply Kierkegaard makes his position quite clear. The object of faith is the absurd or paradox, but only for one who sees it from the outside, for one who does not yet have faith. For the man of faith it is no longer absurd or paradoxical. Thus, in a passage already quoted from the *Journals and Papers*, he writes, "When the believer has faith, the absurd is not the absurd—faith transforms it, but in every weak moment it is again more or less absurd to him. The passion of faith is the only thing which masters the absurd. . . . Therefore, rightly understood, there is nothing at all frightening in the category of the absurd. . . ." Kierkegaard's underlying point is quite clear: Nicolaus has misinterpreted the pseudonyms because, unskilled in dialectics, he has failed to note the fundamental point that their role is simply to illumine faith negatively or from the side of unbelief.

This same point is put equally clearly in a relatively late entry in the *Journals*. The entry is a long one and begins in the familiar way by insisting that for the unbeliever the content of faith is absurd and that "to become a believer everyone must be alone with the absurd." But, suddenly, and in the very midst of these claims, we find this single sentence: "While naturally it is a matter of course that for him who believes it is not the absurd." Now, obviously, the fact of belief cannot alter or dissolve a paradox in what we have already identified as the second, third, and fourth senses of *paradox*; together with the existential sense, these are permanent and inescapable features of Christian belief as such. The very fact of belief, apparently, can change the situation regarding what is a paradox in our last sense because it is possible to revise our conceptions in the light of our claims, and because real belief is, by its very nature, internally consistent and logically coherent. Kierkegaard recognizes this, and the aside quoted above is simply an obvious consequence of the logic of this concept; that, indeed, is why he says ". . . naturally it is a matter of course. . . ." Hence, at least on the logical side, faith does in some sense at least grasp or come to terms with the absurd. That, I think, is why he can write, in the entry quoted in the previous paragraph, ". . . true faith breathes healthfully and blessedly in the absurd."

In this connection, it is interesting to note another journal entry, quoted by Fabro, concerning the "recognizability" of Christ. This, he writes "implies that he is recognizable by his divine authority, even though it requires faith to resolve the paradox." Hence apparently there is, for faith at least, something which can be called a resolution of the paradox.

It would be possible to provide other, similar examples from the journals, but it is, I think, much more important simply to make the point that these writings are quite privileged because in them Kierkegaard no longer feels constrained to look at faith from the side of unbelief. Now he does not need to worry about possibly misleading his reader, and his only concern is to get these matters as straight as possible for himself. We are then, I think, allowed and even obliged to attach special importance to passages such as those we have been considering.

Earlier in this paper we discussed the occurrence and meaning of the words *absurd* and *paradox* in the early pseudonymous works. Before proceeding it is, therefore, important to pause and comment upon one notable and, perhaps by design, almost hidden feature of the *Works of Love*, which follows closely upon these works and which, as Swenson says, represents the centre of gravity of his thought. In fact, it is his fullest and most perfect expression of Christianity and, while dwelling at length upon faith or belief, it makes no reference to the absurd or to a paradox. Instead, it contains twenty-four occurrences of two variants of what is obviously a deliberately formulaic utterance, both of which can be roughly translated as "Christianly understood." The meaning is, I think, unmistakable and clear. There is a Christian understanding of things, and Christian perfection involves attaining that understanding. We shall return to this point later in our discussion of a passage reflecting this same view from one of the late pseudonyms.

These lines laid and perhaps some doubts sown, we proceed now to the late pseudonyms which are openly Christian or, as in the case of Anti-Climacus, Christian "to an extreme degree." The first of these, by H.H., called *Two Minor Ethico-Religious Treatises*, is divided into two distinct parts. "Has a Man the Right to Let Himself be Put to Death for the Truth?" is described as a poetic experiment. It begins with a request to the reader to lay aside "a considerable part of his customary way of thinking" since otherwise the problem discussed will not exist for him "because he has already disposed of it long ago, but in an opposite sense." The meaning of this becomes clear as H.H. asks whether Christ was justified in allowing himself to be put to death. We need not consider what the *philosophers* say but "With *theologians* it is another matter. They set out from faith. In that they do well. . . ." But, he observes, their work "contains nothing for the solution of my problem. The theologians ponder over the eternal significance of this historic fact and raise no difficulty with regard to its historical becoming." The believer is not inclined to do theology "but would rather believe because he *shall* believe, than (as it is senselessly expressed), *because he can comprehend*. This distinction is developed further a few pages later:

> To believe is to believe the divine and the human together in Christ. To *comprehend* Him is to comprehend His life humanly. But to comprehend His life *humanly* is so far from being more than believing, that (if there is no faith besides) it means to lose Him, since His life is what it is for faith, the *divine*-human. I can *understand* MYSELF *in believing*; I can understand myself in believing . . . but to understand faith, or to understand Christ is something I cannot do. . . .

That is not terribly clear. But a brief passage at the end serves at least to put it in perspective. "What I write here, even if I laid it before them, would be for most people as if it were not written, as if it were nonexistent. As was shown above, their thinking ends where mine begins." That is an important clue to our problem and should be kept clearly in mind.

"Of the Difference Between a Genius and an Apostle" asserts that there is such a difference and so makes a number of points. The errors with which H.H. is here concerned are "not confined to heterodoxy but are also found in hyper-orthodoxy. They are in fact those of thoughtlessness." The genius belongs to the sphere of immanence, the apostle to that transcendence. "All thought breathes in immanence, whereas faith and paradox are a sphere unto themselves." The genius may be ahead of his time but his teaching is only a "transitory paradox" which will ultimately be assimilated by the race. The apostle's message, however, is and remains essentially and equally paradoxical in both form and content. "*Authority is inconceivable within the sphere of immanence. . . .*" "To ask whether Christ is profound is blasphemy . . . [and] conceals a doubt concerning his authority. . . ." The son who obeys because his father is a genius is "affected" and does not understand the logic of a command. Similarly, "the whole of modern philosophy is therefore affected, because it has done away with *obedience* on the one hand, and *authority* on the other, and then, in spite of everything, wishes to be orthodox."

The Sickness Unto Death, the first work ascribed to Anti-Climacus, boldly says of God that for Him "all things are possible." Later he writes: "help by virtue of the absurd, that for God all things are possible." The author describes Speculation's success in comprehending as "sewing without making the end fast and without knotting the thread," whereas "Christianity, on the contrary, fastens the end by means of the paradox." He refers to the Christian dogma that sin is a position "—not, however, as though it could be comprehended, but as a paradox which must be believed," and speaks of the "despair of weakness which being offended does not dare to believe."

Toward the end of *Sickness* Anti-Climacus takes up a question which obviously concerned Kierkegaard very much at this point (1848) in his life: the question of the relation of God and man, particularly as posed by the person of the God-Man. Anti-Climacus calls for "a Socratic, a God-fearing ignorance, which by ignorance defends faith against speculation, keeping watch to see that the deep gulf of qualitative distinction between God/and man may be firmly fixed, as it is in the paradox and in faith, lest God/and man . . . might in a way, *philosophice, poetice*, etc., coalesce into one . . . in the System." He laments that:

> the doctrine of the God-Man . . . is taken in vain, the qualitative distinction between God and man is pantheistically abolished—first speculatively with an air of superiority, then vulgarly in the streets and alleys. . . . Never anywhere has any doctrine on earth brought God and man so near together as has Christianity. . . . Neither has any doctrine ever so carefully defended itself against the most shocking of all blasphemies, that after God had taken this step it then should be taken in vain, as though God and man coalesced in one and the same thing—. . . .

But though Anti-Climacus condemns the "slack orators" and "loose thinkers" who equate the multitude with the God-Man and the mob with God, he is apparently not completely at ease with the traditional accounts of the difference between God and man. Indeed, he writes: "Sin is the only thing universally predicated of man which cannot in any way . . . be affirmed of God. . . . As a sinner man is separated from God by a yawning qualitative abyss . . . in one respect man will never in all eternity come to resemble God, namely, in forgiving sins." He also speaks of Christianity as teaching "the likeness (*Ligheden*) between God and man," and of Christian doctrine as "the doctrine of the God-Man, of kinship (*Slaegtskabet*) between God and men." But he will go no further; indeed, he adds immediately "but in such a way, be it noted, that the possibility of offense is . . . the guarantee whereby

185

God makes sure that man cannot come too near to Him." In fact, he concludes God and man "are two qualities between which there is an infinite qualitative difference," and every doctrine which overlooks this is "humanly speaking, crazy . . . in a godly sense . . . blasphemy." There is no escape from paradox since even Christ himself cannot take away the possibility of offense.

This same problem is discussed again in *Training in Christianity*, the second work of Anti-Climacus. It insists that the God-Man is both God and an individual man; this is "the greatest possible, the qualitative contradiction," and, especially, the offence. It attacks "this modern notion about the speculative unity between God and man" which it connects with "regarding Christianity merely as a doctrine" and that "people have forgotten what 'existence' means." Offence has to do essentially with the God-Man which Speculation imagines it has "comprehended." Such folly, however, "one can easily comprehend, for speculation, in speculating about the God-Man, leaves out temporal existence, contemporaneousness, and reality." This is a fundamental misunderstanding:

> Christianity is not a doctrine. All the talk about offence in relation to Christianity as a doctrine is a misunderstanding, it is a device to mitigate the shock of offence at the scandal—as, for example, when one speaks of the offence of the *doctrine* of the God-Man and the *doctrine* of the Atonement. No, the offence is related either to Christ or to the fact of being oneself a Christian.

As does Kierkegaard, Anti-Climacus believes that our intellectual difficulties are primarily spiritual in origin.

Like Kierkegaard's broad-jumper we have spent all our time in preparation and must now be content with a few brief remarks, allowing the reader to draw his own conclusions. But that at least is in the spirit of Kierkegaard.

Kierkegaard was primarily concerned with the absurd or paradox in what we have called the existential sense and his account of this was not, I think, very clear. Many will see this as a grave defect, but it can perhaps be interpreted in another way. As suggested earlier he was attempting a revolution in or, perhaps, on the edge of philosophy. In this connection, think for a moment of Wittgenstein's expression "*a form of life*" and, though it is a somewhat different matter, of Marx's notion of *praxis*, neither of which, let us admit, is very clear. Kierkegaard in fact was attempting to formulate an equally radical reaction to the same sort of philosophy and, further, was attempting to remind us of truths we had in some sense forgotten. He was attempting to drive out a spell, to remind his reader that human existence was

186

different from and more important than mere understanding. That is a perfectly simple point. If his account is unclear to us, that may reflect the extent of our confusion and the accuracy of his diagnosis.

At the outset we suggested that Kierkegaard represented an advance upon traditional theology: He understood that the Christian, at least, must base his conceptions of God and man upon the Incarnation. But his pseudonyms seem so obviously anxious to deny this that we must ask what they were concerned to safeguard and whether this concern was justified.

It is, of course, clear that their first concern is existential. It is equally clear that this emphasis is correct for both human life and Christianity; in both cases *being* really is more important than mere understanding. It is equally clear that the Incarnation is not "humanly possible": It cannot be made intelligible in the light of merely human ideas, and it cannot be understood as *necessary* in the traditional sense of that term with which Climacus appears particularly concerned. The Incarnation was a necessity (in another sense) and not simply a picture book illustration of an eternal truth which mankind would sooner or later discover for itself. On the other hand, the early pseudonyms appear to assume that what is divine can therefore never become a subject of human thought: What God chooses to reveal is, in some curious way, non-assimilable in a way in which other facts are not. Against this one should say that, if the Incarnation happened, the person who knows that it is impossible knows too much. Similarly, Climacus appears to be wrong in his assumption that one can maintain what he treasures as the tension in the life of faith only by treating the Incarnation as, in itself, logically contradictory. A serious Christian is obliged to reshape his conceptions of God and man in the light of this event. Yet that, as anyone who has attempted it will allow, does not reduce this tension, but simply changes its focus or shifts it along the line.

There is also positive evidence that Kierkegaard would have accepted the position we have ascribed to him. He puts Christ at the centre of his life and thought to the almost total exclusion of natural theology. He consistently emphasises the Teacher at the expense of the teaching. He places great stress upon consistency and "consequences" and frequently rejects positions on the grounds that their implications are nonsense or absurd. In general, he assumes that those who have had an experience will find it intelligible and that those who have not will not. Though he prefers the existential sense of "belief," he clearly understands the more familiar one by which to believe p is also to believe the propositions implied by p. Because of his reading of the needs of his time, he chose to emphasize the necessity of faith and the paradox. He always held, nevertheless, that the latter is in some sense resolved in the former. For example, with Anti-Climacus, he knows that there is a true resolution of even the existential paradox in the imitation of Christ in which one achieves true contemporaneity with Him. He also knows that in faith the absurd is no longer absurd: In it one can "resolve" the paradox, and there can be a Christian understanding of things. Finally, there is the fact that, as a believer, he can, for example in the works of Anti-Climacus, speak of the likeness and kinship of God and man.

There is another piece of evidence in *Training* which in its own way is as conclusive as all of the above. It does not even mention the Incarnation. Yet its relevance is obvious, particularly in light of Kierkegaard's conception of "human conceptions" as embodying our rebellion against God.

> Christ never desired to conquer in this world; He came to the world to suffer, *that* is what He called conquering. But when human impatience and the impudent forwardness which ascribes to Christianity its own thoughts and conceptions, instead of letting its thoughts and conceptions be transformed by Christianity—when this got the upper hand, then, in the old human way, to conquer meant to conquer in this world, and thus Christianity is done away with.

Apparently, then, Anti-Climacus, at least, believes that human thoughts and conceptions can be transformed; indeed, if this is not done, "Christianity is done away with."

I conclude with a final remark from Johannes Climacus, not as evidence for my interpretation of Kierkegaard, but as a succinct expression of the larger point I have been attempting to make. In the *Fragments* he speaks of Reason as "capable at most of saying 'yes' and 'no' to the same thing, which is not good divinity." That is the Paradox commenting on the Reason but, I suggest, it could also be Kierkegaard, perhaps in another life, commenting upon a tradition which I have described as following the "way of paradox."

Bibliography

Kierkegaard, *Fear and Trembling*, New York, 1954.

Kierkegaard, *Philosophical Fragments*, Princeton, 1967.

Kierkegaard, *Concluding Unscientific Postscript*, London, 1945.

Kierkegaard, *Works of Love*, New York, 1962.

Kierkegaard, "Two Minor Ethico-Religious Treatises," in *The Present Age*, Oxford, 1949.

Kierkegaard, *The Sickness Unto Death*, New York, 1954.

Kierkegaard, *Training in Christianity*, Oxford, 1946.

Kierkegaard, *The Journals*, transl. A. Dru, Oxford, 1951.

Kierkegaard, *Journals and Papers*, transl. Hong & Hong, Indiana, 1970.

Cornelio Fabro, "Faith and Reason in Kierkegaard's Dialectic," in *A Kierkegaard Critique*, New York, 1967.

N.H. Søe, "Kierkegaard's Doctrine of the Paradox," in *A Kierkegaard Critique*, New York, 1967.

Philosophers, Religion and Conceptual Change

DEWI Z. PHILLIPS

Philosophers often comment on conceptual change without realizing that they themselves may be casualities of it. I want to illustrate this by contrasting some recent and challenging claims made by two very different papers juxtaposed in the Royal Institute volume of lectures on *Talk of God* (Macmillan of London, 1969: Editor, G.N.A. Vesey): "The Concept of Heaven" by Ninian Smart and "Eternal Life" by John Wisdom. But I also hope to shed light on typically careless and confusing uses of standard words in Philosophy of Religion like "myth," "mythic," "literal," "symbol," "symbolic," and "interpretation."

Smart begins by stressing what he calls the organic character of religious belief: It is "impossible to understand a given religious utterance or belief without paying attention to the range of utterances or beliefs it goes with, and they in turn have to be understood in the milieu of religious practice, etc." Though this is true, it is insufficient. One must stress not only the milieu of religious practice, but the wider social and cultural milieux in which such practices are placed. The importance of this emphasis will become apparent later. Clearly, however, religion would be substance-less were there not features of human life whose aspect is changed through their relation to religious beliefs and practices, beliefs and practices which are themselves responses to these same features of human life. To repeat: It is essential to take account of this wider context in order to understand the force of religious belief.

Secondly, Smart wishes to remind us that religious beliefs may change. The changes Smart has in mind result from reflection at a given stage of cultural sophistication. What of religion prior to such reflection? According to Smart it existed at the mythic stage. The mythic is characterised, apparently, by simple belief; belief, for example, in God or gods, in or beyond the sky. But, Smart tells us, these beliefs were not meant literally: "God is mythically represented as dwelling in or beyond the sky, but it would be folly to suppose that this, at the mythic stage, is meant literally, as though God were like a Gagarin." So is the mythic distinguished from the literal. This is not as helpful as it sounds. Such remarks mislead by giving the impression that we know quite well what the literal use is or could be. But to say, "God is above the sky just like the Cosmonaut called Gagarin," is to give us a useless sentence: We cannot make it work in any coherent context. A good example is given by M.O'.C. Drury when he tells of a local resident's reaction to his expression of admiration for a mountain-top glacier corrie lake: "Now wasn't that a queer place to put a lake?" Here was a notion of creation with which Drury could do nothing: He could find no background against which it could do any work! It is misleading, therefore, to distinguish between the mythic and the literal as if one were confronted by two distinct meanings. What is here called *the literal* is a species of confusion which, so far from being an instance of meaning, is a form of words pretentiously alleged to possess a meaning it does not have. We shouldn't say that God is not seen literally, as if that made sense, but that what it means to see God is being misunderstood in this way. One needs to stress the connection between what Smart calls the mythic stage of religious expressions and the various mythologies in human language, which may or may not be related explicitly to mythic expressions in religion. For example: Smart recognizes how often "value-predicates connect up with height—'supreme,' 'a high quality of . . . ,' and so on." Similarly, believers are bidden to lift up their hearts; they respond by lifting them up unto the Lord. If God's being on high were to be called a mythic expression, lifting up one's heart to him might be called a mythic activity. Would it be nonsensical to say that one's heart is not raised up literally?

Smart speaks as though the mythic state of religion cannot survive reflection: "For the mythic way of thinking eschews the distinctions which we are inclined to make." But is this true? Smart's reasoning is based on his belief that hard-headed criticisms tend to reduce the mythic to the literal. Now let us bear in mind that Smart has already told us that the mythic must not be taken literally. It follows that the meaning of the mythic cannot be identified with what is called the literal. If, therefore, reflection reduces the mythic to the literal, it follows also that certain forms of reflection reduce what was not confused prior to the reflection to some form or other of confusion. Does it not follow that the reductionism which may result from such reflection comes, not from the character of the mythic, but from various confused attempts at understanding and grasping this character? When some heard that a man had to be born again before he could enter the kingdom of heaven, they asked how a man, when old, could be born again. The confusion is not in the mythic language of salvation, but in the misunderstanding expressed in the question. There is no necessary reason why the question should lead to a reduction of the original to something other than itself. So why should Smart say, "*Of course*, God is not literally in the sky, and yet this is

191

what the mythic concept seems to be saying once we begin to ask the literal-minded question." But *to whom* does the user of such a sentence seem to be saying this? To the user of mythic language? If the answer is in the affirmative, it means, in this context, that the user of this language has come to think that he needs the confused account of the language he uses, whereas, of course, he does not. But now, the position may be more complicated. This is because the confused account of mythic language may *itself* begin to influence the mythic content and to change its character. How is this possible? Consider the following comments by Peter Winch on the relation between theology and the language and practices of religion:

> Of course, the discussions of theologians affect the teachings of a church; and believers are brought up on these teachings which, in their turn, influence the forms of worship offered to the Church's adherents. Thus the doctrine of Cathar theology that the world of matter is the work of the Devil was connected with the rejection of sacraments in the worship of the Cathar Church. However, the traffic is not one-way. Theological developments are not developed independently of their possibilities of application in the worship and religious lives of believers; and these latter have a certain though not a complete, autonomy. I mean that if a doctrine were felt by believers to be hostile to their practices of prayer and worship, that would create a difficulty for the theological doctrine itself. I emphasize that the traffic goes in both directions and there is give and take. Believers' attitudes to worship may be modified under the pressure of priests, for example, who in their turn are influenced by the theological doctrines in which they are trained in their church. But the attitudes of priests to theological doctrines may also be affected by the resistances they encounter in the attitudes to worship amongst their flocks. Of course, not all believers (or priests) will react in the same way, and thus arise possibilities of schism and heresy.

Winch intends these remarks to question the pervasive view "that the practices of believers are, at the most fundamental level to be explained by the believers' "belief in the truth" of certain theological doctrines." He wants to stress by contrast that

> Worship (which may naturally take many forms) is a primitive human response to certain characteristic human situations and predicaments. . . . These practices will involve certain characteristic uses of language. (Again taking many different forms between which, however, analogies will be discernable). Given the existence of these practices and uses of language, theological doctrines will be elaborated which in their turn will react back on the practices and language of believers. In order to understand the sense of these doctrines (their 'relation to reality') we need to understand their application. This application takes place in contexts such as those of prayer and worship within which language is used according to a certain

192

grammar. This grammar itself imposes limits on what will count as an acceptable theological doctrine, even though, as I have said, a doctrine may itself lead to modifications in the grammar of the language in which belief is expressed in worship. (Peter Winch, "Meaning and Religious Language," to be published with the papers of the Royal Institute Conference at Lancaster on Philosophy of Religion.)

Smart, by contrast, does not similarly allow for the two-way traffic. What he calls the doctrinal use of language is meant to express more abstractly what has to be rescued from the mythic in the face of criticism. Instead of speaking of God as dwelling in or beyond the sky, "doctrinally, God is represented as transcendent, in such a way that *now* the language of heaven is treated as symbolic of transcendence." The movement is one-way in Smart's view: The doctrinal is the refinement of the mythic. But it is extremely difficult to make his remarks consistent, since why does the mythic need to be refined? We have already seen how the mere presence of critical reflection cannot account for any such need. When we look to Smart's other remarks for an answer to this question, we find them involved in circularity and contradiction. Let us try as best we can to outline what appear to be stages in an argument.

Stage one: A mythic use of language untrammelled by critical reflection. (One may question the reality of such a time.)

Stage two: Hard-hearted criticism reduces the mythic to the literal. (We have seen difficulties ascribing meaning to the literal.)

Stage three: The mythic in itself is not meant literally.

Stage four: In the face of criticism, the mythic expression is replaced by the more severe and abstract doctrinal expression.

Stage five: Doctrines are not descriptions. They too have their application to forms of piety and religious practice. (At this point there is some similarity between Winch and Smart's comments on theology, but stage five is contradicted immediately by the next stage.)

Stage six: Doctrinal ideas when expounded nevertheless seem to be descriptive in character:

> The doctrinal idea of God's place, i.e., the notion that God is transcendent, can be explained briefly as follows. It ties in with the context of the doctrine of Creation, as commonly interpreted to mean that God continuously creates and sustains the cosmos, which is thus at all points dependent upon him. This belief implies that God and the cosmos are distinct. For this and other reasons, God does not take spatial predicates (except at the mythic level). Thus God is conceived as lying beyond the cosmos—he transcends it—but not in such a way that it makes sense to say that he is a thousand or a million miles further on.

Here, the mythic seems to be accounted for by these theological truths.

Stage seven: The doctrinal cannot be a wholly adequate substitute for the mythic:

> Though the substitution of a doctrinal idea of God's place for the mythic one sacrifices some of the poetic flavour of the latter, it is still possible to retain the symbolism by continuing to use the mythology in liturgy. By the 'poetic flavour,' I mean that there are suggestions in the idea of God as dwelling in the sky, or beyond it, which are relevant to religious experience and practice, but which are not brought out in such a technical sounding term as 'transcendence.'

Stage eight: The seventh stage is immediately contradicted by the eighth stage. As we saw, the doctrinal is said to be an inadequate replacement for the mythic. Now, however, we are told that although the mythic and the doctrinal may, to some extent, exist side by side, the doctrinal tends to displace the mythic as the central account of where God is. Smart says, "When the mythic undergoes this displacement, it is convenient to refer to it as the symbolic concept of heaven. For it has indeed undergone a change—become a new concept, if you like—by virtue of the principle of the organic understanding of religious concepts and utterances. . . . Since a given concept has to be understood by reference to its organic milieu, some major change in the milieu creates a new concept, in effect." But *what* has become symbolic? Remember that the mythic was not meant literally, according to Smart. Is it the literal misunderstanding which now becomes symbolic, or the mythic itself? In the latter case, what does it mean to speak of the mythic becoming symbolical? Smart, I think, would give the following answer: ". . . this is what happens where the idea of the mythic heaven is no longer taken seriously, but is in essence replaced by a doctrinal concept of heaven, and only retained as a symbolism which points us towards that which is more precisely described by means of a doctrinal concept. This, then, is an argument for distinguishing the original mythic concept of heaven from what we are now calling the symbolic concept."

This seems a poor sort of argument, indeed, quite contradictory. The mythic is replaced by the symbolic, which, in turn, hints at what is more adequately expressed by the doctrinal. But as we saw in stage seven of the argument, the doctrinal was in many ways unable to express what was given in the mythic! The argument seems to be going round in circles: The mythic is replaced by the doctrinal which inadequately expresses what is in the mythic; when this happens the mythic becomes the symbolical which inadequately represents what is given more precisely in the doctrinal. The effect of all this seems increasingly to separate us from the mythic and hence from that which only the mythic can express. But this is not how Smart sees it.

Stage nine: In the final stage of the argument, speaking of the mythic, Smart says that "in the major religions, . . . it has become deeply eroded by the very fact that the major religions have evolved theologies or schemes of doctrine which effectively reduce it to symbolic status." We have already seen, however, that if the two-way traffic between the mythic and the theological is emphasized, this need not follow. It is hard to know how much weight to put on Smart's arguments since it is difficult to detect a consistent thread in them. He goes on to tell us for example: "I am far from saying that myths are unimportant: . . . there may be a way of consistently using the mythic idea of heaven, even within the framework of modern cosmology, etc., but only by using it in a parable way, which almost amounts to giving it symbolic status."

My aim in trying to outline these nine stages in Smart's argument is not to try to extract some consistent thread from them, but to argue that such consistency cannot be found there. I have pursued two main goals: First, to illustrate how a philosopher can himself become the victim of conceptual change without realizing it; secondly, to show how easily terms like "myth," "the literal," and "symbol" become sources of confusion, although they are so often thought to be ideal terms for clarifying what religious beliefs must be. In reading Smart, one receives the impression that philosophers are very much in control of the situation. He speaks of *our* using the mythic; of theologians putting it aside in order to express matters more adequately in doctrinal form; of philosophers learning the whole process and testing it for its consistency. Looking at the whole picture Smart is able to conclude that "in any event, it is almost inevitable that we should here treat the mythic idea as dead for the very question as to its consistency requires us to ask such questions as whether it is possible to locate God in the sky, and such questions belong to a different cultural and intellectual milieu from that in which a mythic idea had its genesis." This picture is, I think, grossly over-simplistic. If the mythic declines, it is not because of its lack of consistency, but because people's values and emphasis on what is important in life erode it. I am not denying that there are forms of religious experience where the symbolism jars and seems inappropriate, but I would also insist that there are other forms where this is not so. Even where the symbolism seems inappropriate, the charge should not be inconsistency, so much as, for example, tawdriness, shallowness, or pursuit of a mechanistic view of religion. To speak, moreover, of the mythic as dead is to ignore the mythology present in our own language. Rather than attaining Smart's picture of programmed consistency, from the mythic via the doctrinal to the symbolic, we reach an overview of the waxing and waning of

195

religious expressiveness which is profoundly influenced by the mythology in our language and by other, various processes. It is essential, I think, to emphasize the two-way traffic between theology and worship. For if we do not, then, as Winch points out, one will misunderstand the relation between theology and religion.

> The difference between them is not like that between a laboratory technician who sets up an experiment without having a clear idea of what he is doing and the scientist who directs him. That is to say, in respect of its religious significance, the unsophisticated believer's worship, the technician's activities differ from those of the scientist in respect of its scientific significance. There is no reason why the unsophisticated believer's faith should not be religiously deeper than that of the theologian.

A theologian does not know more about God than other people, as Tolstoy showed superbly in his short story, *The Three Hermits*.

As well as emphasizing the two-way traffic between theology and religion, we also need to emphasize the many forces at work which may affect the status of religious expressions. The waxing and waning of these expressions is to be understood in this context. It may well be that the notion of doing something about this in the sense of wanting to secure the sense of the language, is itself confused. Thus, the conservative theologian who exhorts believers to hold fast to the old faith, may underestimate the extent to which such constancy depends on conditions outside the control of individualistic response. Similarly, the liberal theologian who exhorts believers to make their faith intelligible in the language of their times, may underestimate the extent to which the very language of our times militates against the intelligibility of the faith and leads to our concern with the meaning, however vague, of being called *religious*. What needs greater emphasis than Smart gives it is the way in which philosophical reflection may itself fall prey to these various pressures. Even if he were right, the questioner who wanted to locate God would not have revealed the inconsistency of the mythic expression of God and gods living in or beyond the sky. Instead, his question would be a symptom, a misunderstanding of the mythic. These misunderstandings are partly concealed by the superficial similarities between the surface grammars of various areas of human discourse. But to say this is not enough: One must also stress that the elevation of one such area of discourse or human activity at any given time, due to startling advances or discoveries, creates a prestige for it which tends to make it, at a certain intellectual level, the paradigm of intelligibility for other areas of discourse and activity. The rise of modern science is an obvious example. During such periods of the pre-eminence of a paradigm the character of other areas of discourse may change. They may be

196

enriched or they may be impoverished. The latter may well have been the fate of the mythic in religion. The popularity of the anthropology of religion may well be revealed as a profound interest in something which used to be with us, but which we now see only through a glass darkly.

The final irony is that the picture Smart presents to us is itself a contributing factor to the decline of mythic expressiveness in religion. Theological speculation of a certain kind itself contributes to the decline of the mythic, since a certain kind of philosophical theology — given that it has a certain prestige in the life of the church—may itself become a type of pre-eminent paradigm. I do not refer to philosophizings in the style of Feuerbach which are attacks on religion, but to sympathetic attempts by philosophers to explain religious belief. Unphilosophical believers are hardly likely to look to Feuerbach for a paradigm of rationality. Of course, in so far as these questions are themselves of philosophical interest, the task cannot be avoided. It arises naturally within a philosophical movement. The consequences to which I have called attention are, nevertheless, undeniable and, therefore, can themselves become a matter of philosophical interest. Such an interest lies behind the present paper, since I have been arguing that Smart's arguments can be met at different levels. One can, as I have already done to some extent, engage in philosophical disagreement with Smart about the notion of the mythic, of the literal, and so on. But one can also—and this has been my main interest—see in his not untypical mode of writing on conceptual changes from the mythic, through the doctrinal, to the symbolical, *as itself an example of conceptual change in two ways.* First, if I am right, it is a product of misunderstanding. Seeing the mythic decline, he has misunderstood both the character of the decline and the nature of what has been said to decline. Secondly, and more importantly for present purposes, the very type of philosophizing born of such misunderstandings becomes *itself* an agent for conceptual change; becomes itself a new force among several others which erodes the language of the mythic.

In Smart's error, however, one has but *one* example of this phenomenon. John Wisdom's essay, "Eternal Life" offers another example, I suggest, of a very different kind. Here, the cultural surroundings are similar to those we have encountered in Smart's paper. Wisdom, too, recalls those who have said that there is a God above and a way to eternal life. Those who have spoken of the latter have sometimes meant to imply that there is some kind of duration after death and sometimes not. In both cases, however, they have meant to assert a hope in the face of the despair felt by many at the thought that life ends in death. As he looks back at history, Wisdom

197

concludes that the hope of life after death has brought comfort to millions. The difficulty now is that in a critical spirit people have said that they do not know what these words mean. Some words of the Buddha, it is true, have brought comfort without speaking of life after death, but by and large, Wisdom thinks, those who have said that there is a way to eternal life without implying that there is life after death, have brought comfort to relatively few. Wisdom appreciates why Spinoza wanted to distinguish between "eternity" and "duration," but cannot get much out of what he means by "eternity." He finds similar difficulties with those who speak of truth as ineffable or of eternity as being within them. And yet, Wisdom is not content to let these words go. He feels that there is something important about them that eludes him. Someone may speak as follows:

> I no longer believe what the words 'There's a God above' used to mean to me when I was a child. I no longer believe what the words 'There's a God above' still mean to many. Indeed the words 'God exists' no longer mean to me anything which I believe. And yet I can't dismiss them from my mind. When I look back on all that has been said about God, then I feel that though much of it has been fake or doubtful or obscure, still the words 'There is a God above' may yet with further thought guide us to some truth which is still of great importance for our lives.

Wisdom refers to a Mr. Kollerstrom's attempts to give an account of "There's a way to life eternal" without implying anything about duration after death. Wisdom is not clear whether he is confronted by someone preparing new meanings or someone using old words in order to grope towards new meanings. Once again one couldn't say what truth is being conveyed Mr. Kollerstrom relates a dream in which he envisages possible outcomes which his life may have had. Speaking of the dream he says,

> But everything that is spiritually my own, everything of true worth that I have found for myself, derives from that great dream. Still it enriches and instructs me; without it my life would have been a husk. Though the gifts of the gods may blast or wither us, if we can at least hear them, they will transform us.

Wisdom is confronted, then, with all these examples of talk about God or the eternal, and with all such expressions of belief. He has no scheme of things in terms of the *mythic*, the *doctrinal*, or the *symbolic*. He cannot see clearly what such words come to, but he has a philosopher's suspicion that they mean something important. He does not claim to know what to do with these words or how to categorize them. His is the perplexity which is often a prelude to the dawning of an aspect—to seeing old things from so fresh a perspective that one sees *something new*. (One suddenly sees the hypocrisy in Judas' smile.) Wisdom sums up his relation to the words as follows:

> There are occasions when a person engaged in an enquiry, perhaps a person trying to gain an understanding of certain bewildering phenomena in nature, finds in his mouth certain words . . . without yet knowing what he means by them. We know that in such circumstances it may happen that the words of which he may himself say that he doesn't yet know what he means by them nevertheless help him to grope his way towards a concept which turns out to be just what he needs for that understanding of things which he is struggling to attain.

In this context a new aspect does dawn for Wisdom upon the questions he has hitherto been asking. Confronted with Mr. Kollerstrom's dream, Wisdom kept asking, in the face of what he calls the old story, equally old questions:

> It's the old story. It is time that though Mr. Kollerstrom's dream was somewhat extraordinary I have some idea of what it was like. But does it provide evidence for some truth, some doctrine, some proposition? And, if so, how so? And what is the truth, or what he regards as the truth, for which he thinks it provides evidence?

But may not *this* have been the mistake, to think that one is concerned here with propositional truths and descriptive doctrines? Wisdom begins to suggest this towards the end of his paper. He reminds us that what happens in a dream may make us see the whole of our lives differently. We are here beginning to take account of expressive uses of language, among them, the mythic, which we have already encountered in this paper.

The difference between Ninian Smart and John Wisdom—two men who reveal so much about our time—in relation to conceptual change should now be apparent: I have argued that Smart is an unconscious victim of such change; Wisdom is a quite conscious victim. In this context Wisdom propounds Socratic ignorance. The sense in which Wisdom is lost for want of a meaning cannot be explained without reference to the same factors which fashion Smart's viewpoint. But there is an essential difference: These factors cannot fashion or affect Wisdom's viewpoint, since *he has none*. He offers us a glimpse of a quest, not a glance at a goal. What he expresses eloquently in his paper is the character of his philosophical predicament, the character of his lostness. A new aspect begins to dawn, but it is not divulged. Wisdom writes "Unfinished" at the end of his paper, but this seems to indicate more than that he simply takes his paper to be incomplete. "Unfinished" belongs, in an important way, to the very essence of the paper; it powerfully evokes a sense of the quest and the state of being which Wisdom is depicting.

199

A philosopher can no more complete another's speculations than a composer can complete the composition of a fellow composer. What I say now, therefore, refers to a possible development. In seeing the possibility of revealing new aspects, Wisdom might well have considered the mythic in religion and its connections with the mythology in our language. Had he done so, would he not have seen that his characterizations of these early beliefs in childhood and later, might well need revision? The so-called *literal* hopes and fears could in some cases turn out to be what Wisdom calls *fake*, *doubtful*, or *obscure*, but they might themselves be understood in this way because of pressures from alien, irrelevant paradigms of intelligibility, including prestigious philosophical paradigms. Clearing away this confusion will reveal the mythic for what it is. We are reminded of what was already before us. We may find that the mythic, like much else, is "that known, because not looked for." Having looked for it, however, we may see it as it is for the first time. It may well be that we have to experience what it is to be lost, like Wisdom, before such a rediscovery is possible. Consider these lines from T.S. Eliot's "Little Gidding" in his "Four Quartets":

We shall not cease from exploration
And the end of all our exploring
Will be to arrive where we started
And know the place for the first time.

This may well be the experience of a philosopher who has to reflect upon religious belief in the midst of conceptual change. He rediscovers neither new meanings, nor old words used to express new meanings. No, he rediscovers the old, old story which these old words always did express. To rediscover such a story is to reveal what a properly human religion can be like. To the wise philosopher of religion such revelations are infinitely precious. Dreams of transcendence yield to the deepest needs of men and women. The old story triumphs over commentaries in blinding jargon and over systematic misinterpretation.

Notes on Contributors

RICHARD BOSLEY grew up in a Mormon community, then took his B.A. in classical literature at the University of Utah. He continued his training in Latin and Greek at the University of California, Berkeley while taking a master's in philosophy. He later wrote his doctorate in Germany at the University of Göttingen under the noted Aristotelian scholar Gunther Patzig, having first studied Medieval Arabic in the Middle East. He is the author of *Aspects of Aristotle's Logic*, (Assen, Van Gorcum, 1975), of a philosophical novel on the problem of universals to be published by a Canadian Academic Press, and of articles and reviews for such journals as *Mind*, *Canadian Journal of Philosophy*, *Notre Dame Journal of Formal Logic*, *Dialogue*, *Ajatus*, etc. Several of his plays on historical and philosophical themes have been performed at annual meetings of the Canadian Learned Societies. Richard Bosley is Associate Professor of Philosophy at the University of Alberta and has been Visiting Professor at the University of Pittsburgh. He works extensively on ancient and medieval philosophy and on the lessons for metaphysics and epistemology of early and recent philosophies of language. He is married to a Welsh actress who is also a specialist in French literature. He has two sons.

CATHERINE DAFOE, the Editorial Assistant for this Volume, specializes in social geography and perceptual studies for geography. Before pursuing a career as a geographer, she gained working experience in several parts of British Columbia and Alberta as a restaurant manager and a purchasing agent for an electronics firm. She has also worked with small and large Canadian stores. Both her interest in perceptual studies for geography (raising questions about conceptual relations between geography and modes of perception) and her fondness for science fiction have brought her to the study of philosophy as a specialized discipline. Catherine Dafoe has ancestors from the Maritimes, but lives with her daughter in the West.

J.J. FRANCIS FIRTH, born in Barrie, Ontario, graduated from the honour course in philosophy at Saint Michael's College in the University of Toronto in 1939, the same year he entered the Congregation of Basilian Fathers. He obtained his M.A. in philosophy from the University of Toronto in 1942 and his Licentiate from the Pontifical Institute of Mediaeval Studies in 1944. For sixteen years he taught at Saint Basil's Seminary in Toronto, first church history, then theology. He taught patristics for five years in the religious studies program of the University of British Columbia, and for three of those years also the history of mediaeval philosophy in the same university. In 1969 he obtained the doctorate in mediaeval studies from the Pontifical Institute of Mediaeval Studies in Toronto. His thesis, a critical edition of the *Liber poenitentialis* of Robert of Flamborough, a practical manual for the priest hearing confessions composed at Paris in 1208-1213, has been published through the publications department of the same institute. In addition he has published brief articles or notices in *Traditio* 16 (1960) and 17 (1961) and in *Mediaeval Studies* 30 (1968) in connection with the same work. Since 1969 he has been Assistant Professor of Philosophy at Saint Joseph's College in the University of Alberta.

WAYNE GRENNAN was born in Halifax, Nova Scotia, where he now teaches philosophy at Saint Mary's University. He originally graduated in engineering, then took a B.A. in philosophy with first class honours at Dalhousie University. Since being granted the M.A. by Dalhousie for a thesis on "The Causal Relation," he has worked at Oxford University under Basil Mitchell, Nolloth Professor of the Philosophy of Religion, on a doctoral dissertation entitled "Wittgensteinian Fideism: Conceptual Relativism in Philosophy of Religion." He has received awards from Canada Council and the Killam Foundation for his studies. Professor Grennan has also taught at Saint Thomas University (Fredericton, New Brunswick) and at Dalhousie University where he was a Visiting Fellow. He has work appearing in *The Thomist* and *Sophia*. A version of this paper "Can Faith Be a Christian Virtue?" has been presented at a Congress of the Canadian Philosophical Association. Wayne Grennan is married and has two sons.

JOHN KING-FARLOW is Professor of Philosophy at the University of Alberta. Currently, he is a founding editor of the *Canadian Journal of Philosophy*, Secretary of the Canadian Philosophical Association, Counselor of the Association of Philosophy Journal Editors, Canada's member of the editorial board of the microfilm organization, *Philosophy Research Archives*, and trustee of The Philosophy Information Service. Author of *Reason and Religion* (London, 1969) and co-author of *Faith and the Life of Reason* (Dordrecht, 1972), he is also co-editor with Yvon Lafrance of the francophone Canadian series *L'Univers de la Philosophie* (Montréal and Paris, 1973-77), co-editor with W. R. Shea of the *Contemporary Canadian Philosophy Series* (Neale Watson Academic Publications, 1976-1977), and co-editor with Roger A. Shiner of *New Essays in Philosophy of Mind* (Alberta, 1975). John King-Farlow holds degrees from Oxford (M.A.), Duke (A.M.), and Stanford (Ph.D.), has studied more briefly in France, and held staff appointments at universities in Canada, the United States, England, and Australia. His papers and reviews have appeared in English and French in the journals of many countries, including *Mind, Analysis, Philosophy, Dialogue, Philosophia, Philosophy of Science, Zeitschrift für allgemeine Wissenschaftstheorie, Review of Metaphysics, Laval Théologique et Philosophique, Rassengna Internazionale di Logica, Religious Studies, Theoria, Sophia, Australasian Journal of Philosophy,* etc. His verse has appeared in literary magazines of several countries. Advent Books of London published his poem *The Dead Ship* in 1968.

JOHN LESLIE was born in Britain but has now taught for many years at the University of Guelph, Ontario. His philosophy of Cosmic Optimism is reflected in a passion for climbing mountains which is keenly shared by his wife. Professor Leslie studied psychology and philosophy at Wadham College, Oxford University, where he later wrote a thesis on "*THE THEORY THAT THE WORLD IS AS IT IS, BECAUSE IT IS BEST THAT IT SHOULD BE SO.*" He has subsequently published articles on Cosmic Optimism and its implications in *Studia Leibnitiana,* (1971), *Idealistic Studies,* (1971) *Philosophy,* (1976), and *The American Philosophical Quarterly,* (1970, 1972, 1976). He is also the father of two children. John Leslie is much valued and employed as a Referee for the Canadian Philosophical Association's annual Congress, to which he has presented papers of his own. He is nearing the completion of a book, *Values and Necessity*. In this work he hopes to demonstrate the soundness and wisdom of Cosmic Optimism as a complete philosophical system.

C.B. MARTIN is Professor of Philosophy at the University of Calgary where he has served as chairman. When he taught for many years at the University of Sydney, before coming to Canada, he was counted among Australia's outstanding philosophers and widely considered to be that country's most gifted philosopher of religion. His work on the thought of the British Empiricists, especially on that of John Locke, and his causal analysis of the peculiarly difficult concept of memory have also brought him international recognition. His book, *Religious Belief* (Cornell University Press, 1959) remains the best known of his many writings: It may offer the most devastating attacks on Judaeo-Christian concepts and beliefs since David Hume posed his sceptical questions two centuries earlier. He has contributed to such periodicals as *The Australasian Journal of Philosophy*, *Mind*, *The Philosophical Review* and *The Canadian Journal of Philosophy*. C.B. Martin remains a strong advocate of the view that the rejection of traditional religious beliefs should increase rather than remove human concern for political and social morality. He is actively interested in the traditions, problems, and goals of Canadian Indians in the Province of Alberta.

ALASTAIR McKINNON is MacDonald Professor of Moral Philosophy and chairman of the Philosophy Department at McGill University. A native of Ontario, he holds the Bachelor of Divinity degree from McGill, the M.A. from the University of Toronto, and the Ph.D. from the University of Edinburgh. He is author of *Falsification and Belief* (Mouton, The Hague and Paris, 1970) and of articles and reviews in a number of scholarly journals. Alastair McKinnon has been a pioneer in using computer technology to provide a better understanding of outstanding philosophers' writings; this work has led to the publication of a concordance to Wittgenstein's *Philosophical Investigations* and of still more ambitious indices to the texts of his favourite philosopher, Kierkegaard. With M. Venant Cauchy, Université de Montréal, he is co-founder and co-editor of *CLIO*, a journal which serves those who wish to extend the compass of such research. Alastair McKinnon is a former director of the Canadian Philosophical Association who has served the Association in several other capacities. As a teacher at McGill since 1950 he has contributed to many and varied parts of intellectual and academic life in one of Canada's oldest universities. He stands among the best known Protestant philosophers of religion in North America. His essay in this volume, "Paradox and Faith: A Kierkegaardian Contribution to Religious Thought," reflects all three of his major interests: the philosophy of religion, the writings of Kierkegaard, and the value of employing computers to assist human eyes and intellects.

JAY NEWMAN was the second doctoral graduate in philosophy from Toronto's new York University. Since receiving that degree he has been teaching at the University of Guelph, Ontario. He received his master's degree from Brown University. Professor Newman has done much research and has published work on one of the nineteenth-century's most important intellectual figures, Cardinal John Newman, a man whose conversion to Catholicism startled the English-speaking world. While holding to his native Jewish tradition, Professor Newman has published papers which challenge philosophical appraisers of most Western religions in such periodicals as *Religious Studies, Journal of Value Inquiry, The Thomist, Sophia, Proceedings of the American Catholic Philosophical Association* and *Laval Théologique et Philosophique.* He is much interested in continental philosophy, Ethical Relativism, and the philosophy of history, and is also concerned with promoting dialogue between philosophers in schools traditionally associated with French Canadian and English Canadian universities.

DEWI Z. PHILLIPS currently holds a joint appointment at Carleton University's Department of Religious Studies in Ottawa and at the Philosophy Department of the University of Wales in Britain. Since 1971 he has been Professor of Philosophy and head of the department with the University College of Swansea. He has also taught at Queen's College, University of Dundee, Scotland and at the University College of North Wales, Bangor. He holds degrees from the University of Wales and from Oxford University. His striking and internationally controversial writings on religion, ethics, and philosophy in literature include his books, *The Concept of Prayer* (1965), *Moral Practices* (1970), *Faith and Philosophical Enquiry* (1970), *Death and Immortality* (1970), *Sense and Delusion* (1971), and *Philosophizing about Religion* (published in Welsh, 1975). From 1968 to 1974 he served as General Editor of the famous series, *Studies in Ethics and the Philosophy of Religion* for Routledge and Kegan Paul. Dewi Z. Phillips is a strong believer in Canada's national policy of encouraging members of ethnic groups to take their traditional language and culture seriously: He and his three sons are fluent in Welsh.

CARLOS G. PRADO was born in Guatemala, but later became a Canadian citizen. From 1960 to 1963 he served with Guatemala's Mission to the United Nations in New York. In 1964 he received a master's degree in philosophy from the University of California, Berkeley. In 1970 he received the doctorate in philosophy from Queen's University, Kingston, Ontario for research on *Perception in D.M. Armstrong's Materialist Theory of Mind.* In 1972 he was a spokesman for Canadian philosophy and for Canadian editors of philosophy journals at the Inter-American Philosophers' Congress in Brazil. He is currently Associate Professor of Philosophy at Queen's University, having also taught at Chaminade College in Hawaii. Dr. Prado has published work on philosophy of religion and philosophical psychology in scholarly journals of several countries: *Mind* (U.K.), *Noûs,* (U.S.A.), *Theoria* (Sweden), *Dialogue* (Canada), *The Australasian Journal of Philosophy,* etc. He has addressed the Canadian Philosophical Association, the Canadian Association for Study of Religion, the Canadian Association for Latin American Studies and other learned groups and bodies. He is currently revising a book on the tenability of religious beliefs.

F(rancis) E(dward) SPARSHOTT was born in England in 1926 and educated at the King's School, Rochester, and the University of Oxford (B.A.,

1950). Since 1950 he has been teaching at the University of Toronto, where he is now Professor of Philosophy at Victoria College. He has served as a trustee of the American Society for Aesthetics and as president of the Canadian Philosophical Association. He is the author of the following books on philosophy: *An Enquiry into Goodness and Related Concepts* (Toronto and Chicago, 1958); *The Structure of Aesthetics* (Toronto and London, 1963); *The Concept of Criticism* (Oxford, 1967); and *Looking for Philosophy* (Montreal, 1972). Besides serving on the editorial committees of *Ethics* and *Philosophy in Literature*, F.E. Sparshott has long remained active as a writer of poetry and a noted judge of verse and fiction. He has advised the Governor-General on literary awards. At intervals he also publishes work on ancient philosophy and the Greek classics. He makes his home in Toronto with his wife and daughter.